Looking Into the Abyss

THEATER: THEORY/TEXT/PERFORMANCE
Enoch Brater, Series Editor

LOOKING INTO THE ABYSS

Essays on Scenography

Arnold Aronson

The University of Michigan Press
Ann Arbor

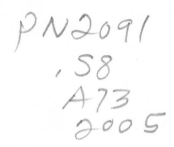

2008   2007   2006   2005   4   3   2   1

A CIP catalog record for this book is available from the British Library.

Library of Congress Cataloging-in-Publication Data

Aronson, Arnold.
     Looking into the abyss : essays on scenography / Arnold Aronson.
         p.   cm. — (Theater—theory/text/performance)
     Includes index.
     ISBN 0-472-09888-8 (cloth : alk. paper) — ISBN 0-472-06888-1
(pbk. : alk. paper)
     1. Theaters—Stage-setting and scenery.   I. Title.   II. Series.
PN2091.S8A73   2005
792.02'5—dc22   2004027782

In Memory of
Ruth Bayard Smith

Acknowledgments

Several of the essays in this volume were first presented as papers at various meetings of the International Organization of Scenographers, Theatre Architects, and Technicians (OISTAT). I owe a debt of gratitude to my many friends in that organization too numerous to single out, and particularly to my colleagues on the History and Theory Commission. My involvement in OISTAT came about through my editorship of *Theatre Design & Technology,* the journal of the U.S. Institute for Theatre Technology, from 1978 to 1988. I am particularly grateful to those in USITT who supported me and sent me to the various meetings at which many of these papers were presented, especially Dr. Joel E. Rubin and Sarah Nash Gates. The late Edward F. Kook, a founder of USITT, urged me (literally commanded me) to write about designers, so I owe much of my career to his prodding.

Several essays in this collection reflect the crucial input of the editors who published them in their journals and books. I would especially like to thank Helmut Grosser and Karin Winkelsesser, former and present editors of *Bühnentechnische Rundschau* for translating and publishing two of these articles. It has also been a pleasure to work with Claude Schumacher of *Theatre Research International,* Theodore Shank and Adele Shank of *Theatre Forum,* Vera Gottlieb and Paul Allain of *The Cambridge Companion to Chekhov,* Deborah Geis and Steven F. Kruger of *Approaching the Millennium,* Stuart Hecht of the *New England Theatre Journal,* Sarah Weiner of the Wallach Art Gallery, and Marc Hacker of the David Rockwell office. I thank Enoch Brater, who was editor of *Theatre Journal* at the time "Postmodern Design" was published and, as the advisory editor of Michigan's theater book series, encouraged me to pursue this book. And I am grateful to Rebecca Mostov, Marcia LaBrenz, and particularly LeAnn Fields of the University of Michigan Press, who made this possible.

I owe a great deal to my students Megan Smith and Anne Gridley and to my son Isaac for his support and help in putting this book together.

The first thing my late wife, Ruth Bayard Smith, would turn to when opening a book was the acknowledgment section in order to see how the author thanked his or her spouse. Thus, writing this is particularly hard. Over the years I have become so used to submitting my work to her for advice and editing that I find myself at a loss without her invaluable input. Ruth did, in fact, read most of these pieces when they were first being written, but if the final versions and recent creations contain infelicities, awkward locutions, or vague referents (my most consistent fault in her opinion), it is because of the lack of her keen eye and editorial skill. Without her patience, support, and love through the all the previous years, none of this would have been possible. This book is dedicated to her memory.

Contents

Introduction

The title of this collection (and of one of the essays within it) comes from Friedrich Nietzsche's *Beyond Good and Evil,* in which he warns, "Whoever fights monsters should see to it that in the process he does not himself become a monster. When you look long into an abyss, the abyss also looks back into you."[1] This collection is about looking into that abyss we call the stage. Among Webster's definitions of abyss are "an immeasurably deep gulf or great space" and "intellectual or spiritual profundity." It is, in fact, precisely such a "great space" we encounter when we confront the stage. Even the tiniest stages—the mountebank's trestle of the Middle Ages, for instance, or the minuscule platform of Caffe Cino, the first off-off Broadway theater—are boundless; like Hamlet's nutshell, they contain "infinite space." To look into such a expanse is potentially frightening, especially if, as Nietzsche suggests, it looks back into you. And the stage most definitely returns the gaze.

We are spatial creatures; we respond instinctively to space. Our arrival into the world, the moment of birth, is a spatial experience as we emerge from a safe, enclosed environment into the vastness of an unknown expanse. Every time we confront a stage we are, in a sense, confronting the space—the abyss—we first confronted at birth. The stage, regardless of its configuration, functions as an optical focal point and creates the impression that we are looking through this lens into a boundless space beyond. In fact, for most spectators, it is the apprehension of space that may be the most profound and powerful experience of live theater although, admittedly, it is one that is most often felt subconsciously. And yet the spatiality of the stage is rarely addressed by critics or theater theorists. It is as if the meaning and import of a Greek or Elizabethan tragedy, a medieval mystery play, a Noh drama, a French farce, or a grand opera could exist—could be analyzed and understood—completely separate from the stage and theater for which it was initially composed, or from the theatrical environment in which it is being experienced at the present moment. And the same holds true for all the visual and physical elements we lump together under the rubric of design. How many spectators, even theater professionals, can truly read a stage? Brecht wanted an audience that was as knowledgeable as the one at a sporting event, an audience that understood the rules, the nuances, the strategies, the potentialities. But who in a theater audience is truly aware of the impact of the color of a wall or the placement of a door, the effect upon dramatic rhythm of the ground plan, the psychological response to the texture of a costume (something the Russian designer Alexandra Exter was keenly aware of), or the quality of light? And yet, we are living in what is increasingly touted as a visual society.

Critics and theoreticians who deal with theater tend to come from the world of literature and therefore are prone to attribute the profundity of theater primarily to its language and the ideas expressed by that language. And, of course, there is a rationale for this; we do not quote the arras that probably hung at the rear of Shakespeare's stage, we quote his words; we may be interested in the quality of the door *slam* at the end of *A Doll's House,* but I would venture that most spectators pay little attention to the quality of the *doors* that may be visible on Ibsen's stage. Yet theater is, first and foremost, a visual art. The very word *theater* comes from the ancient Greek *theatron,* the name given to the area in which the audience sat. (Fifth-century Athenians had no single word for the totality of the physical components of the "theater.") *Theatron,* in turn, comes from the root *theasthai,* meaning "to see." The *theatron,* the place where the audience sits, is thus "the seeing place." We still say, "I'm going to *see* a play." (And despite the fact that today we often call the equivalent of the *theatron* by its Latin name, *auditorium,* we do not go to the theater to "hear a play.") But beyond that particular locution, the visual component of theater is largely ignored, and is even viewed with suspicion. We are told, for example, that a musical production is not successful if the audience leaves "humming the scenery." Why? Why is the pleasure of the eye considered not merely inferior to the pleasures of the ear, but somehow unseemly? Part of the blame no doubt lies in a certain Puritan heritage and its Old Testament mistrust of graven images. And certainly the Western scholarly tradition that has valorized Aristotle, who relegated spectacle to the lowest rung on his hierarchy of component elements of tragedy, is a contributing factor. But we must bear in mind that Aristotle was writing about how to compose a tragedy, not how to stage one. It is hard to disagree with his general principle that spectacle as a substitute for good plotting or character was an indication of a poor poet. But at the same time, because there is no extant commentary from Aristotle or his contemporaries on staging, tragedy seems to be equated with the poet's text alone, and there is no sense that scenography might play a significant role in the creation of drama. As I suggest in the essay "Behind the Screen Door," the *Oresteia* is at least in part made possible by the technological, physical, and scenic elements of the stage. Moreover, it is clear that Aeschylus was fully aware of the potentialities of the physical stage in shaping the rhythms of the tragedy and in manipulating audience response to the work. Of course, it is not Aristotle but his neoclassical apologists who laid the foundations of modern dramatic aesthetics and developed literal rules of playwriting based upon a kind of fundamentalist reading of *The Poetics*. It is with these theoreticians that drama enters the world of literature and leaves the physical stage behind. (But it is also true that this prejudice has ancient roots. The three original Muses of Greek mythology, Calliope, Euterpe, and Erato, were associated with forms of poetry. The six who were subsequently included with the group were also from the liberal arts and sciences: oratory, history, tragedy, comedy, choral song and dance, and astronomy. The visual arts held no place in this particular pantheon.)

Interestingly, the Sanskrit treatise on theater, the *Natyasastra*, which is, in essence, one of the first discourses on reception theory, devotes several chapters to the spatial and visual components of the theater. Bharata Muni understood the importance of the physical theater, and the entire *veda* is an exploration of the way in which each and every component of the theater contributes to the reception and understanding of the drama.

Other factors, of course, contributed to the denigration of visuality in Western theatrical history. The cultural divide between high and low art that emerged in the nineteenth century also relegated the world of spectacle and visuality to the popular theater, while valorizing the literary theater of high culture. Scenic spectacle and technological effects became the realm of melodrama, Grand Guignol, music hall, circus, and, in its own way, naturalism. It was this foregrounding of the image over the word in these forms that led Stéphane Mallarmé to urge the symbolists to "detheatricalize the theater." As I note in the essays on Joseph Urban and David Rockwell, the association with the popular and spectacular can lead to a dismissive critical response, especially in the world of architecture where theatricality (i.e., spectacle and emotional manipulation through imagery) is still an undesirable epithet. Yet the symbolist rejection of theatricality did not mean the elimination of the visual within theatrical work. The symbolists, after all, pioneered the use of scrims and experimented with the color and quality of light, and their stage designs turned to medieval and Pre-Raphaelite motifs and a subtle visual palette carefully integrated with the spiritual intent of the

theatrical work. What the symbolists and others in the late nineteenth century were rejecting was the excessive spectacle and effects of the melodramatic and naturalistic stage. In other words, it was "design for design's
sake," as it were, that was objectionable, not design itself. And yet, once
design became self-effacing, it became, in a sense, invisible. This remains
true to the present. Robin Wagner's minimalist design for *A Chorus Line* in
the 1970s (which consisted of little more than a white line on the stage floor
until the final scene) was achieved through a painstaking process of elimination and was highly regarded by cognoscenti, but the production was commonly described as taking place on a bare stage. His decidedly nonminimal-
ist settings for the New York production of *Angels in America,* on the other
hand, were criticized by some for being excessive.

Visuality was historically a fundamental basis of Western philosophy—
the idea of philosophy as a contemplative act. Hannah Arendt, for instance,
noted that the "predominance of sight is . . . deeply embedded in Greek
speech, and therefore our conceptual language."[2] But visuality, not surprisingly, is perceived as the realm of painting (and related arts), and because
painting, like language, was most commonly associated with representation,
reference, and meaning, the two—image and language—were understood
as occupying a similar sphere and thus were often seen as either redundant
or competing for the same social and cultural space. As literary critic W. J.
T. Mitchell explains,

> Words and images seem inevitably to become implicated in a "war of
> signs" . . . in which the stakes are things like nature, truth, reality, and the
> human spirit. Each art, each type of sign or medium, lays claim to certain
> things that it is best equipped to mediate, and each grounds its claim in a
> certain characterization of its "self," its own proper essence. Equally
> important, each art characterizes itself in opposition to its "significant
> other." Thus, poetry, or verbal expression in general, sees its signs as
> arbitrary and conventional—that is, "unnatural" in contrast to the natural
> signs of imagery. Painting sees itself as uniquely fitted for the representa-
> tion of the visible world, whereas poetry is primarily concerned with the
> invisible realm of ideas and feelings.[3]

For much of the twentieth century, however, the visual aspect of philosophy has been under attack, and in the poststructuralist era vision, or at least
the hegemony of sight, has been largely rejected. This, too, has no doubt
contributed to the limited attention paid to the visual aspects of theater by
the high theorists of the latter twentieth century. To focus on the visual in

the theater would be to grant it a kind of autonomy and objectivity. And because vision and sight are not only physiological phenomena but cultural constructs, to discuss (contemplate) the theatrical image would also require an acceptance of certain cultural norms, a step that is not only difficult in a multicultural society, but anathema in a postmodern world.

The problem, of course, is that critics (both literary and dramatic) have equated the scenic element of theater with painting or other plastic arts and understood it as a (corrupt) subset of (pure) visual art. The misconception becomes clear when one looks at Mitchell's description of poetry versus painting, for instance: "Poetry is an art of time, motion, and action; paint-ing an art of space, stasis, and arrested action."[4] Scenography, however, is an art of time, motion, action, *and* space, that is, an amalgamation of the two. (Nonetheless, I suggest in "Can Theater and Media Speak the Same Lan-guage?" that the problem of film and video projection in the theater is a result of the essentially painterly qualities of those media that clash with the unique scenographic qualities of live theater.) It is difficult to deal with an image or spatial construct that is unstable—images and space that are not merely transformed through the mechanical devices of the stage but also by the presence and movement of live actors whose own performances are unstable. Furthermore, even if one is willing to revert to such analytical sys-tems as semiotics and phenomenology—both particularly well suited for theater—one is confronted, on the one hand, with the paradox of signs and signifiers that are identical yet differ in meanings and representational codes, and, on the other, tangible space and objects that, in most theater forms, can only be experienced at a distance or through some form of mediation.

Theater artists and educators like to claim that theater is the ultimate art form or quintessential liberal art because it subsumes almost all other arts and even social and hard sciences. But from an analytical standpoint, this renders it impure, contradictory, amorphous, and virtually ungraspable. Critics who deal with theater much prefer to render it into its component elements and deal with them separately—primarily focusing on the literary while con-signing the rest to the realm of craft. (Acting, because of its particular rela-tionship to representation, and because of the postmodern obsession with *écriture* and the body, has provided a fruitful site for some theoreticians. While design and space would seem equally attractive subjects, they are still more often understood as incidental by-products of the theatrical event, not integrally related to the realization of theater.) Even theater artists them-selves have sometimes condemned theater for its protean qualities. Richard Wagner's *Gesamtkunstwerk* was a response to the lack of a single visionary in the creation of this particular art, and Edward Gordon Craig suggested

replacing the unreliable actor with marionettes in a similar attempt to exer-
cise absolute control over the presentation of the work. The very hetero-
geneity of the theatrical makes it unlike almost any other art form and therefore not as easily analyzed.

Visuality, of course, does not have to be limited to the elaborate illusionistic settings, clever machinery, and spectacular tricks of the melodrama or
the pictorial realism of a Charles Kean or David Belasco. Shakespeare is
praised for creating images in "the mind's eye" through language. The
scenic elements of the Tudor stage may have been few, but the imagistic
aspect was paramount. As Martin Jay has noted, the word *image* "can signify
graphic, optical, perceptual, mental, or verbal phenomena."[5] But again, we
tend to privilege the evocations of verbal imagery over the physical recre-
ations or representations of scenographic efforts. We praise Shakespeare's
simple verbal rendering of the dawn in *Romeo and Juliet* while smiling indul-
gently at Belasco's attempts to achieve a specifically California sunset
through stage lighting technology in *Girl of the Golden West*. But the fact is
that in either case, the material world is referenced, and the meaning and
intent of the performance is integrally tied to the success of the particular
evocation.

Much modernist drama has tried to remove theater from the context of
the "real world." Tangible landmarks are eliminated; action occurs in a
void. But such a thing does not exist. Samuel Beckett may have set each of
his plays in an increasingly abstract space, but there was always a signpost—
from the literal tree by the side of the road in *Waiting for Godot* to the human
mouth that is all that remains visible in *Not I*. The great designer and teacher
Ming Cho Lee knows that he will always encounter a student who wants to
set a play in "a void." For this student he has a simple question: "OK. What
color is the void?" Theater is visible—we see something, and that something has a shape, a color, a texture. Even if everything is stripped away,
there is still the stage itself, staring back at the audience. Absence of design
is still design. Any arrangement of space or objects, any movement through
or across that space, is design. And if we remove the stage through the elimination of light or through, say, the medium of radio, then there is design in
the mind's eye. The old adage applies: all that is needed for theater is two
boards and a passion. Well, those two boards exist in space, and the passion
unfolds in that space through time.

This collection of essays is not in any way a definitive, let alone exhaus-
tive, examination of the spatiovisual aspect of theater. It is intended more as
the opening of a dialogue that will, I hope, bring the physical aspect of theater back into its proper place as an element as integral to the performance

as the spoken word, and perhaps lead those interested in the theater to become more aware of their role as "seers" of theater.

Scenography

The subtitle of this collection is "Essays on Scenography," not "Essays on Design." *Scenography* is at once an ancient and recent term. Aristotle refers to *skenographia:* scenic writing. So while he may not have addressed the issue, he understood that theatrical production involved several kinds of writing, and one of them was the text and vocabulary of the physical theater. But the Renaissance theoreticians did not pick up on that particular word. In the West, words such as *design, decor, scenery,* and their linguistic equivalents emerged. In Europe in the latter half of the twentieth century, however, the word *scenography* increasingly emerged as the term of choice. It implies something more than creating scenery or costumes or lights. It carries a connotation of an all-encompassing visual-spatial construct as well as the process of change and transformation that is an inherent part of the physical vocabulary of the stage. In that sense, it bears some relation to the French term *mise en scène.* British scenographer Pamela Howard recently wrote a book entitled *What Is Scenography?* that begins with answers to the titular question from some fifty scenographers from around the world. What is both maddening and delightful is that no two answers are alike, and many are wildly contradictory. Despite this lack of agreement on the meaning of the term, I still find it far more useful, more encompassing, and more inclusive than the word *design,* which, particularly in the United States, refers to a very specific and limited aspect of the spatiovisual experience of performance. Howard, somewhat like Bharata Muni, includes everything from the space to the text, to the performer, to the audience as elements of scenography. This may be extreme in that it seems to subsume all aspects of theater, but it is better to err on the side of inclusiveness than to focus on the narrowly defined.

Both the economic system of American theater production and the long-established structure of American theater education, however, have tended to reify design. Students are generally taught as set designers or costume designers or lighting designers. Although design students may collaborate with directors, they rarely are educated as directors, or vice versa. Producers, in turn, hire design "teams" whose members may work in virtual isolation, bringing their work together only in the technical rehearsals. This isolation has only increased with the advent of faxes, e-mail, and other forms of electronic exchange that allow communication without presence. It is significant, I believe, that many of the rather limited number of American designers who might be called scenographers find it necessary to do much of their work abroad.

Organization of this Book

I have divided this collection into two parts. The first, "Thinking about Scenography," contains somewhat more general essays on the role of scenography in the understanding and experience of theater, although they remain rooted in the actuality and process of production. With the exception of two essays, "Postmodern Design" and "New Homes for New Theater," all the essays in part 1 were initially given as papers at conferences, largely gatherings of practicing designers and architects. The intention was to open a dialogue between artists and critics (and, ideally, audiences). Too often these days, the vocabulary of poststructuralist discourse seems of limited value for the work of practicing artists, not because the material is irrelevant, too rarefied, or complex—indeed, many cutting-edge theater artists read widely and deeply in contemporary theory—but because theater artists and those who write about the art seem increasingly to talk past each other, as if residing in vastly different spheres. I hope that these essays may help to rejoin these worlds.

Part 2, "Scenography in Context," takes a look at the work of specific designers or groups, or the scenographic response to certain playwrights. Whereas the first part of the book is arranged chronologically by date of composition, the second part is arranged chronologically by artist and thus provides a journey of sorts through the twentieth century. (Several of these pieces were "commissioned," but they nonetheless reflect topics and individuals whose work lies at the heart of modern and postmodern theater.) Unlike the first part, all but one of these essays (the one on the Wooster Group) were written initially for publication. But the aim was similar: an attempt to refocus or resituate the discussion of theater within the realm of the spatial, visual, and physical.

In pulling these essays together, I discovered that I cited certain authors, even certain quotations, repeatedly in different contexts. Perhaps this is an inevitable by-product of gathering over a decade's worth of essays that were presented to very different audiences. Most notable in this regard was Gaston Bachelard, whose *Poetics of Space* I find essential for an understanding of the way in which we comprehend the spatiality of the stage. But I also discovered, a bit to my surprise, that I mentioned the futurist Filippo Tommaso Marinetti several times. References to the Wooster Group and its productions reappear in several essays beyond the one devoted specifically to the group. This is in part a result of my long-standing admiration for their work, an ongoing project of investigating the relationship of the performer, text, space, technology, society, and spectator. I have tried to minimize the repetitions where possible, and ask the reader's indulgence for the rest. I also note that many of these essays deal with the increasing influence of the digital age. Since most of the essays were written in the 1990s, this is perhaps inevitable. I firmly believe that the new technologies are transforming the very structure of our thoughts and perceptions, in turn affecting the way in which we create and understand art. Some of the essays may seem a bit naive in the face of rapidly changing technologies, but I hope that the underlying ideas are still valid.

Notes

1. Friedrich Nietzsche, *Beyond Good and Evil: Prelude to a Philosophy of the Future,* trans. Walter Kaufmann (New York: Vintage, 1966).
2. Hannah Arendt, *The Life of the Mind,* quoted in *Sites of Vision: The Discursive Construction of Sight in the History of Philosophy,* ed. David Michael Levin (Cambridge: MIT Press, 1999), 5.
3. W. J. T. Mitchell, *Iconology: Image, Text, Ideology* (Chicago: University of Chicago Press, 1987), 47–48.
4. Mitchell, *Iconology,* 48.
5. Martin Jay, *Downcast Eyes: The Denigration of Vision in Twentieth-Century French Thought* (Berkeley and Los Angeles: University of California Press, 1994), 9. See also Mitchell's introduction to *Iconology.*

PART I Thinking about Scenography

Postmodern Design

Seventeenth-century court society meets Bela Lugosi and George Lucas. . . .
—Description of Anne Bogart's production of *Life Is a Dream*

Bob Wilson . . . used to say, "Your work is so good but oh, it's so ugly all the time." And I thought so too. The imagery that I was dealing with was not making pretty pictures, it was a dialectical examination of the problematics of seeing.
—Richard Foreman

The postmodern reply to the modern consists of recognizing that the past, since it cannot readily be destroyed, because its destruction leads to silence, must be revisited: but with irony, not innocently.
—Umberto Eco

Although Western drama from Ibsen and Strindberg to the present is often lumped together under the rubric of "modern drama," it is rare to come across a mention of "modern design." If design styles are discussed at all, they are usually mentioned only when plainly related to identifiable art movements such as constructivism or surrealism or various branches of realism: suggestive realism, poetic realism, photorealism, and so forth. If there is no clear-cut movement known as modern design, how is it possible to talk about "postmodern design"? Nonetheless, certain design characteristics definable as "modern" may be discerned across a broad spectrum of performances throughout the twentieth century, while increasingly over the past two decades, a new style has emerged that is fundamentally different in approach and aesthetic values, that has certain similarities to postmodern architecture, and that challenges the standard ways of seeing conditioned by nearly a century of modern design. This new style can be called, rightfully, "postmodern."

Modern stage design has been characterized by the presence of a strong

From *Theatre Journal* (March 1991).

metaphorical or presentational image or related series of images—the "pretty pictures" that Foreman talks about. There was a singular quality, a unity, even a monolithic aspect to these images, what Adolphe Appia termed an "organic unity." Moreover, the image often became identified with the style of a designer, thus allowing the elevation of the designer-artist to a position of equality, if not dominance, among the theater's creative personnel. Fredric Jameson, one of the leading theoreticians of postmodernism, could have been referring to this prominence of the designer when he identified a key characteristic of modernism as "the invention of a personal, private style, as unmistakable as your fingerprint . . . which can be expected to generate its own unique vision of the world."[1] Similarly, Jean-François Lyotard's definition of modernism, though intended for a broader sociopolitical context, can encompass this sense of organic unity: "A metadiscourse . . . making an explicit appeal to some grand narrative."[2] Modern design functions by visually and metaphorically placing the specific world of the play within some sort of broader context of the world of the audience; it is a kind of metanarrative that attempts to encompass the world within a unified image. But Appia's organic unity seems impossible to grasp in the postmodern world. A kind of panhistorical, omnistylistic view now dominates stage design; the world is seen as a multiplicity of competing, often incongruous and conflicting elements and images, and the stage has come to represent this view.

If modern design moved the stage picture away from the specific, tangible, illusionistic world of romanticism and realism into a generalized, theatrical, and poetic realm in which the pictorial image functioned as an extension of the playwright's themes and structures (a metanarrative), then postmodern design is a dissonant reminder that no single point of view is possible, even within a single image. We are confronted with what Charles Russell calls "an art of shifting perspective, of double self-consciousness, of local and extended meaning."[3] Through the use of discordance, ugliness, and juxtaposition—what postmodernists would call rupture, discontinuity, disjuncture[4]—the spectator of postmodern design is constantly made aware of the experience of viewing and, at the same time, in the most successful examples, made aware of the whole history, context, and reverberations of an image in the contemporary world. It should also be noted that modernism assumes the presence of a single viewer or reader whose perceptual mechanisms are shared by all viewers within the society. Moreover, the object is still central in modernism. Postmodernism shifts the work of art from the object to the transaction between the spectator and the object and further deconstructs it by negating the presence of a representative objective viewer.

If one tries to describe modern design by looking at all that has been associated with "modern drama," the result will be confusing at best. The hodgepodge of design styles associated with modern drama ranges from detailed realism to total abstraction and thus has little apparent stylistic consistency or theoretical basis. Moreover, with only a few notable exceptions, it is not easily correlated with specific developments or movements within modern art. Although there is a strong tradition in the late nineteenth and twentieth centuries of fine and plastic artists designing for the stage—from Paul Sérusier and Picasso to David Hockney and David Salle—these artists have shown, for the most part, a surprising inability to transpose their radical ideas onto the three-dimensional space of the stage in a manner as innovative as their art. Modern art on the stage has tended toward flat representation of the superficial stylistic qualities of particular artists. It is an ironic testament to the overwhelming strength of the stage space that it can dominate and subjugate anything put upon it and create a more or less homogeneous look. The frontal relationship of spectator and performer in most presentations, the usual need for visibility and audibility, and the "reality" imparted by the presence of human beings in most stage productions exert a tremendous pressure on the shape and format of design, thereby limiting innovation. The collaborative nature of theater, the existing architecture of theater spaces, and the economic pressures of both commercial and noncommercial theater also contribute to the essentially conservative nature of the art. These reasons help explain why avant-garde artists have had little impact on the development of stage design, and why evolutions in the art of stage design must be measured in fairly subtle ways. A stage set is still a stage set; there are only a limited number of ways in which the visual elements of a production can relate to the performers and the spectators.

For all intents and purposes modern design began with the theoretical writings of Adolphe Appia and Edward Gordon Craig, starting with Appia's work in the 1890s. In response to the scientific realism that typified the naturalistic drama of the 1870s and 1880s and the two-dimensional but detailed realism of painted sets typical of nineteenth-century romantic realism, Appia and Craig called for a theatricality characterized by simplicity, suggestion, abstraction, and grandeur within the context of a three-dimensional sculptural setting that would unify the performer and the stage space. Important in this modern concept was the plasticity or transformability of the stage through light and, in some cases, movable scenic elements such as Craig's famous screens. Paramount in this approach was the sense of aesthetic pleasure and harmony expressed by Craig in his essay "The Artists of the Theatre of the Future." "It is idle to talk about the distraction of scenery," Craig wrote, "because the question here is not how to create some distracting scenery, but rather how to create a place which harmonizes with the thoughts of the poet."[5] The image, according to Craig, proceeds from the "mind's eye." In other words, the scenic artist responds intuitively to the ideas evoked by the playwright; the result will be a visual image at one with the playwright's thoughts. This idea was well summarized by the French scenographic scholar and critic Denis Bablet:

> In [Craig's] view, the presentation of a drama must reveal to us the inner life, the very essence of this drama. The complete picture offered to us by the production must at each moment correspond to the various phases of the dramatic action. The decor is not an autonomous frame, the objective presentation of a place in which the action would be as if projected after the event. . . . By being directly in harmony with the movements of the actors, with the suggestions of the play, and possibly with the music, it becomes integrated with the life of the drama and participates in its revelation. The interplay of line, color, objects, and lighting effects produces in the public a visual emotion which is in harmony with its auditory emotion and which strengthens it.[6]

This approach, which could easily apply to Appia as well as Craig, was echoed in the United States by Robert Edmond Jones, who is generally considered the father of modern American design. Like Craig, Jones refers to the "mind's eye" (attributing the phrase to Hamlet) and goes on to explain:

> Stage-designing should be addressed to this eye of the mind. . . . A setting is not just a beautiful thing, a collection of beautiful things. It is a presence, a mood, a symphonic accompaniment to the drama, a great wind fanning the drama to flame. It echoes, it enhances, it animates. It is an expectancy, a foreboding, a tension. It says nothing, but it gives everything.[7]

Recurring motifs of musicality (including harmony and unity) and spirituality suffuse the writings on design by these artists and, by and large, this attitude has pervaded modern design. In the modern mise-en-scène the text, the performance, and the scenography unite ideally into a seamless, beautiful whole. Other basic principles of modern design also emerged in these writings and works. First of all, the stage was not illusionistic—it was identified as a stage or as a space for acting, not as some other place such as a room, a forest, and so on. If identity of space was required, it was to be established through dialogue, action, reference, or through suggestive rather than explicit scenery. Scenery consisted of platforms, ramps, steps, screens, walls, and curtains. Scenery might also include three-dimensional elements that *suggested* objectified places such as castles, landscapes, or rooms but were in and of themselves nonspecific. Whereas a naturalistic set was a physical manifestation of a psychological and sociological study, the new, modern decor was the spiritual essence of an object—scenery as Platonic shadows. Three-dimensional space, which was essential since the performer was three-dimensional, was created or enhanced by sculpting the stage with light. This was especially true for Appia.

Another characteristic was a visual and conceptual unity. The design embodied a fundamental concept or metaphor of the production, and through the use of a single or unit set, or through the use of transcendent motifs, the design provided a structural unity to the whole production. The idea of unity was a response to the fragmentary nature of much nineteenth-century Romantic design in which coordination among the visual elements was sporadic and haphazard. The disunity of design in the nineteenth century, however, was simply the result of contemporary stage practice rather than the result of any consciously thought-out aesthetic. Performers, for example, generally provided their own costumes; theaters relied upon stock scenery. Unintentionally, then, the costume and decor of the nineteenth century provided a peculiar kind of continuity with the experiential world of the spectator, whereas modern design functioned not as an extension of the world but as a *metaphor* for something other. In the postmodern practice, if we follow Ihab Hassan's schemata, this becomes metonymy.[8] But with the new emphasis on stage-as-stage, or with the dominance of a visual motif typical of modern design, the set, in fact, could become the dominant element of a production, setting the whole tone and shaping the interpretation of the script as well as determining the rhythm and movement of the performers.

These principles dominate the work of modern designers from Appia and Craig through Josef Svoboda and Ming Cho Lee. In recent years, however, the modern approach has seemed insufficient or inappropriate for revivals of opera and classical theater. The attempt to embrace the classics on the modern stage, indeed the perceived need to "save the theater," as costume designer Laura Crow has put it, requires that we "make them of today."[9] As director Peter Sellars has said, we can speak only of what we have seen in our own lifetimes and thus must employ a "system of contemporary references."[10] The result is often a seemingly vulgar and alienating collage of styles, periods, and references—a very conscious lack of unity among the visual elements of a production. It is this intentionally radical disruption of pleasing aesthetic synergy that is a cornerstone of postmodern design. One definition of postmodern design, then, is the juxtaposition of seemingly incongruous elements within the unifying structure of the stage frame, the purpose of which is to create a referential network within the mind of the viewer that extends beyond the immediately apparent world of the play. A postmodern design will often make reference to other productions, to other works of art, and to an extra- or nondramatic world. Unity derives from the very presence of a stage, a theater, performers, and, perhaps, the visual style of the designer.

This, of course, is a central premise of virtually all postmodern art—the "presence of the past" or what Hassan calls "present-ification"[11] and Jameson calls "pastiche." The latter is defined as "the imitation of a peculiar or unique style, the wearing of a stylistic mask, speech in a dead language."[12] Postmodern design virtually reeks with the presence of the past, and it often pastes together a collage of stylistic imitations that function not as style but as semiotic code. Whether or not this is a "dead language," though, is certainly debatable.

Certain developments in modern scenography can be dated from landmark productions that heralded a new approach: one thinks of Robert Edmond Jones's *The Man Who Married a Dumb Wife* (1914) or Ming Cho Lee's *Electra* (1964). Postmodernism has not produced such a work, though an almost textbook example of this approach—albeit a not very radical one—can be found in John Conklin's designs for Wagner's Ring Cycle at the San Francisco Opera (1983–84).[13] In a way, Conklin is closest in spirit to the architects generally associated with the postmodern movement. Charles Jencks in *What Is Post-Modernism?* notes that the "enjoyment of difference" that is so typical of the postmodern sensibility leads to a style whose content "is the past seen with irony or displacement. . . . We now have the luxury of inhabiting successive worlds as we tire of each one's qualities."[14] This could well describe Conklin's 1983 setting of Valhalla in *Das Rheingold*. The facade of Valhalla was depicted as an amalgam of four eighteenth- and nineteenth-century architectural sources. The base was modeled after a section of a women's prison; above this was a re-creation of an eighteenth-century idealistic project by Etienne-Louis Boulee; the midsection was based on Leo von Klenze's Konigstor, a neoclassical version of the Propylaea; and the whole thing was topped off by a copy of Gottfried Semper's Dresden Opera House.

The implications and repercussions are stunning. First of all, the collec-

1. Model of Valhalla in *Das Rheingold,* San Francisco Opera, 1999 revival designed by John Coyne, based on original 1983 design by John Conklin. The upper section is based on the Dresden Opera House, the midsection on Leo von Klenze's Konigstor in Munich (itself based on the Propylaea), and the base is modeled on a nineteenth-century women's prison. (Photo courtesy San Francisco Opera.)

tion of architecture is an anthology of sorts of nineteenth-century German sensibility—in other words, the environment in which Wagner worked and created the opera—so the production is immediately rooted in historical ground without any attempt at an "historically accurate" setting. Semper was not only an architect, but played a crucial role in preserving Wagner's career following the Revolution of 1848, so the reference to Semper has connections to Wagner the man as well as to the opera. The Dresden Opera House was destroyed in World War II, and thus the representation makes reference to Germany's more recent history and the appropriation of Wagner by the Nazis while at the same time providing an obvious image for the destruction of Valhalla. The references to prisons, visionary architecture, and the classical world, of course, reverberate within the context of the Ring Cycle. Finally, Conklin's arrangement of architectural elements results in an opera house sitting atop a fort. "The gods," explains Conklin, "live over a fort in an 'opera house' because they are 'opera singers.' Valhalla symbolically is a set!"[15] So the gods, who are depicted through opera and are, of course, impersonated by opera singers, are placed within a replica of an opera house that resembles a heavenly palace, all set within a real opera house. The set reverberates with references to opera-as-opera, stage-as-stage, to the historical and social context of the work and the composer, and so on. Ironically, these references may escape the viewer since the unity and style of Conklin's setting may strike many spectators simply as an unidentifiable classical facade of some kind. Even those who may recognize the Dresden Opera are unlikely to recognize all the other references. But the quotations and connections are important to Conklin and, he claims, give the work an enhanced "power." Just as no one can see a Wagnerian opera (or any historical theatrical work, for that matter) in a sociopolitical or cultural vacuum, the designer cannot present a "pure" or virginal setting.

A more blatant juxtaposition of images and references occurred in Robert Israel's design for the same opera cycle three years later at the Seattle Opera. In his *Siegfried,* the forest was painted on flats, and as Fafner strode through the forest, the flats fell over. Israel believes that a central theme in contemporary theater is the tension between illusion and reality (which he sees as an implicit metaphor for moral struggle), and this concept is fully exploited in this conceit. In Israel's design, this nineteenth-century opera used the nineteenth-century technique of painted scenery. Yet in the contemporary world it is virtually impossible to fool anyone through scenography; even the most cleverly done trees are perceived as signs of trees. Nonetheless, the audience can delight in the illusion or at the naïveté of illusion. The act of the falling flats is like the magician showing us how the trick is done, or like the puppeteer removing the screen so as to expose the strings; the mechanics once exposed only serve to reinforce the illusion while seemingly admitting the spectator into the world of the manipulator. Everyone acknowledges the illusion; everyone knows that everyone knows. And yet, in this case, the falling trees/flats functioned as metaphor. Fafner is powerful, and in the midst of theatrical delight there is a real sense of danger. Where Conklin's set could be seen as postmodern in its careful amalgamation of architectural and scenic styles and periods, Israel's becomes postmodern in its blend of illusion with the destruction of illusion.

An alternative approach can be seen in the work of West German choreographer Pina Bausch, who imports "real" objects into the stage world, thereby reducing them to signs.[16] In *1980,* for instance, the large stage floor was covered with sod that was actually watered during the course of the performance, filling the auditorium with the damp smell of suburban lawns. In *Arien* she covered the entire stage with two inches of water. Such elements affect movement and rhythm no less than Appia's rhythmic steps. At the same time, of course, the semiotic understanding of the elements is thrown askew; the phrase *organic unity* takes on mind-boggling repercussions in such a context. The water or the grass is "real"; the performers do not act *as if* they were walking through these elements—they *are* walking through them. Yet the settings do not represent a lawn or a river; they represent a stage covered with "found" objects that may evoke any number of associations in the minds of the spectators. Historically, stage design has asked the spectator either to suspend disbelief (in post-Renaissance illusionistic theater) or to accept the stage as an essentially neutral, though perhaps emblematic and special, place. Certain modern designs have tried to combine the two tendencies, but much postmodern design seems to thwart both processes. Found (i.e., real) objects are placed on the stage, yet the framing device of the stage does not permit the spectator to view the object as object or the stage as stage. Normal perceptual mechanisms are circumvented. The stage is stripped of its vocabulary (or at least its conventional Western vocabulary) so that a reading of signs consistent with an understanding of the concrete world outside the stage becomes difficult if not impossible. The result is akin to what Jameson calls "the waning of affect" in which "all feeling or emotion, all subjectivity, has vanished."[17]

The historical roots of postmodern design can be traced back at least to the production of Alfred Jarry's *Ubu Roi* at the Theatre de l'Oeuvre in 1896. In his preshow speech to the audience Jarry described the set they were about to see. "We have a perfect decor," he stated,

> for just as one good way of setting a play in Eternity is to have revolvers shot off in the year 1000, you will see doors open on fields of snow under blue skies, fireplaces furnished with clocks and swinging wide to serve as doors, and palm trees growing at the foot of a bed so that little elephants standing on bookshelves can browse on them.[18]

The scenery, painted by Jarry, Pierre Bonnard, Édouard Vuillard, Toulouse-Lautrec, and Sérusier, was further described by Arthur Symons:

> The scenery was painted to represent, by a child's conventions, indoors and out of doors, and even the torrid, temperate, and arctic zones at once. Opposite you, at the back of the stage, you saw apple trees in bloom, under a blue sky, and against the sky a small closed window and a fireplace . . . through the very midst of which . . . trooped in and out the clamorous and sanguinary persons of the drama. On the left was

painted a bed, and at the foot of the bed a bare tree and snow falling. On the right there were palm trees . . . a door opened against the sky, and beside the door a skeleton dangled.[19]

The grotesqueness of the imagery, the juxtapositions of objects, and the collage of chronological periods would seem to qualify this famous production as the first postmodern design a mere three years after Appia's first published work. Perhaps all that keeps *Ubu* from achieving this status is the use, primarily, of painted scenery in an essentially illusionistic, if illogical, manner, just as the storyline of the play, though grotesque, is a fairly straightforward narrative. Both plot and decor preserved, in their own fantastic ways, the essential unity, harmony, and moral structure of nineteenth-century drama and production.

As with so much else, precedent can also be found in the work of the dadas. Although much of their work involves incongruity and juxtaposition, a particularly coherent example can be seen in the late dada ballet *Rélâche*. The Erik Satie–Francis Picabia piece, performed by the Ballets Suédois, included, among other things, a wall of silver disks acting as reflectors for lightbulbs, a tableau vivant recreation of Lucas Cranach's *Adam and Eve,* and René Clair's film *Entr'acte.*

A more theoretical framework, however, can be found in the work of Bertolt Brecht, whose maxim, "Show that you are showing," embodied the scenographic approach to his alienation effect.[20] While Brecht acknowledged and even emphasized the need for aesthetic beauty on the stage, and often stated his love for particular images and objects, the basic aim of his alienation technique was to distance the spectator from the event in order that the viewer might reach decisions about the problems raised in the play. "It's more important these days," wrote Brecht in the mid-1920s, "for the set to tell the spectator he's in a theatre than to tell him he's in, say, Aulis."[21] Scenographically this was achieved through the use of techniques that would not allow the spectator to become enmeshed in an illusionistic world. The lighting instruments, the scenic elements, the structures were to be shown. Furthermore, there was a mixture of detailed realism in props and costumes with emblematic settings. In an essay on the pictures of Brueghel, Brecht noted that Brueghel combined incongruous and contradictory elements but in so doing was able to reinforce the themes of the painting, not distract from them. "Whenever an Alpine peak is set down in a Flemish landscape," Brecht noted, "or old Asiatic costumes confront modern European ones, then the one denounces the other and sets off its oddness, while at the same time we get landscape as such, people all over the place. Such pictures don't just give off an atmosphere but a variety of atmospheres. Even though Brueghel manages to balance his contrasts he never merges them into one another."[22] The desirability, even necessity, of conflating images is reinforced in a later essay in which Brecht notes that modern knowledge forces us to see history in different ways: "The farmer was not aware throughout the centuries of his need or potential need for a Ford car. The rapid social and economic development of our period alters the audience swiftly and radically, demanding and facilitating ever new modes of thought, feeling and behavior."[23] Here seems to be justification for a major tenet of postmodernism—the juxtaposition of historical periods achieved in this case through the introduction of icons of contemporary society in the world of the classical production. Russian-born designer George Tsypin would seem to reinforce this view. "Straightforward updating offends me," he explains, but

> when we look at paintings from the Renaissance period, we see all the biblical characters painted in Renaissance clothes; in medieval manuscripts you can see all the characters wearing medieval clothes. We live in a period in which all the myths and all classical literature is treated that way—as if it is happening right now. That is partially the reason that design seems to be a mix of different languages. In my designs I try to achieve a certain fusion of different elements. It's not just a juxtaposition of different styles.[24]

This can be seen again in Tsypin's design for JoAnne Akalaitis's production of *Leon and Lena (and Lenz)*, adapted from Georg Büchner's play *Leonce and Lena* and his story "Lenz" at Minneapolis's Guthrie Theater. Although an early-nineteenth-century story, it was reconceived in terms of a young man from a rich family "on the road." The locale became the Midwest, and a highway jutting out from the back of the stage and projecting over the auditorium became a dominant image. German romanticism became entangled with images of American loneliness—the classic open highway (complete with a sunset) and Jack Kerouac. In a similar vein, Tsypin created a mysterious setting for Peter Sellars's production of *The Count of Monte Cristo*. Strange black objects that continually moved about the stage, spewing out and swallowing up performers and later combining to form a ship, were actually Napoleonic armoires.

Further influences on the development of postmodern design can be found in the works of John Cage and Richard Foreman. In an interview in 1965 Cage was asked how he would present classical theater today. He responded that he thought of "past literature as material rather than as art."

> Our situation as artists is that we have all this work that was done before we came along. We have the opportunity to do work now. I would not present things from the past, but I would approach them as materials available to something else which we were going to do now. They could enter, in terms of collage, into any play. . . . Now as material it can be put together with other things. They could be things that don't connect with art as we conventionally understand it.[25]

Cage had been using this approach of quoting past art in a collagelike framework long before this statement. His musical compositions and his theoretical writings and teachings were crucial in the development of Happenings in the late 1950s, and his work with choreographer Merce Cunningham had a profound effect on developments in modern and postmodern dance. For the Cunningham dances, Cage's music and Robert Rauschenberg's designs were generally created with no reference to the choreography—the three elements were combined in performance. Consequently, the methodology and the final results were as far from the Appia-Craig model as possible. Cage-inspired Happenings (also influenced by dada, Bauhaus, and Antonin Artaud, among others) frequently used found objects for their scenography and action with the result often being a collagelike rendering of contemporary culture, though generally without any ostensible social, political, or literary intention. Nonetheless, it had profound effects on both art and theater and helped to release theatrical design from a single-minded, metaphor-bound, imagistic approach.

An example of this idea of quotation (though one that Cage would undoubtedly find too contrived and self-consciously artistic) may be seen in the concept for a 1989 production of Brecht's *Mahagonny* directed by Jonathan Miller. As described by the designer by Robert Israel, the boxing ring walls were to have murals based on Giotto's *Massacre of the Innocents*. While the image of dead babies in the Renaissance mural clearly related to the death in the boxing ring of Brecht's play, the quotation of the Giotto, Israel believed, was "also, on some level, a defacing of the Giotto, because it is placed in a boxing ring." The mural was "defaced" even further by tracing compositional diagrams—such as the ones found in art books—over the figures, and in some cases overlaying new diagrams on top of this. "It becomes a real defacing of the art in every way," continued Israel, "and a defacing of the illusion because it is a wall decoration. At one point part of it is replaced by an upside down picture of Chairman Mao which is also defaced."[26] The production is not a quote in the sense of creating a decor "in the style of . . ." It is a reverberant reference to styles of art, periods of history, and human events that still functions as scenic decoration. Furthermore, it forces the audience to be aware of technique (i.e., presentation) as well as content.

Richard Foreman, who was one of the most innovative and influential avant-garde theater artists of the late 1960s and 1970s, embodied most of the concepts of postmodern design in his original works staged in his loft and similar off-off-Broadway spaces. On a basic level, Foreman's scenography is "ugly." This is not meant facetiously. The homemade quality of his sets and the generally somber colors were a conscious attempt to thwart the usual slickness of commercial production, which, he felt, lulled the audience into a complacency. In true Brechtian fashion this "showing" of the techniques and materials of the setting kept the spectator from entering the scene and denied traditional aesthetic pleasures. A notable element of Foreman's scenography was the juxtaposition of incongruous elements and the mixture of objects of wildly differing scales. In addition, embedded within a particular setting could often be found smaller versions of the set (or sets already seen or soon to be seen). These might be painted on walls or exist as models placed at points within the set. Thus, the spectator was allowed to view the same space from various perspectives and in different ways, and even in a sense to move through time not by narrative device but through visual manipulations and juxtapositions, all while remaining in a fixed location. Scenographic techniques were borrowed from the Renaissance and baroque theater, notably the use of a sort of wing-and-groove scenery, and reference to historic theater was reinforced by the use of a print of the Mnemonic Theatre of 1617 in his advertising posters. Finally, Foreman employed framing devices. While sound, light, and gesture were often used to frame an action, object, or image, the stage was often filled with literal frames that evoked Renaissance paintings while at the same time segmenting and focusing spectator attention. The proscenium-style arrangement of most of his productions allowed an amazing control and manipulation of space, depth, and focus. Foreman set out to accomplish no less than a nearly total revision of modes of perception learned by most audiences through the whole modern tradition of Western theater.

When Foreman began creating his own theater in 1968, the reaction against the proscenium that had been brewing for nearly a century was reaching its apex. Much of the most significant and innovative theater of the twentieth century had involved explorations of nonproscenium space: thrust, arena, annular, and environmental. The twentieth-century *metteur en scène* has attempted to create a three-dimensional environment that would replicate the "real" world or would physically implicate the spectator in the stage experience. Foreman's aggressively frontal mise-en-scène was thus seen at the time as almost reactionary (though nothing else about his productions were). However, virtually all postmodern design has been frontal, if not actually proscenium. (Several postmodern productions have been mounted by Liviu Ciulei, Andrei Serban, and Foreman, among others, at the thrust-stage Guthrie Theater and the theater-in-the-round of Washington, D.C.'s Arena Stage.) Postmodern design, at least so far, has been pictorial design. Nonproscenium production tends to suggest a connection between the world of the stage and the world of the auditorium and, by implication, the world beyond. Such staging implies continuity and sameness between image and viewer. But postmodern design is discontinuous and requires a perceptual interruption. In order for the image-design to have an impact, however, the contrasting elements must be connected in the mind of the viewer. Thus, somewhat like the Brueghel pictures that Brecht described, they need the unity and cohesion of a frame to encompass them. It is no coincidence that many of the postmodern designers frequently refer back to the Renaissance, a period in which the scientific desire for unity clashed with an appetite for diversity and a delight in incongruity. The single frame of the late-Renaissance proscenium arch sequentially enclosed the world of neoclassical tragedy and the multiplicity of fantastic images of mythological and allegorical intermezzi within an evening's performance. But where Renaissance stage design was suffused with a contemporary sensibility, multiple periods, styles, or genres were relatively discrete, though ultimately unified and encompassed by a single frame. Postmodern design tends to blend all periods, styles, and genres within a momentary image within a single frame. (A costume with a period silhouette but made of contemporary fabrics is a common device; anachronistic props are employed; contemporary expressions or gestures enter into classical dialogue, etc.)

Nonetheless, postmodern design keeps a certain distance; it requires a viewer, not a participant; it is often ironic. It may be possible to achieve this in a nonproscenium environment, but postmodernism is inherently theatrical, and the proscenium (or proscenium-like arrangement) remains the prime semiotic embodiment of theatricality in our visual vocabulary. It provides the best forum for "the dialectical examination of the problematics of seeing," as Foreman stated. What remains unclear, however, is whether these postmodern characteristics constitute a style of design. Jameson claims that in pastiche "stylistic innovation is no longer possible, all that is left is to imitate dead styles."[27] The bold designs of Israel, Tsypin, Adrianne Lobel, Michael Yeargan, and others are certainly more than mere imitations and pastiche, but it is difficult to state categorically what their style is. It is, though, most definitely different from what has constituted modern design.

Notes

1. Fredric Jameson, "Postmodernism and Consumer Society," in *Postmodernism and Its Discontents,* ed. E. Ann Kaplan (London: Verso, 1988), 17.

2. Jean-François Lyotard, *The Postmodern Condition: A Report on Knowledge,* trans. Geoff Bennington and Brian Massumi (Minneapolis: University of Minnesota Press, 1984), xxiii.

3. Charles Russell, "The Context of the Concept," in *Romanticism, Modernism, Postmodernism,* ed. Harry R. Garvin (Lewisburg, Pa.: Bucknell University Press, 1980), 192.

4. See, among others, Ihab Hassan, "Toward a Concept of Postmodernism," in *The Postmodern Turn* (Columbus: Ohio State University Press, 1987), 84–96.

5. Edward Gordon Craig, *The Art of the Theatre* (London: William Heinemann, 1911), 22.

6. Denis Bablet, "Edward Gordon Craig and Scenography," *Theatre Research* 11.1 (1971): 11.

7. Mordecai Gorelik, *New Theatres for Old* (New York: Samuel French, 1949), 179–80.

8. Hassan, "Concept of Postmodernism," 91.

9. Laura Crow, interview by the author, June 28, 1989.

10. Will Crutchfield, "The Triumphs and Defeats in Sellars's Mozart," *New York Times,* July 25, 1989, national ed., 11.

11. Quoted in Linda Hutcheon, *A Poetics of Postmodernism: History, Theory, Fiction* (New York: Routledge, 1988), 20.

12. Jameson, "Postmodernism and Consumer Society," 16.

13. The work of Robert Wilson is sometimes classified as postmodern, and his production of *Einstein on the Beach* (1976) is sometimes cited as a crossover work that introduced a wider audience to his style. But Wilson's scenography, more than most, is a true theater of images. The pictures, though sometimes bizarre or surreal (he was acclaimed by former surrealist Louis Aragon as the heir to that tradition), are strikingly beautiful. They are, furthermore, self-contained and generally self-referential. Moreover, rather than alienating, the work is mesmerizing, often inducing a trancelike state in the audience. The image within the frame of a Wilson production is highly structured and complete and rarely refers overtly to any other work of theater or art. His productions, in fact, can be seen as a culmination of the theories of Gordon Craig. Even Wilson's work with Heiner Müller might be viewed, not as an example of postmodern design, but as the creation of a container in which a postmodern play sits (surprisingly comfortably).

14. Charles Jencks, *What Is Post-Modernism?* (New York: St. Martin's Press, 1986), 56.

15. Arnold Aronson, *American Set Design* (New York: Theatre Communications Group, 1985), 19–20.

16. German design has been a major influence on postmodern design, just as the designs of the Berliner Ensemble were a major influence on American design in the 1960s.

17. Fredric Jameson, "Postmodernism; or, The Cultural Logic of Late Capitalism," *New Left Review* 146 (July–August 1984): 61.

18. Roger Shattuck, *The Banquet Years,* rev. ed. (New York: Vintage, 1968), 206.

19. Shattuck, *The Banquet Years,* 207.

20. Bertolt Brecht, "Showing Has to Be Shown," trans. John Willett, in *Poems, 1913–1956,* ed. John Willett and Ralph Manheim with the cooperation of Erich Fried (New York: Methuen, 1976), 341.

21. John Willett, *Caspar Neher: Brecht's Designer* (London: Methuen, 1986), 98.

22. *Brecht on Theatre,* ed. and trans. John Willett (New York: Hill and Wang, 1964), 157.

23. *Brecht on Theatre,* 159–60.

24. George Tsypin, interview by the author, June 22, 1989.

25. Michael Kirby and Richard Schechner, "An Interview with John Cage," *Tulane Drama Review* 10.2 (1965): 53.

26. Robert Israel, interview by the author, June 23, 1989.

27. Jameson, "Postmodernism and Consumer Society," 18.

One Hundred Years of Stage Lighting
Why We Cannot Light as Appia Did

> Daylight is not at our command. Although we can dim it (drapes, colored glass, etc.) we cannot control daylight itself and modify its proportions at will. We must, therefore, turn to artificial light created by ourselves, i.e., stage lighting. For our eyes, this light is to the simple light of day what, for our ears, the art of sounds is to shouting. It will be the aesthetic ruler of brightness—capable of modifying its vibrations.
>
> —Adolphe Appia, "Eurhythmics and Light," 1912

> Now, God be praised, that to believing souls
> Gives light in darkness, comfort in despair!
> —Shakespeare, *King Henry VI, Part 2*

The images we create upon the stage are inevitably codified reflections of the world around us, and thus informed by contemporary sensibilities. The conventions and scenic techniques developed by theater artists at any given moment in history are employed to create a theatrical milieu that we in the audience accept as a sign or representation of our environment. The scenic illusionism of the nineteenth century, for instance, was, among other things, an inevitable product of the industrial and scientific revolutions, the growth of antiquarian studies, and a concomitant fascination with technology and spectacle. The subsequent abstract and symbolic scenography of Adolphe Appia and Edward Gordon Craig in the late nineteenth and early twentieth centuries, on the other hand, was a reflection of new psychological explorations of the inner workings of the mind, a discovery of Asian arts and philosophies that emphasized the spiritual and the emblematic, and new developments in scientific inquiry that would soon lead to attempts to explain the cosmos as part of a unified system.

Presented at the conference "Aspects of Theatre Lighting since Adolphe Appia," Amsterdam, November 1993; published (in German) in *Bühnentechnische Rundschau,* October 1994.

Light is obviously a part of the visual environment of the stage and a powerful, if often subtle, factor in spectators' overall perceptions of the theatrical event. While much of the history of stage lighting, of course, is integrally tied to developments in technology, lighting, no less than scenography, is informed by shifting perceptions of the everyday world. The way in which we light the stage is indicative of how we see light in our daily lives. The theoretical and aesthetic approaches to stage lighting developed by Appia were inevitably shaped and controlled by the way in which he and his late-nineteenth-century contemporaries perceived light. Appia's singular genius lay in his ability to take the new technology, electric lighting, and use it as the primary tool of his new artistic vision that would transform the stage for the next century. Ironically, while the technology of producing light has not changed significantly in the past one hundred years, the way in which we see has altered radically. We no longer see the world as Appia saw it. Consequently, we can no longer light the stage in the way that he did.

The new technology allowed the stage designer to replicate the diffuse light (and shadows) and angles of sunlight, to suggest the effects created by man-made light fixtures and to generate well-controlled special effects. Even in the nontheatrical world of everyday life, the new electric lighting attempted to duplicate the angles and intensity of the sun. In such an environment, something like footlights became anathema; they were seen as an unnatural form of lighting that defied logic and offended the sensibilities. There was no equivalent of footlights in the natural world, hence they became an anachronism on the electrified stage. Semiotically, they became unreadable; they could not be understood as a sign for any form of recognizable extratheatrical lighting—and thus they shattered the fragile illusionism of the stage and disrupted what Appia called "organic unity." The fundamental basis of Appia's lighting reform emerged from an attempt to create a scenographic vocabulary that matched, at least on an emblematic level, the perceived structures of the natural order. In his "Comments on the Staging of *The Ring of the Nibelungs*" (1891–92) Appia stated:

> the current use of fixed footlights must be irrevocably done away with and replaced by portable strip lights completely subordinated to lighting from above with the single aim of creating artificially the *diffused light* of day. . . . For exterior settings, the light will *always* come *from above* save for some few exceptions; the height of the characters is taken as the maximum angle and all comes from the same direction. For the interior setting the light will enter very obviously through the openings (never hor-

izontally) reinforced extremely subtly by footlights or by special instruments to provide diffused light.[1]

These guidelines would become systematized and codified in the United States by Stanley McCandless and put into practice by Jean Rosenthal and Abe Feder and serve as the basis for several generations of designers. I quote this passage not because of the emphasis on footlights but because Appia proposed a system of stage lighting that mimicked natural light by emanating from identifiable sources at logical angles in a relation to human beings. It was a radical idea. But the world that he mimicked—those perceptions—no longer exist. Even daylight, which Appia (as quoted above) suggests we cannot significantly control, is different than it was a century ago.

As an audience we learn how to read light on the stage just as we learn how to read any stage convention, from the irrational placement of furniture in a naturalistic box set to the emblematic colors of Beijing Opera and the mudras of Kathakali. Just as we in the West have learned to accept both box sets and fragmented walls as differing signs for realistic interiors, so have we have learned to accept warm and cool colors, forty-five-degree angles, backlighting, accents, and so on as realistic lighting emanating from plausible and motivated sources. But just as an uninitiated Westerner, say, may find the semiotics of Noh or Kathakali unfathomable because they are based on alien cultures, values, and perceptions, I contend that we have a generation for whom the semiotics of lighting in our own theater is equally bewildering. The rules that were formulated by Appia and systematized by McCandless make little sense in our light-saturated world.

When Adolphe Appia first began to consider how light could transform the stage in the 1880s, and when he began to write about it in the 1890s, humankind saw the world differently. Light and darkness were still inexorable powers that shaped the rhythms and patterns of everyday life in a way that seems almost primitive to us today. Consider, for example, the startling fact that in Appia's day it was still possible to see stars in the heavens even in the most urban cities of Europe and America; and by traveling only a short distance into the countryside one could be immersed in the utter darkness of night. By contrast, there are few places in the contemporary industrialized world in which the night sky is not polluted by the glow of lights from cities, highways, shopping centers, factories, airports, stadiums, and virtually every aspect of modern life. In the early 1990s, for example, Mt. Wilson Observatory in southern California, one of the major astronomical observatories in the United States, was faced with the prospect of closing because the nearby city of San Diego was contemplating a new street lighting system whose glow would virtually obliterate Mt. Wilson's view of the night sky.

Our ancestors, as recently as two or three generations ago, were as familiar with the night sky as we are with, say, television; they knew the phases and movements of the planets, stars, and moon and could tell the time, the seasons, and navigate by these elements. How many people today can identify constellations, differentiate between planets and stars, or identify the seasons by the location of these bodies? Humankind seems to have an intrinsic need not merely to illuminate the darkness but to eliminate it. "Lighten our darkness, we beseech thee, O Lord; and by thy great mercy defend us from all perils and dangers of this night," reads an evening prayer from the *Book of Common Prayer*. Similarly, this plaintive cry from the Brihadaranyaka Upanishad: "Lead me from the unreal to the real! / Lead me from the darkness to the light! / Lead me from death to immortality!" Poet Dylan Thomas may have "rage[d] against the dying of the light," but all we need do is flip a switch. However, in the process of eradicating night we have lost yet another link with the natural rhythms of the cosmos; we have severed our connection with the natural darkness that, by rights, should occupy some half our lives.[2]

What have these observations to do with stage lighting? The art of lighting began as an attempt to replicate the natural light of the sun that illuminated performances from ancient times through the Renaissance. It began as an attempt to brighten the gloomy interiors of Renaissance theaters and to enhance the spectacle of nighttime festivals at court. But if light is the antithesis of darkness, if lighting design is the transformation of invisibility into magical visibility, then how does one learn to light the stage in a world in which darkness does not exist? *Without darkness we cannot see the light.*

In Appia's time, so-called artificial light (what an odd term!) was still something special. Its very existence was reason enough to notice it. In theaters that we would consider pits of darkness—even Appia commented that "our stage is normally a dim and undefined space"[3]—observers commented on the brightness, the effects, the "reality" of artificial light. When Richard D'Oyly-Carte first introduced electric light in the auditorium of London's Savoy Theatre in October 1881, a newspaper story related that "as if by the wave of a fairy's wand the theatre immediately became filled with a soft, soothing light, clearer and far more graceful than gas. . . . [The audience] gave a cheer."[4] A few months later, when D'Oyly-Carte introduced electric light to the stage itself, the *Times* noted that "the effect was pictorially superior to gas, the colours of the dresses . . . appearing as true and distinct as by daylight."[5]

But even in the everyday world it was not all that long ago that night-time lighting was sufficiently unique that it could attract spectators the way moths are attracted to flames. As recently as the 1960s new stores announced their openings and drew in customers by mimicking Hollywood premieres: searchlights swept the skies, and the curious came from miles around to find the source of the light and to see what certainly must be a special event, for why else would such light be used? Today, in a world saturated in a brilliant luminescence, such effects would barely be visible amid the competing stimuli, and even if they were noticed, they would hardly pass the threshold of curiosity.

We now live in a world in which the most banal enterprises employ flashing, moving, dancing lights in a profusion of colors, a world in which laser light shows no longer raise an eyebrow, a world in which stasis is anathema and the senses are no longer stimulated but assaulted. The once miraculous fantasy of lights that made up such attractions as Times Square, Piccadilly Circus, and Coney Island, the sort of display that, as the Italian futurists demonstrated, could inspire an avant-garde movement, is now unremarkable. "Fire + fire + light against moonlight and against old firmaments war every night," proclaimed Filippo Tommaso Marinetti, in his futurist manifesto, "The Variety Theatre."

> great cities to blaze with electric signs. . . . electric signs dim die under a dark stiff hand come to life again continue to stretch out in the night the human day's activity courage + folly never to die or cease or sleep electric signs = formation and disaggregation of mineral and vegetable center of the earth. . . . transformation of the streets into splendid corridors to guide push logic necessity the crowd toward trepidation + laughter = music hall uproar. . . . tubes of mercury red red red blue violet huge letter-eels of gold purple diamond fire Futurist defiance to the weepy night the stars defeat warmth enthusiasm faith conviction will power penetration of an electric sign into the house across the street.[6]

The energy and technology that Marinetti exalted in 1913 now exists in rock concerts, music videos, video arcades, and even shopping malls, in the frenetic rhythms of television commercials, and the seductive cadences of Hollywood's techno-ballets of slaughter and mayhem. For the generations raised on the flickering light-box known as television, for a generation attuned to the pulsating assault of discos and MTV and anesthetized by the frantic pace of image-driven films, how are the comparatively tame images of a stage play or even a musical possibly to be comprehended? Although even a simple, single-set drama may now employ several hundred lighting instruments and modulate through dozens of computer-controlled light cues, the visual language hardly registers on the benumbed retinas of contemporary audiences. The relatively static and monochromatic lighting typical of most stage dramas is virtually below the threshold of visibility.

In a 1912 essay Appia seemed to warn of this danger. "First of all," he explained, "we shall learn that, merely 'to make visible,' is not to light in this sense at all, and that, on the contrary, in order to be creative or plastic, light must be an atmosphere, a luminous atmosphere."[7] A few years later he proposed that "like the actor, light must become active."[8]

Though Appia's scenography was in part a response to the pictorial realism and naturalism of the nineteenth century, the Appian approach and the naturalistic aesthetic were related through much of the twentieth century. In order to sculpt space—that is, create the illusion of three-dimensional space within the cubic framework of the proscenium stage—light had to obey the rules of nature. As his comments on the Ring suggest, source and directionality still prevailed within the semiabstract sphere of Appian light-space. In general, light on the stage, whether in a naturalistic context or in an abstract setting, created the illusion of light from a knowable source that obeyed the rules not only of physics but of ordinary human observation.

But ordinary observation today reveals a different order. In a city of skyscrapers, for instance, where does light come from? Light is reflected at bizarre angles off glass-skinned buildings. City dwellers may find themselves in shadow or darkness at midday because natural light is blocked by man-made structures, while at night they may be bathed in light as bright as that from the sun. From discos, to airport walkways, to shopping malls, to hotel atriums and chic restaurants, to the grotesquely theatrical world of Las Vegas nightclubs and casinos, lighting emanates from "unnatural" angles, from hidden or invisible sources, and, increasingly, from beneath the floor. Moreover, it moves. Thus, architects and illuminating engineers in our culture have obliterated any true sense of darkness and our ability to comprehend it, while simultaneously eliminating logical and knowable motivation from lighting. And yet this approach to light is so commonplace in our society that we seldom pay any heed. It is significant, I think, that the leading design textbook in the United States begins its section on lighting with this sentence: "While each one of us reacts to our environment in a unique manner, it is generally true that *we take light and lighting for granted*" (emphasis added).[9] Light is no longer associated with day nor with experiential sources.

Interestingly, the more-or-less neutral space of platforms, steps, black drapes, and open stage inspired by Appia as the perfect environment for his "organic unity" has become the source of a disjunctive, discordant, nonharmonious system of light. In this Appian stage space that was exploited by expressionism and embraced by modern dance—a stage space that became emblematic of twentieth-century theatrical performance—light has become the most visible, most dynamic, and most compelling force; it even, on occasion, surpasses the performer. Largely because of modern dance, light has drifted from its moorings, as it were. It is no longer tied to motivational sources but has taken on a physical force, making it a performer within the dance. Light is a force that draws dancers toward it; it is a force that pushes dancers across a stage; a wall of light may act as resistance against a dancer or create a sort of curtain through which the audience must struggle to see.

Almost any production nowadays, whether dance, opera, musical theater, or drama, reveals lighting design practices that would have been incomprehensible only a few years ago. Instead of the wash of light that permeated the stage (with appropriate accents and highlights), we now encounter high-contrast lighting and selected visibility. A performer may be illuminated in the midst of total or partial darkness; details are selected out and highlighted while all else is concealed. Backlight, no longer purely functional, has now become an end in itself, a visible element of the stage picture. Building upon the innovations of Josef Svoboda, smoke or mist is often employed so that very long, narrow, diagonal shafts of backlight may be seen. We have what the late lighting designer Richard Nelson described as shafts of light "blazing against darkness."

We are in a world of postmodern lighting. Just as postmodern scenography derives from an amalgam of elements drawn from historical sources, theatrical images, and the kaleidoscopic content of the everyday world presented in a panhistorical, omnistylistic pastiche, postmodern lighting is a veritable cauldron of lighting techniques placed in the service of a production. From the time of Appia until the near present, light was the subtle thread that guided us through the narrative structure or unified discourse of the theatrical work of art; the lighting designer in a sense was our Virgil, guiding us through the darkness. But in postmodern design, light on the stage obeys the logic of light in urban spaces, of television and cinema, of rock concerts. Light may emphasize juxtaposition and contrast rather than organic unity. Light, in fact, is no longer about unity but about transition. *How* we get from one place or moment to the next has become more important than what it looks like when we are there.

We are, historically, in a period of political and social transition, and lighting design inevitably reflects that sense of instability. It is a light that ebbs and flows, startles and surprises. What we don't see becomes as important as what we do see.

When limelight and the electric arc lamp were introduced, many observers were dismayed by the effects. The critics objected not to the instruments per se, but to the disruption caused by the harsh white light in the midst of the yellow effulgence of the gas-lit stage. A Swedish critic complained about the lighting effects in an 1897 production of Strindberg's *Master Olaf:* "the red light in the first *tableau,* the glaring sunshine after the death of the mother. Here a stagey element was introduced, which seemed brutal, just because it seemed to have so little to do with the rest."[10] This discordant image, so disruptive to fin de siècle sensibilities, might be described by postmodernists as "rupture" or "disjuncture," but this unintentional discontinuity, caused by the use of a still-imperfect technology with no understanding that its aesthetic rules differed from those of gas, has become an intentional aesthetic in late-twentieth- and early-twenty-first-century lighting design.

Compared to the "primitive" technology of one hundred years ago, light on the stage today utilizes computers, electronics, and more efficient lamps. But the method of production would not be unrecognizable to Appia or David Belasco. The very aesthetics (or more properly, lack of aesthetics) of the nineteenth century, however, are now being replicated and exploited in a visually disjunctive manner to create a vision that more accurately reflects the perception of our world. The unmotivated, the inorganic, and the disunified that were unintentional hallmarks of nineteenth-century lighting are now the aesthetic realities of light in the contemporary world.

Notes

1. *Adolphe Appia: Essays, Scenarios, and Designs,* trans. Walther R. Volbach, ed. Richard C. Beacham (Ann Arbor: UMI Research Press, 1989), 94.

2. A recent article in the *New York Times* ("City Lights Alter Rhythm of Life on Long Island Sound," July 29, 2003) noted that the significant amount of light along the Long Island Sound from the northeast megalopolis was disrupting the feeding and mating habits and life cycles of many forms of marine life.

3. "Actor, Space, Light, Painting," Appia 184.

4. Terence Rees, *Theatre Lighting in the Age of Gas* (London: Society for Theatre Research, 1978), 170.

5. *The Times,* December 29, 1881, quoted in Rees, *Theatre Lighting.*

6. Filippo Tommaso Marinetti, "The Variety Theatre," trans. R. W. Flint, in Michael Kirby, *The Futurist Performance* (New York: E. P. Dutton, 1971), 185–86.

7. "Eurhythmics and Light," Appia 150.

8. Appia, "Actor, Space, Light, Painting," 184.

9. W. Oren Parker and R. Craig Wolf, *Scene Design and Stage Lighting,* 6th ed. (Fort Worth: Holt, Rinehart and Winston, 1990), 362.

10. Tor Hedberg, quoted in Gösta M. Bergman, *Lighting in the Theatre* (Totowa, NJ: Rowman and Littlefield, 1977), 276.

New Homes for New Theater

One characteristic of twentieth-century theater has been the search for new forms of theater space, a search born out of the Romantic and avant-garde notion that the past had to be destroyed in order to make way for the new. Since the time of the symbolists in the late 1880s the space of the proscenium stage has been alternately foreshortened and deepened, shrouded with scrims and opened to the very bricks and mortar of the theater itself. The proscenium stage has also been challenged, variously, by thrust and arena configurations and by all aspects of environmental theater. During the first third or so of the twentieth century, in the first flush of the technological age, visionaries proposed spherical theaters, endless theaters, and total theaters, while others suggested placing audiences on moving conveyers, rotating rings, or suspending them on cantilevered platforms. Theater has moved into the street, the factory, onto urban rooftops, open fields, beaches, even the sky and the sea; it has, on occasion, even rediscovered its roots in the marketplace. It has incorporated projected images, movies, television and will, no doubt, incorporate holograms as soon as that technology becomes feasible. Yet for all this, the proscenium still dominates, a relic of the Renaissance. Even in non-Western countries the proscenium—or at least a variant of the end-stage—has frequently supplanted traditional and indigenous stages, thereby creating cumbersome, even ludicrous, marriages of form and content.

The proscenium is, without doubt, the most awkward and irrational stage space ever conceived. Derived in part from the illusionistic painting as well as the need to mask the technology that supported illusion, it functions psychologically and architecturally to distance the spectator, and impedes the involvement of an audience in the act of theater. It creates distorted and obscured sight-lines for all but a few, even in an age in which perspective

From the catalog of "Phenomena: The International Festival of Performance, Puppet, and Visual Theatre," Jerusalem, 1996.

scenery is rarely if ever used. It forces the performers into unnatural configurations whose formality and conventions are appropriate only in certain forms of theater. Why does a form of theater architecture, created in another time, for a different set of circumstances, still dominate? More important, is there an alternative?

We must begin with an understanding of the physics of theater. All theater is composed of the equivalent of molecular building blocks that compose the larger whole. Just as molecules in nature combine in different configurations to create a vast array of elements with differing properties and effects, so too do the molecules of theater combine for diverse results. The fundamental building block of the physical theater is the platform or trestle stage. This is the simple raised platform on which performers act. Its very existence differentiates it from the surrounding space, thereby making it special or even magical. It also determines the audience configuration. Placed in an open space—a field, say, or a market square—it encourages spectators to treat it as an arena stage. Placed against a wall, it becomes a thrust; placed within an existing room, it may become an end-stage. The next step up the molecular ladder, the next level of complexity, is the booth stage, in which a curtained backstage is added to the platform. This simple step has enormous implications. It creates, of course, a hidden space that, semiotically, becomes an ever-changing multiplicity of concealed and implied worlds. A word, a gesture, or an image within this configuration transports the spectator to an entire universe of the imagination. On a simple mechanical level it creates enormous possibilities for the actors in terms of entrances and exits, as well as creating the opportunity for that most fundamental theatrical force: concealment and revelation. It also creates a more frontal relationship with the audience by eliminating any possibility of an arena configuration, and even limiting the thrust arrangement.

All known theater has built upon these elemental structures. Place a booth stage inside an arena and you have the Elizabethan theater; put a platform in a tennis court and you have the Hôtel de Bourgogne; a roofed platform in a hall creates the Noh stage. The environmental theater of the 1960s and 1970s tended to be little more than a series of platform stages scattered through the audience instead of in front of them. Even the futuristic proposals of Frederick Kiesler, Andreas Weininger, Jacques Polieri, and others for spherical theaters consisted of little more than platform stages suspended inside globes.

The fundamentally frontal arrangement of virtually all theaters is almost impossible to avoid; human perception is based upon direct apprehension, and only simultaneity in multispace configurations can subvert this confrontational process. At the same time, frontality functions as a mirror. When we face a stage, we are facing a reflection of ourselves and our society. What distinguishes the theaters of a particular period or culture is the way in which the arrangement of these elements reflects the spatial configurations of the society at large. The world of the Athenians, for instance, centered around the agora. It was a world in which everything—commerce, politics, social interaction—occurred in open air at the heart of the city. It was a society that was, in Hegel's description of the classical, a place "in direct communication with the world of external Nature."[1] The ancient Greek theater evolved in this open, interactive space, and when it was removed to the Acropolis, it maintained its basic configuration and performer-spectator configuration. The center of the Renaissance world, however, at least politically, was to be found in ducal palaces and churches—large, imposing edifices that were closed off to the outside world. Both sorts of edifices accommodated large numbers of people, but these gatherings were in enclosed, dark spaces, usually rectangular in shape (the nave of a church, the great hall of a palace). Hegel, again, is instructive in his description of the Romantic (modern) artwork as addressing itself "to the inward mind, which coalesces with its object simply and as though this were itself. . . . It is this inner world that forms the content of the romantic."[2] In theatrical terms this means that the platform stage is removed from the open air and from the market place—from the truly public sphere—and is situated instead inside a hermetic world.

The Japanese theater that originated in the liminal space of a dry riverbed, the Elizabethan theater that borrowed the site of the bear-baiting pits, the Indian processional performances of the Ramlila that transformed the town into a living theater are all examples of theaters as reflections of the society that spawned them. The physical theaters and the structures of performance are metaphorical and symbolic representations of their time, culture, and society.

While we must acknowledge that some historical structures serve us well in the "culture industry"—the baroque opera house, the nineteenth-century picture-frame proscenium, the thrust stage and flexible-space theater are all essential for the popular performance of museum-quality historical theater forms—we must also acknowledge that these forms are neither representative of our time nor conducive to the creation of contemporary theater. So the question remains: What is? The fantasies of spheres and domes were actually sentimental images of a futuristic age that existed only in literature or art, and fit a popular conception of the world of the future. (They thus served well as theaters for the world's fairs of the first two-thirds of the twentieth century or the utopian dreams of Disney World.) To create alternative or new spaces today based on such romantic imagery will lead only to gimmickry. But if the Theater of Dionysus was a replica of the agora— the "home" of Athenian society—and if the church was the "home" of medieval world, and the great hall the abode of power in the Renaissance, then we must seek our "home." Where does the society of the late twentieth century live? The answer might provide a blueprint for a theater.

I would like to suggest that the home of our society is, in fact, the home, that is, the house. Never before in history has the private home been such a dominant force in architectural aesthetics. It goes beyond the homes of the wealthy and the powerful to incorporate vast segments of the population. Contemporary humanity lives not in the market square or the church or the halls of central authority, but in discrete and often highly individualized homes. Each home is a miniature, segmented universe, its rooms, basements, attics, garages, patios, and porches the equivalents of galaxies, solar systems, nebulae, and intergalactic strings. Each of these microcosms essentially replicates that of its neighbors and its counterparts around the world. Modern society consists of compartmentalized units that, when combined, form neighborhoods, towns, cities, and nations. The philosopher of this world is Gaston Bachelard, whose treatise *The Poetics of Space* is a key to understanding this phenomenon. "The house," he says, "shelters daydreaming, the house protects the dreamer, the house allows one to dream in peace. . . . [It] is one of the greatest powers of integration for the thoughts, memories and dreams of mankind."[3] Isn't this a definition, of sorts, of theater?

The search for new forms of theater space should lead us to the house. I am not, of course, suggesting the simple transference of performance into homes, though this certainly has been done. Rather, we must seek the elements of "homeness" (as Heidegger might say) in theatrical presentation. As Bachelard has noted, each space, each corner of the house has particular associations. Cellars and attics contain mystery, fearsome dark corners, dusty memories. They create a vertical structure of polar opposites. Kitchens are associated with food, nourishment, comfort; parlors or living rooms with family; bedrooms with sleep, sex, loneliness or warmth, fear of the dark or pleasurable dreams, and so on. Our theater is likewise a repository of dreams, emotions, memories, and evocation; it should also be a gathering place for society to come together to dream and remember. But how can one dream in sterile halls whose configuration and decor are echoes of another time, place, and culture? It would be like trying to dream inside someone else's head.

The theater, thus, must seek a physical form that evokes, if not replicates the house. Some theater artists have done this to one degree or another. Japanese director Tadashi Suzuki, when looking for a home for his theater company, sought out an old farmhouse because of its quality of having been lived in, and its connection to the people, society, and land. The Bread and Puppet Theater abandoned New York City in the 1970s to move to a farm in Vermont. Italian director Luca Ronconi created a theater piece in the 1970s called *XX* for which a twenty-room house was constructed in the theater with the audience segmented into different rooms (during the course of the performance walls were removed). Maria Irene Fornes's play *Fefu and Her Friends* is set in a house, and the audience moves from room to room. Many other examples could be cited.

The "house theater" must take into account the compartmentalized structure of the home, its multiple levels both below and above the ground, its sustenance of discrete yet simultaneous activity, its ability to provide absolute privacy or a place for communal celebration, its embracing of all human activity from the sacred to the profane and from the inspired to the banal.

In dealing with the home in contemporary society, acknowledgment must be made of the so-called communications revolution. In the privacy and even solitude of our homes we are connected, via electronic and digital devices, to the entire world. One can communicate with almost anyone in any place at any time; never before has the population of the world been so closely connected while so utterly isolated. The new theater must take into account this means of communication as well as this strange sense of dislocation.

What does the "house theater" look like? It may already exist in the theaters and productions produced in abandoned factories, warehouses, piers, ballrooms, train stations, and the like—the decaying "outbuildings" of a societal farmstead, as it were—evoking the ghosts of the past while creating possible theaters for the future. (The Wooster Group, which employs sophisticated video technology in its theater in a converted industrial garage, is a prime example.) It may exist in the virtual rooms of cyberspace, as in the "online" performances of artists like Laurie Anderson. We have been conditioned to think of theater as a communal event that occurs in a purpose-built structure and that any innovative or new form must look new, that is, futuristic. It must, in other words, resemble a theater that we know, only different. But a new form of theater "merely" has to transform our perceptions by making us see the work in a fresh way. Theater as home, house as theater, may be the way in which that occurs.

Notes

1. G. W. F. Hegel, *Introductory Lectures on Aesthetics,* trans. Bernard Bosanquet (London: Penguin, 1993).

2. Hegel, *Introductory Lectures on Aesthetics,* 87.

3. Gaston Bachelard, *The Poetics of Space,* trans. Maria Jolas (Boston: Beacon Press, 1994), 6.

Theater Technology and the
Shifting Aesthetic

In 1992 the rock group They Might Be Giants issued a compact disc entitled *Apollo 18*. It consisted of seventeen tracks ranging from about one
minute to three and a half minutes in length, plus an additional twenty-one
tracks of one to ten seconds each. In at least one regard I think this particular work was as revolutionary as the Beatles' *Sgt. Pepper's Lonely Hearts Club
Band* was in 1967. (I realize that for someone of my generation that is a blas-
phemous, heretical statement.)

Sgt. *Pepper* was significant not only for its music but because it announced the arrival of the "concept album" in which all the songs were
woven together in what appeared to be a seamless whole. It laid the
groundwork for rock operas while sounding the death knell for old-style
rock 'n' roll. Now, from a musical standpoint, *Apollo 18* broke little ground.
Its tunes have not entered broad public consciousness, and the performers
never became pop icons. But on the liner notes for this album was the nota-
tion, "The indexing of this disc is designed to complement the Shuffle
Mode of modern CD players." In other words, this CD was to be played in
an electronically determined random order; pure chance was to replace
conceptual organization. This is the antithesis of *Sgt. Pepper*. Not only are
we—the artists—it seems to say, *not* determining the order in which you
hear this music, but every hearing of it will be different (up to the statistical
limits, whatever that might be). If modernism is typified by a sense of a
beautiful whole or aesthetic unity, then *Apollo 18* was a stunning declaration
of postmodernism with its elements of rupture, dissociation, and pastiche.
More significantly, however, for the first time in history that I am aware of,
an artist working in the popular culture, willingly, even eagerly, relin-
quished control of the reading and apprehension of the work of art. It may

Presented as the keynote speech at the New England Theatre Conference, November 1996; published in *New England Theatre Journal* 8 (1997).

be argued that the order in which one listens to the tracks on a pop music album is irrelevant, but the fact is that the artists lay down the tracks in a certain order. In the days of that ancient medium of vinyl records or tape, skipping tracks or rearranging the playing order was difficult and could even damage the recording. So, like any good vaudeville show, popular songs were programmed strategically to make sure that you would listen to the whole album. But with the advent of CDs and shuffle mode, the listening audience has been subverting intentional order. From an aesthetic standpoint, this probably has little effect; shuffle mode is mostly employed for dance music or background listening, not for a serious session with *Parsifal,* but it is, nonetheless, a conscious alteration of the artist's intent. In this, John Cage's desire to free the audience from authorial manipulation seems to have been achieved on some level.

Now, let me fantasize about what I might do in this electronic playland. With my multidisc CD player I can arbitrarily mix (or purposefully program) tracks from, say, Miles Davis, the Rolling Stones, Beethoven's Ninth, klezmer music, and Mozart's *Don Giovanni.* While this is playing in the background I get on the World Wide Web and download an image of Leonardo's *Last Supper* that I then proceed to alter by replacing the heads of the disciples with those of the 1996 New York Yankees, whom, let us imagine, I have also downloaded from the Yankees' home page. I then change the whole color palette and send the new image to a friend in China. Next I retire to my "home entertainment center" to watch movies—perhaps some Buster Keaton, *Casablanca,* and Antonioni's *The Passenger.* At various moments I freeze the image, reverse, forward frame by frame, zoom in, adjust the color, change the quality and volume of the sound. I could go on. My version of cyberhell, of course, belies my old-fogeyness both in terms of the content I have chosen and my lack of imagination in terms of what to do with it. The term *polymorphous perversity* pales as an attempt to describe the possibilities of this universe.

But I think it serves to make the point that our relationship to art is in the process of a rapid and radical shift. We used to be trapped in a spatiotemporal framework controlled by the artist and, to a degree, by the producer. To see a work of visual art, for example, I had to go to a museum or at least look in a book, which meant access to a library or bookstore. To see a movie I had to wait for it to appear at a movie theater or on television—in either case, I had to be available at the designated time. A movie seen once might never be seen again. If it became a "classic," it might show up at a revival house, but if not, it was relegated to the vaults of memory. Today, however, I can see virtually any image, read any text, and hear any sound at any time and in almost any place. More importantly, I can rip these works of art out of their frames and restructure them, retexture them, refashion them to suit my taste or my perverse sensibilities. Art is no longer an artist's creation to be seen, observed, savored, pondered, analyzed, critiqued, or even reviled by an audience. It is raw material for the private amusement and constructions of consumers functioning in isolation from each other.

Musical sampling is perhaps the most obvious and blatant example of this phenomenon. Fragmentary quotations of a musical composition are captured—can we say stolen? enslaved? is borrowed, appropriated, or acquired more correct?—and become compositional units within a new piece. This is not the same thing as quoting a motif as homage or inspiration; it is an announcement that the tone, timbre, texture, style, structure, in fact, the very originality of one artist is mere fodder for another. All work is equal; all work is equally available.

Theater, at least by any standard definition, still requires an audience to assemble at a particular place, and time and the ability of the spectators to exert any control over the performance is almost nonexistent; so how does this particular discussion of new technology relate to theater? I would argue that the relationship of technology to the theater is neither direct nor obvious. The mere addition of video monitors or remote tilt-and-pan spotlights—the typical sort of nods toward modern technology in the theater—does not, in and of itself, create new forms of theater. Technology, rather, alters our perceptual mechanisms; it changes the way we see and, more importantly, the way we think. An example may be drawn from one of the landmark American theatrical designs of the last half century, Robin Wagner's setting for *A Chorus Line* in 1975. It consisted entirely of a white line on the floor (and a black surround), capped by a stunning exclamation point of Mylar mirrors in the final scene. To arrive at that apparently simple design took an enormous amount of work and thought, a process of stripping away all that was not essential. In terms of theatrical design I believe it ranks along with John Cage's *4'33"* and Robert Rauschenberg's *White Painting* as revolutionary way stations on the highway of twentieth-century art; it forced a whole reconsideration of the role and function of design and even the visual and spatial properties of the stage. Yet to the casual observer, the design's utter simplicity, other than that last scene, was decidedly "low tech." It was, nonetheless a result of technology. It was a reflection of a new sensibility in which notions of beauty were informed by the aesthetics of technology. This was an era in which sleek exteriors hid miniaturized—and therefore seemingly simplified—technology whose external form no longer gave a hint as to its function. Stereos were housed in matte black boxes or sleek chrome, automobiles were stripped of extravagance and anything that protruded or that appeared merely decorative, buildings were covered in a skin of glass—often dark or reflective. Power came from the invisible. We entered the era of ostentatious nonostentation. High tech and minimalism were one and the same. *A Chorus Line* came almost exactly midway between the first man on the moon and the first personal computer. The white line was not only a barrier to be crossed by would-be chorus members but a threshold of a new technological era.

Too often today producers or directors believe that it takes modern artifacts to make a modern production. This goes back at least to the projections used by Erwin Piscator in the 1920s as well as to the contrivances of nineteenth-century melodrama, not to mention the seventeenth-century machine plays of the French stage. More recently it has shown up in the use of video in theater. In the 1987 London production of *Chess,* for example, also designed by Robin Wagner, two walls of video monitors presented the audience with a panoply of shifting images. They served as an occasionally pleasant distraction from an otherwise unspectacular musical, but they seemed to be little more than a gimmick. For the typical audience, this was simply a reminder of the far more sophisticated world of technology that existed right outside the theater doors. (It should be noted that in the original conception of director Michael Bennett the monitors were a crucial part of the overall concept and the stage was starkly bare. When Bennett became ill, Trevor Nunn took over and introduced furniture and a more literal sensibility into the production. He retained the video monitors but never used them conceptually.)

Piccadilly Circus or Times Square, the Strip in Las Vegas, the Ginza in Tokyo, sections of Hong Kong and Seoul are blazing infernos of brilliant, moving light and images that shift as fast as an eye can blink. In an era in which images from the David Letterman show could be projected over Times Square on the Diamond Vision screen, and then an image of that image rebroadcast to millions of homes on television, thereby creating reverberations of images and audiences, how can a pathetic bank of monitors on a theatrical stage do anything except remind an audience of what it—the stage—is not. At best it is an example of "gee whiz naturalism," as when an actor turns the faucet on the onstage kitchen sink and water comes out and we are somehow awestruck. We are amazed at the banality. Technology on the stage is actually an enactment of absence—it reminds us of the unseen world that now comprises our everyday experience.

If current generations live in a world barraged by overwhelming light, sound, and movement and a dizzying array of mediated imagery, then no wonder the theater, with its simplicity, cannot attract new audiences. The most elaborate Broadway spectacle cannot compete with the technology right outside the theater door in Times Square. But again, it is not merely a matter of fast-paced images or technical gizmos—it is a new way of thinking, a new way of seeing. In semiotics one talks of the reader's or viewer's "competence." You must be able to recognize a sign in order to read it. The stereotypical individual who goes to a museum of modern art or an avant-garde play and responds to the work by saying, "That's not art" or "That's not theater," is not merely expressing conservative taste. Such a "reader" is literally incapable of decoding the sign structure and therefore is incapable of recognizing it as a form of art. Theater, by definition, requires the inter-action between a live actor and a live audience. It is time-bound and space-bound. No matter how fast it moves, it is slower than the cyberkinetic world in which it precariously lives. We have audiences who are no longer com-petent, a generation of spectators who, when they see theater, do not recog-nize what they are seeing. The question, then is not simply *what* can be done about this, but whether anything *should* be done about this. In other words, does one reeducate the audience or reeducate the theatrical creators?

Part of this inability to see comes from a radical shift in the structure of our worldview, a structure now informed by technology. Most theater is still constructed on a linear model, something akin to what the late French philosopher Gilles Deleuze called an arboreal model—a structure, like a tree, based on roots and branches—that is, a hierarchical model in which everything is connected in a particular order and relationship. Deleuze advocated in its place a rhizomatic structure—an ever-expanding network capable of sprouting a complete form at any point, a structure in which no one point is superior to any other, a structure capable of almost infinite replication making eradication difficult if not impossible.

A rhizome doesn't begin and doesn't end, but is always in the middle, between things, inter-being, *intermezzo*. The tree is filiation, but the rhi-zome is alliance, exclusively alliance. The tree imposes the verb "to be," but the rhizome is woven together with conjunctions: "and . . . and . . . and . . ." In this conjunction there is enough force to shake up and uproot the verb "to be." Where are you going? Where are you coming from? What are you driving at? All useless questions. To make a clean slate of it, to start over and over again at zero, to look for a beginning or a foundation—all imply a false conception of voyage and movement (methodological, pedagogical, initiatory, symbolic . . .) But Kleist, Lenz, or Büchner have another way to travel, as if moving or setting off in the

middle, through the middle, entering and leaving, not beginning or end-
ing. . . . The middle is not at all an average—far from it—but the area
where things take on speed. *Between* things does not designate a localiz-
able relation going from one to the other and reciprocally, but a perpen-
dicular direction, a transversal movement carrying away the one *and* the
other, a stream without beginning or end, gnawing away at its two banks
and picking up speed in the middle.[1]

Some recent observers of the cultural scene have seen house music as the
epitome of the Deleuzian world. The component elements of the disc
jockey, the record, the sound equipment, the dancers, the room, and, of
course, the mediated music are inseparable and ultimately indistinguishable.
The dancers losing all sense of self and of boundaries become, in Deleuze's
famous phrase, a "body without organs"[2]—a creation in which ideas can
move freely without the interference of boundaries or hierarchies. Energy
flows through this body, unimpeded and undifferentiated.

The World Wide Web, of course, is a paradigmatic rhizome with its horizontal proliferation of sites expanding exponentially. The Web is a "place"
(such a spatial referent is meaningless in a virtual world) in which home
pages of a local kindergarten, a virtual sex club, the White House, and the
Institute for Medieval Studies are separated by the click of a mouse. (The
very fact that almost anyone who reads this will understand references to
home pages, mouse clicks, and webs suggests that we are in a very different
referential world than we were not so long ago when Edward Albee essentially invented the game of Trivial Pursuit when Martha quoted a Bette
Davis line to open *Who's Afraid of Virginia Woolf?*)

Just as the theocratic worldview of the Middle Ages, neoclassical sci-
entificism in the Renaissance, and the theory of relativity at the start of the
twentieth century all affected the theater of their day, so must this new technology affect us today. But how? Because theater exists in time in the experience of a community within a bounded space, it cannot evaporate into the
ether to be reinspirated through the pores like the Hellenistic concept of
pneuma. Nor, of course, do we have remote controls in the theater. We
enter the theater building, we take our seats, and just as Richard Wagner
desired a century and a half ago, we project ourselves across the mystic
chasm into the ideal world depicted on the stage. And despite the occasional
attempts at such forms as environmental theater, we are still dealing with a
single-focus linear event that bears little resemblance to present-day experience or knowledge.

I think some theater has begun to respond in small ways. Tony Kushner's

Angels in America, for instance, though old-fashioned in its thematic and character approaches, is nonetheless structured around dozens of scenes that function not unlike windows on a computer screen. Any one scene is present beneath the surface of any other, and any one can be foregrounded through hypertextual reference. French-Canadian director Robert LePage's *Needles and Opium* captured this new sensibility, as do many of the post-modern plays of Mac Wellman or the creations of Anne Bogart with her Saratoga International Theatre Institute. The opera productions of director Peter Sellars with designer George Tsypin are more a product of Foucault and Deleuze than Einstein and Freud. But it is the Wooster Group that has most successfully responded to this brave new world. Especially in *Brace Up!*—their translation (into the 1990s) of *The Three Sisters*—they incorporated video not only to connect a multiplicity of genres and aesthetics (*Godzilla* and Chekhov to name only the most blatant), but also to link on- and offstage space while dissolving the boundaries that separated these worlds, and to bridge the presence and absence of performers. Their use of video brought offstage actors into an onstage mix, retained the presence of actors who could not be physically present (as when Willem Dafoe was off making a movie), allowed actors to interact with themselves (as Michael Kirby did in *L.S.D. (. . . Just the High Points),* and poignantly and eerily kept the brilliant actor Ron Vawter an essential component of the show after he had died of AIDS.

Should we get rid of old-fashioned theater? Of course not. Cars, airplanes, and space shuttles have not eliminated walking. But it is worth noting that walking and running can now be pleasure and sport as well as utilitarian activity. Likewise, older forms of theater cannot have the same impact or utility in this age as they did in a previous time. Thus, I believe that certain institutions such as Broadway or regional theaters will become our Kabuki or Beijing Opera, preserving popular forms as entertaining spectacle, maybe even becoming pastiche entertainments in the same way. In the next millennium, *Cats* will still be running ("*Cats,* now and forever" warns the ad), but it will include not only Grisabella and friends but the Garfield balloon from the Macy's Thanksgiving Parade, and perhaps Norma Desmond flying in on a helicopter. Another theater will feature "all chandeliers, all the time." While this admittedly facetious vision may not come to pass, Broadway seems already headed toward an institution of revivals and spectacles for tourists rather than a vital cauldron of new creative ideas. The new theater no longer has much to do with the sites we once associated with the form.

We are victims of Aristotle or at least victims of Renaissance critics and their more recent apologists. For many people theater equals dramatic text. So we look at medieval theater and pronounce the *Second Shepherd's Play* acceptable but other dramatic texts of the Middle Ages naive and boring; or we see Italian Renaissance drama as a stultifying knock-off of Seneca, whom we see, in turn, as a knock-off of the Greeks. We look at Noh texts or commedia dell'arte scenarios with confusion. We are, in other words, incapable of seeing these mere fragments as parts of a larger, far more sophisticated theater. These were theaters in which the performance went well beyond the limits of a "play" to encompass hours and even days or weeks of multiple events in multiple locations in a festival performance context. In trying to comprehend them we are incompetent audiences; we do not recognize the theater. We cannot read those events any better than the new cyberspectator can read contemporary theater.

What if the revolution has already occurred and we missed it? What if new forms of theater have emerged as a result of new ways of thinking and because we are trapped into habitual patterns of perception, we cannot see it? Laurie Anderson and George Coates are creating performances on the Web, the Super Bowl rivals the festival of Dionysus, and modern revolutions are dependent on faxes and e-mail. Are rock concerts, discos, sporting events, and political rallies our theater?

If theater requires a live performer and a spectator, then there will never be a direct analogue of shuffle mode or remote controls. But I think something strangely equivalent is happening. The days of a monolithic theater appealing to a wide swath of the populace have passed, at least for now. We now have many small, intimate theaters aimed to narrow audiences based on ethnicity, gender, sexual preference, location, politics, and so on. They are, in a sense, like tracks on a compact disc or sites on a DVD. We no longer have to listen or watch under the strict control of a cultural hierarchy—we can pick and choose and structure our own culture. This is but one result of the shifting aesthetic wrought by technology.

Notes

1. Gilles Deleuze and Félix Guattari, "Rhizome," in *On the Line,* trans. John Johnston (New York: Semiotext(e), 1983), 57–58.
2. Deleuze and Guattari, "Rhizome," 2.

Behind the Screen Door

One of the most iconic images of American popular culture of the 1990s came, of course, from television: Jerry Seinfeld's apartment door bursting open with Kramer grasping the doorknob and sliding into the room as if the door were dragging him by its own sheer will. A manic force was thrust, as if from some other cosmic sphere, into the relatively calm, if absurd, world of Jerry Seinfeld. This is a comic rhythm we know well from more than half a century of television sitcoms: Ed Norton, only slightly less antic than Kramer, invading the phlegmatic arena of Ralph Kramden in *The Honeymooners,* or the deceptively benign Ethel Mertz (a sly reference to Kurt Schwitters's branch of dada perhaps?) apprehensively opening the door to Lucy's frenzied domain in *I Love Lucy.*

In the world of sitcoms, but equally true in drama since ancient times, the door is a barrier: a bulwark against the chaos that lurks just beyond. But it is an easily transgressed border, and the forces of disorder slip in with ease to disrupt the illusory status quo. At the end of each episode, harmony and balance are temporarily and tentatively restored; the door is closed again until next week, and the homes and lives of the characters are left in fragile limbo.

Our stages, our movies, our television shows depict rooms with doors; characters come and go, opening and closing doors. Yet we rarely notice, unless the action is intended to draw attention to itself: a character makes a broad comic entrance; someone hides behind a door; a squeaking door induces terror. What is theater, after all, if not a series of exits and entrances? The word *enter* may be the most common word in a commedia dell'arte scenario—the plays were essentially a series of comings and goings, making the text a catalog of doors, as it were. The word *exeunt* marks the rhythm of Shakespeare, and when Antigonus "exits pursued by a bear," he exits, lest

Presented in a much shorter form at the Congress of OISTAT, Pittsburgh, 1997. Published in revised form as "Türen und das Theater" in *Bühnentechnische Rundschau,* vol. 6 (1999). Expanded and presented at the Conference in Honor of Professor Don B. Wilmeth at Brown University, October 2003.

we forget, through a door. The door marks a beginning and an end; it punctuates comings and goings. Similarly, the fundamental language of computers is a binary one consisting of 0s and 1s; a digital doorway is open or closed. A commedia scenario, or a television sitcom scenario, is also a binary system—the doorway opens and information flows in, it closes and the information flow ceases. A classic example is the stateroom scene from the Marx Brothers' film *A Night at the Opera*. In this scene, Groucho discovers that his cabin is barely larger than a closet. Moreover, he discovers three stowaways in his steamer trunk: Chico, Harpo, and Alan Jones, who plays the romantic lead in the film. Over the next few minutes cleaning personnel, waiters with trays of food, a manicurist, a plumber, and others enter the cabin. The door opens repeatedly and each time more chaos invades the cramped space. According to our metaphor, there is ultimately an information overload and the system crashes: the door to the cabin breaks open and everyone inside spills out into the hall. The door sets up a rhythm—it is a visual equivalent to a metronome—that not only regularizes the action but sets up expectations. Once we understand the structure, we eagerly await the next opening of the door and the next flow of information. But just as important, the door establishes a boundary; it establishes a demarcation between the cramped, confined space of the cabin and the much larger world of the ship. It also marks the bounds between order and chaos, between a world of rules and a world of alogical action. To go through the door is to pass from one state of being, or one world, to another.

In the following I would like to consider three aspects of the door. First, what did introduction of the door on the stage do to create tragedy? Second, why, in the special universe of sitcoms, are the doors to New York apartments always unlocked? And finally, are the doors we see on television the same as those we have encountered onstage for the past twenty-five hundred years?

We do not think of the door as an invention, yet I would suggest that it is the most profound technological and scenographic development in the history of theater. It is such an obvious device that it is hard to conceive of theater without it. Yet when Greek tragedy emerged at the end of the sixth century B.C.E., there were no doors on the stage. Of course there were doors in ancient Athens, but in a society that conducted much of its business, both commercial and political, in the open air, the door did not loom so large. And strange as it may seem, it was decades before someone thought of putting a door on the stage. Predoor tragedy was a very different kind of drama than that which would follow in the postdoor era. There were practical implications in the introduction of doors, changes to the structure and rhythm of the drama; but there were also profound implications on a metaphoric, symbolic, and philosophical level as a result of this seemingly simple and innocuous development.

The introduction of the door delineated two separate spaces: the world seen, and the world unseen; the known and the unknown; the tangible and the implied. In the words of Jim Morrison of the 1960s rock group, the Doors, "There are things known and there are things unknown, and in between are the doors." (This may have been a reference to Aldous Huxley's famous book on hallucinatory drugs, *The Doors of Perception,* whose title, in turn, was borrowed from William Blake.) Psychologist Carl Jung described the dream as "the small hidden door in the deepest and most intimate sanctum of the soul, which opens into the primeval cosmic night that was soul long before there was a conscious ego."[1] The theater functions as a kind of collective dream for the society. It is a door into the soul of humankind. On some level, I believe, doors on the stage, even in seemingly benign farces, echo this opening onto the inner world of the soul. Every time a door opens on the stage, a cosmos of infinite possibility is momentarily made manifest; every time a door closes, certain possibilities are extinguished and we experience a form of death. The creation of a boundary on the stage, ironically, made virtually boundless what the dramatist could achieve.

Theater is, in large part, about presence and absence. Perhaps one of the most elemental forms of theater is the game of peek-a-boo that we play with babies. They can watch with glee for hours on end as we hide and reveal our faces, while they swing back and forth on an emotional pendulum between the terror of loss and giggles of surprised delight and relief. We do this as adults, only we call it theater. The curtain hides a world and we are curious, anticipatory; the curtain opens and we applaud and gasp with delight. But even more powerful than the curtain—which is virtually an anachronism in the contemporary theater—is the door. Behind the closed door lies the possibility of pleasure as well as the terror of the unknown; the open door symbolizes both promise and loss. Poet W. H. Auden seemed to understand this quality of the door.

> We pile our all against it when afraid,
> And beat upon its panels when we die:
> By happening to be open once, it made
> Enormous Alice see a wonderland
> That waited for her in the sunshine, and,
> Simply by being tiny, made her cry.

There is an old theater adage, usually applied to Ibsen's *Hedda Gabler,* that if a gun appears in the first act, it must go off by the last. Likewise, I would suggest, if a door is closed in the first act, it must be opened by the last, or vice versa. August Strindberg's *A Dream Play* is largely structured around a locked door, and modern drama is often said to begin with Nora's slamming of the door at the end of Ibsen's *A Doll's House.* Although that particular door is one we never see, her passage through it marks a profound transformation for the character, for the drama, and for society. Chekhov's masterpiece, *The Cherry Orchard,* essentially begins with Madame Ranyevskaya and her entourage returning home, entering the house through a door. And the play ends as the characters leave, closing the door behind them, inadvertently leaving the butler, Firs, locked alone onstage to die.

We actually know, more or less, when a door was first used on the Greek stage. It was around 460 B.C.E. How do we know this? Because Aeschylus's trilogy, *The Oresteia,* dates from 458 and is so radically different from what came before that something must have occurred to alter tragedy. That monumental occurrence was the door. None of the extant plays prior to the *Oresteia—The Persians, Seven against Thebes, The Suppliants, Prometheus Bound*—requires a door or any sort of scenic structure. *Prometheus Bound,* for instance, takes place on a rocky mountaintop, *The Suppliants* on an open field. All available evidence suggests that most of the pre-Oresteian drama was "doorless." Imagine, if you will, the "predoor" Theater of Dionysus in the early part of the fifth century B.C.E., newly constructed on the hillside of the Acropolis. The *theatron* consists of wooden benches embedded in the rocky slope beneath the Parthenon, and they overlook a terraced flat area, the orchestra, where the actors and chorus will perform. There is no structure on this flat stage other than, perhaps, an altar. A temple to the god Dionysus sits behind the orchestra, and a vista of the countryside is visible beyond. Unlike our modern experience of theater, in which we sit enclosed in darkness peering into an artificially illuminated box, the ancient Greeks sat in the bright Mediterranean morning sun in springtime watching mythological stories being reenacted against the glorious background of the landscape that was for them the center of the universe.

The Persians, for example, begins, as most Greek tragedies do, with the entrance of the chorus. How do they enter? There are no wings, no doors, no curtains. We see them coming up a long path from behind the orchestra. This takes some time, and we can observe them coming into view, as if over a horizon, perhaps beginning their song as they approach the stage— the anapests are a marching rhythm. They finally arrive on the stage and sing and dance. Toward the end of their first choral ode we see another actor coming up the pathway behind the orchestra. In case we don't see him, or in case we don't know who it is, the chorus tells us: "But lo! she comes, / A light whose splendor equals eyes of gods, / The mother of our king, I kneel" (151–53).[2] And they go on for seven more lines. While the queen is certainly deserving of a lavish introduction, the length of the choral speech is determined by the distance the actor must traverse. The chorus is, in essence, vamping, covering from the moment the audience first sees the actor until he arrives on the stage. As the various characters proceed up these paths, we might experience feelings of anticipation, expectation, doom, horror, or optimism. What we cannot experience, however, is *surprise*. Entrances in the early Greek theater were processional—they unfolded through time. And exits took on the qualities of a final musical chord fading off into inaudibility.

But the introduction of a scenic structure onto the stage, and with it the door, fundamentally altered the rhythm of the tragedy. Now characters could appear suddenly and disappear quickly. A processional rhythm was replaced with what we might now call a cinematic rhythm by the simple introduction of the door. Instead of a continuous action happening in essentially real time, the door—and the illusion it created—allowed an intercutting of scenes that had the effect of telescoping time and space. Dramatists were no longer confined, if indeed they ever had been, to real time onstage. The *Oresteia* is the first extant play that requires a door. There are specific references to a palace, there are entrances and exits in and out of the palace, there are sounds from within, and references to action within. *The Libation Bearers* and *The Eumenides* change locales during the course of the action, almost with abandon: *Choephori* begins at the tomb of Agamemnon, shifts to the exterior of the palace of Clytemnestra and Aegisthus, then to the interior, and finally to the exterior again; *Eumenides* begins outside the Temple of Apollo at Delphi, moves to the interior of the temple, then to the Temple of Athena in Athens, and concludes at the court of Areopagos. It is almost as if Aeschylus, having been given a new toy, cannot play with it enough. The door creates the possibility of multiple locales; but more important, it actually creates drama. The audience learns of the murder of Agamemnon and Cassandra aurally—by Agamemnon's anguished cries from behind the door. A twelve-line choral ode follows, and then a remarkable event occurs. The door opens, revealing a tableau of Agamemnon dead in his bath, wrapped in a purple robe, Cassandra dead on top of him, and Clytemnestra standing triumphantly over them.

This scene is possible only because of the door. Without a door the cries of murder would have to have come from somewhere down the hillside and the bodies carried up the long pathway to reveal their deaths; or they would have to be killed in plain sight. While there was no explicit prohibition against violence on the stage in ancient Greece, violence was rare for purely practical reasons: the Greek dramatists understood that the physical act of murder could not be realistically re-created on the stage. And even if it could, it is not as satisfying as giving way to unfettered imagination. Behind a door we can envisage anything. The screams conjure up far greater horror than any murder that could be reasonably re-created on the stage. The door hides; the door reveals. And it also hides again. On the vast open stage of pre-Oresteian drama, how were dead bodies disposed of? Either they had to be carried off—an awkward solution—or they unceremoniously became actors again, got up, and walked off the stage. But once the door was introduced, it could close after the scene of revelation and the bodies were simply gone with only the audience's memory of the carnage remaining.

That simple facade and doorway transformed the way in which audiences perceived the theater. The space behind the facade, of course, had not changed—it was the same Athenian countryside the audience had seen the previous year when they came to the festival when there was no facade. But now, illusion came into play. If the door in *Agamemnon* represented the palace at Argos, then anyone emerging through the door was understood as coming from the palace. Thus, the audience imagined the various rooms of the palace, even though they remained unseen. That also meant that the world beyond was not Athens but Argos. This sense of imaginary worlds becomes even richer in Shakespeare's day. When Hamlet enters through the door for the first time, he is in the palace at Elsinore. More important, we accept that he has just arrived from the university, and we believe that if we could somehow go through that same door, there would be a waiting carriage and a road that would take us back to Wittenberg. That is what a door can achieve.

When we go to the theater, regardless of genre, we are watching a transformation. An ordinary human being is transformed into Medea or Hamlet, or the ghost of a warrior, or a dancing cat. But equally important, an essentially ordinary space is transformed. The simple stage can become the "vasty fields of France," the front of a palace in Thebes, or a suburban living room. The stage, regardless of its shape or configuration, is a magic circle transforming everything within it. But entering into a magic circle is not a simple matter. In Goethe's *Faust,* Mephistopheles must be invited within Faustus's room:

Faust: A knock? Come in! Again my quiet broken
Mephistopheles: 'Tis I!
Faust: Come in!
Mephistopheles: Thrice must the words be spoken.
Faust: Come in, then!

$$(4.1-5)^3$$

The very process of entering transforms him—in this case Mephistopheles takes on human form. This is a metaphor for the theater. We invite actors into our rooms, as it were. The actors enter the stage through a door and they are transformed. On the classical French stage the start of the play was preceded by three loud knocks on the stage floor. Ostensibly this was a signal to the audience, but it could also be understood as a ritualistic summoning of spirits from the nether regions—spirits who would then enter through the door as the curtain rose, magically transformed into actors. And herein lies the answer to the question of the "open door policy" of television sitcoms. Kramer and his cohorts are descendants of commedia dell'arte masks. And these masks, in turn, are most likely descendants of medieval devil clowns. (Harlequin's patchwork costume probably evolved from the patched linings of jackets worn inside out by the lords of misrule.) These devil clowns can trace their ancestry to the imps and tricksters of folk performance and ritual. In other words, Ed Norton, Fred and Ethel, Eddie Haskell, and a host of others similar characters are devils. They are thus excluded from the domestic sphere under normal circumstances and can only enter by ritual invitation. But like the open window through which Dracula enters, the unlocked door provides a sort of permanent passport that eliminates the need to knock. These devils may come and go at will.

But where are they entering from? In reality, it is from backstage, a very unglamorous and even chaotic world with virtually no relation to the illusion the audience sees onstage. Yet the powerful symbolism of the stage implies a world beyond—unseen, yet present. When we see an actor entering through a door, we understand that he or she is coming from, say, outside the house to the inside, or from one room to another, or, to quote a stage direction from Shakespeare's *As You Like It,* from "another part of the forest." Now in the real world we do not get from one part of the forest to another by going through doors, but doors on the stage do not have to be literal. They become signs of passage, and as such take on a life and function of their own, different, to a degree, from the way they function in real life. In our homes, doors separate one room from another, or the inside from the outside; in the theater they represent a passage between the onstage world and the off. On Shakespeare's stage, for example, there were, in all likelihood, one or two doors in the upstage wall. Almost all entrances and exits were made through these doors. Sometimes this would be logical in terms of reference to the real world: when Hamlet enters Gertrude's chamber, it makes perfect sense to come through a door; when Falstaff enters Mistress Quickly's tavern, of course he enters through a door. But look at act 4, scene 4 of *King Lear,* for example: "The French Camp; Enter, with drum and colors, Cordelia, Doctor and Soldiers"; or the very opening of *Macbeth:* "Thunder and lightning. Enter three Witches." They entered through a door.

The door is a theatrical convention. In Restoration England, the theaters were built with a pair of doors on either side of the forestage through which actors entered and exited, and making an entrance or exit was the epitome of an actor's vocabulary. Throughout the eighteenth century managers, in order to accommodate more patrons (and make more money), kept reducing the size of the forestage, first eliminating one set of doors and finally both sets. The actors protested vehemently; they wanted their doors. At Covent Garden Theatre in 1810 the management relented briefly and had the doors restored, but they were soon taken away again. The theater went from the theatrical to the realistic. The only doors to be found now were within the scenery, which, more often than not, depicted drawing rooms. If the door is part of the architecture of the stage, we are in a theatrical environment; if it is part of the scenery, it is illusionistic.

The door is a threshold, a liminal space that marks a boundary between two spaces yet belongs to neither. French philosopher Gaston Bachelard in *The Poetics of Space* discusses the "dialectics of outside and inside." "The door," he exclaims, "is an entire cosmos of the half-open. In fact," he continues, "it is one of its primal images, the very origin of a daydream that accumulates desires and temptations: the temptation to open up the ultimate depths of being, and the desire to conquer all reticent beings."[4]

Thresholds carry magical significance. As children, and secretly as adults, we exert great effort not to step on the doorsill because of ancient superstitious beliefs that live on in us that suggest great misfortune if we step on the sill. Since ancient Egyptian times, many cultures have maintained the practice of carrying the new bride across the threshold. This was done in part to protect the bride from the spirits who guarded the house, since she was a stranger coming into her husband's domain. Many cultures had threshold gods that protected one's comings and goings; in some cultures amulets or good-luck charms are buried beneath the doorsill; and many Jews today still have mezuzahs on doorjambs to remind one of the presence of God, who, in turn, will protect the house and those who enter, recalling Psalm 121: "The Lord shall preserve thy going out and thy coming in from this time forth, and even for evermore." Doors, of course, are symbols of salvation. In the New Testament, in the Book of John, Jesus says, "I am the door: by me if any man enter in, he shall be saved."

A passage between two spaces—two worlds—that the door signifies is a dangerous one. That is why, for instance, evil spirits are often depicted as living beneath bridges in fairy tales. The Bible is replete with instances of sinners or nonbelievers who die as they cross a threshold, of evil waiting outside doors, of rites of purification at doorways, of guardians or keepers of the threshold, and so on. The doorway is often a place of sacrifice, or a place to deposit items for safekeeping.

Almost all cultures believe in a heaven, underworld, or some such abode for spirits and the deceased. In almost all cases, the passageway between the world of the living and the dead is marked by a door or gate. The Egyptian otherworld had 12 doors; Valhalla had 540. The duchess of Malfi, in John Webster's play, says, "I know death hath ten thousand several doors / For men to take their exits" (4.2). Heaven, Hell, and Eden all have doors or gates. Book IX of Dante's *Purgatorio* is devoted to the Gate of Purgatory in which the angel of the Lord sits upon the sill of adamantine stone and presents the traveler with two keys that would allow him to pass through.

Thus, entering onto the stage is not merely a passage but a profound— can we say life-threatening?—event. While Western theater has lost the ritual aspects, and much of the terror, of this entrance (although the elevated heart rate of many performers just prior to their entrances and the phenomenon of stage fright may be vestiges of this ancient sense of mortality), the idea of onstage and offstage is so powerful an image that it has suffused the language. It is preserved in various classical Asian forms, notably in the Noh theater of Japan. In the Noh, the story often involves gods and ghosts and recollected events. Here characters do not enter into an illusionistic space. Rather, they enter through a curtained door, proceed down an oblique runway, the *hashigakari,* past three symbolic trees representing Heaven, Earth, and Man before entering onto the rectangular stage where the story will be enacted. The entrance through the curtain transforms an actor into a character who is filled with a spirit. And the character remains until the actor once again passes through the door at the end of the play. There is almost a literal passage from one world to another. The Japanese Kabuki theater uses something similar. But here the lavishly costumed lead actor makes a grand entrance through a door in the wall of the auditorium and then walks down a runway, the *hanamichi,* through the audience, stopping part way down for applause and, in earlier times, to accept gifts. Here, the entrance through the door signals the very theatricality of the presentation. Coming through the door is a way of saying, "Look at me."

The door can establish either a comic rhythm or a tragic one. French critic and sociologist Roland Barthes discussed the tragic implication of doors in his essay on the plays of seventeenth-century writer Jean Racine. Noting that when characters leave the stage in a tragedy, they are often going to their death, Barthes described the door between the onstage and offstage space as "a tragic object that menacingly expresses both contiguity and exchange, the tangency of hunter and prey."[5] It is not just in Racine that exiting through the door is to confront death: Agamemnon, Cassandra, Clytemnestra, and Aegisthus, as already mentioned, Oedipus's wife and mother Jocasta, Baron Tuzenbakh in *The Three Sisters,* Hedda Gabler, all exit through a door to their deaths. In Shakespeare, on the other hand, death, in the form of opposing characters, often *enters* through the door, leaving havoc on the stage, though we should remember that poor Rosencrantz and Guildenstern exit, to die in England.

In farce, doors are not gateways for death but for chaos. Here is a typical description from Georges Feydeau's *All My Husbands:* "The living room of Barrilon's house. There are French doors leading to the garden and an archway leading to the front door. There are several doors leading to various bedrooms, and to the rest of the house."[6] Behind these doors lovers, mistresses, spouses, bumbling crooks, and others will hide. Entrances and exits are timed with exquisite precision. We laugh because *we* know who has just exited or who is hiding in a closet, but a duped spouse does not. Honor, dignity, marriages are saved, or not, by the timely click of a door latch. Perhaps no one was more adept at the ingenious use of a door than the great silent-film clown Buster Keaton. In many of his movies, somewhat as in the farces of Feydeau, everything depended upon the timely use of a door. For *The High Sign* (1921), for example, Keaton devised a house of doors (including ingenious trapdoors), and the climax is a madcap attempt by Keaton, the woman he loves, and her father to stay out of the clutches of a gang of murderers who chase them through the house. The doors in this version of Keaton's world protect the good and destroy the evil. The threshold gods have been propitiated and work their magic well, if comically. Once again we are in a binary world: information is admitted through a passage, or it is not.

But despite the centrality of doors in early-twentieth-century movie farces, and, I might add, despite the necessity of doorways and gatekeepers on the modern-day Internet, the door is increasingly rare on the living stage. Something shifted in the twentieth century. The symbolist artists and poets of the late nineteenth century are partly responsible, and Freud definitely is. Both began to question the absolute authority of external reality. There are perceived truths and inner truths that cannot be contained by walls and cannot be reached through doors. The dichotomy of inside and outside began to disintegrate as the two worlds melded together. I think another culprit is, in some way, Chekhov. Yes, he gave us houses with rooms and doors, but he also tried to break down the distinction between spaces, between the visible and the invisible. Strindberg may have given us locked doors, and Ibsen slammed ones, but Chekhov's stage directions are always telling us about the outside, even when we are inside. The opening directions of *The Cherry Orchard* mark a transition: "A room that still goes by the name of the nursery. One of the *doors* leads to Anya's room . . ." But then he seems to lose interest in rooms. The directions continue, "It is dawn and the sun will soon come up. It is May. The cherry trees are in flower, but in the orchard it is cold."[7] Here, in 1904, in a few simple sentences, Chekhov has dissolved the separation of inside and outside. Once this happens, what use is a door? Andrei Serban directed a landmark production of *The Cherry Orchard* at Lincoln Center in 1976, designed by Santo Loquasto. There were no walls, and thus no doors—just furniture on a vast stage with ethereal trees in the background [see photo on p. 127]. European designers such as Adolphe Appia and Edward Gordon Craig early in the twentieth century radically altered the look of the stage, using simple suggestive settings of platforms, steps, curtains, and fragmentary semiabstract pieces instead of the detailed settings of the nineteenth century. Now the stage was not necessarily another place in the illusionistic sense. It was a stage. But a stage without doors. In 1904, the same year that *The Cherry Orchard* was produced, Craig went to Berlin to design a production for Dr. Otto Brahm, Germany's leading director at the time. The production was the seventeenth-century English play *Venice Preserved* by Thomas Otway. Central to the action is a door; but Craig designed a set without a door. The collaboration of director and designer fell apart, but the death knell for the door was clearly at hand. Just as the actors at the start of the nineteenth century were bereft without doors—they did not know how to enter or leave the stage—drama as a whole lost a certain kind of theatricality. In what is arguably the most famous play of the twentieth century, Samuel Beckett's *Waiting for Godot,* two tramps wait by the side of road near a tree. For ambiguous reasons they cannot leave; they are destined to wait. Several times throughout the play Gogo and Didi repeat the exchange: "Let's go. / We can't. / Why not? / We're waiting for Godot." The final two lines of the play and the final stage direction:

Vladimir: Well? Shall we go?
Estragon: Yes, let's go.
They do not move.

Much has been written about the metaphorical and philosophical reasons for their stasis, their inability to leave. But there is a very practical explanation as well: they cannot leave because there is no door! (Of course, Beckett the ironist followed *Godot* with *Endgame* in which there *was* a room with a door, and still characters remained trapped.)

Our theater has become, in some ways, like modern pop music that does not know how to end—it just repeats over and over as it fades out. Without doors, there can be no grand exit, and thus there is no finality. The societies that produced theaters with doors as major elements tended to be strong, confident societies. We are living in a time of uncertainty, and that produces a theater without doors.

But comedy cannot exist without doors. (Aristophanes, remember, emerged after the introduction of the door.) Both farce and domestic comedy rely upon doors for their comic rhythms. This leads to the final question: are the mediated doors of television sitcoms—the ones visible on a screen—and the three-dimensional doors of live theater the same?

Television exists in a different relationship to the spectator than does the stage. Not only do the spectators and performers in live theater share a tangible space, but the objects in that space are, relatively speaking, fixed. Our spatiotemporal relationships to anything from a prop to a wall are kinesthetically real, based upon our knowledge of the world. Even if we are confronted with movable scenery, the mechanism is understood, at least in principle. And we can observe the spatiality of the stage transforming so that our relationship to any object (and its illusionistic implications) remains visible. Whether we are dealing with forced perspective, a box set, the poetic essentialism of the New Stagecraft, or the visual pastiche of postmodern scenography, we are still confronting tangible, knowable space in the real world, and it will obey the natural laws of optics, time, and space. It is, if you will, a Newtonian stage.

On an obvious level, the physical relation to the TV is different. The image is isolated in a box within a room within a house where it becomes one object among many. (This is even more true of televisions found in bars, waiting rooms, airports, etc.) Even with plasma screens and home entertainment centers, the human still tends to be larger than the image. The scale of the spectator and the scale of the viewed image are seldom unified. At the very least, the image becomes isolated. Like a painting hung on a gallery wall, it has no imagistic, architectural, or necessary relation to its environment. But in most gallery settings the paintings are usually the visual focal points. Moreover, they are foregrounded against the wall. Television, because of its technology as well as its physical relation to the spectator's environment, tends to eliminate what Walter Benjamin described as "aura" in "The Work of Art in the Age of Mechanical Reproduction." Distance is eradicated. Whereas Stanislavsky may have wanted the spectators at *The Three Sisters* to feel as if they were guests at the Prozorov household, TV is commonly described as bringing its characters into the viewer's home. We do not project ourselves into the apartments of our favorite sitcom characters; rather, we sense them as somehow part of our living space. Television is not something contemplated at a distance; distance—crucial for aura—is generally lacking. (The stage, it may be argued, also creates an isolated image separate from the spectator, but the unity of shared experiential space and the implications of live presence contribute to a kind of transparency and the creation of an aura.)

Distance on television is dissolved in another crucial way—through the movement of the camera or the constant shifting of perspective. (*The Honeymooners* was a transitional show, as it were, and is in many ways closer to theater than subsequent TV programs. It is viewed from the single perspective of one camera, and any change in point of view is limited to panning and close-ups. *I Love Lucy*'s great innovation was the three-camera setup that allowed for multiple—that is, shifting—points of view.) The instability of the image not only eliminates aura but, in the case of the door, reduces its historical, symbolic, and emblematic values and associations. The door's size, relative to the viewer, is subject to change. Moreover, the threshold aspect of the door is easily violated because the camera is capable of moving through it. We can peer through keyholes, move through open doors, glide into adjoining halls and rooms. It is arguable that Aeschylus already did this. When the bodies of Agamemnon and Cassandra are revealed, are we inside the palace or outside? Aeschylus used the door for revelation, but dissolved the Bachelard-like dichotomy of inside and outside. The door, at that moment, became a door *on a stage,* not a door in a palace. The system of references had changed, but not the relationship of the physical setting to the audience, nor the information value of the door. The door of Seinfeld's apartment may be a threshold for Kramer to violate, but it is not a real threshold for the spectator. We may easily pass through the door for a scene in the hall, to move to another apartment, or to enter the larger city through which the characters move.

Lev Manovich, a new-media theorist, posits Paul Virilio as the Benjamin of the postindustrial age. Virilio creates two categories, Small Optics and Big Optics, the former based on geometric perspective—that is, on human vision and world experience—and the latter based on real-time transmission of information at the speed of light. Big Optics, according to Virilio, is displacing Small Optics. The concepts of near and far, horizon, distance, and space—the geometry of human vision and art, to paraphrase Manovich— are dissolving, creating a "claustrophobic world without any depth or horizon."[8] This effect of digital technology has been described by art historian Jonathan Crary as "the process by which capitalism uproots and makes mobile that which grounded, clears away or obliterates that which impedes circulation, and makes exchangeable what is singular."[9] While Crary is focusing, of course, on the socioeconomic factors, his notion of clearing away that which impedes circulation might be applied somewhat literally to the door. The door can be a useful impediment for comic purposes in the sitcom, but it can also impede the movement of the camera. But the audience of television or film expects—in a way it does not in the theater—to be able to move through doors, windows, walls, and space in general. Television space knows no boundaries.

The door is necessary in television as an indexical sign; it tells us that we are in an environment analogous to the one in which we are sitting while watching. It is a convention—comic in sitcoms, melodramatic in cop shows—that establishes scenic and dramaturgical rhythms as it has since Aeschylus. But unlike the door of the theater, which has seeming permanence, the door of the television is merely iconic, and its solidity and Euclidean basis is ephemeral.

On the stage, a door is a sign of the liminal, the unknown, the potential, the terrifying, the endless. On the screen, a door is a sign of a door.

Notes

1. C. G. Jung, "The Meaning of Psychology for Modern Man," in *Psychological Reflections: A Jung Anthology,* ed. Jolande Jacobi (New York: Pantheon, 1953), 46.

2. Aeschylus, *The Persians,* trans. S. G. Benardete, in *Aeschylus II,* ed. David Grene and Richmond Lattimore (Chicago: University of Chicago Press, 1956).

3. Johann Wolfgang von Goethe, *Faust,* trans. Bayard Taylor (New York: Modern Library, 1950).

4. Gaston Bachelard, *The Poetics of Space,* trans. Maria Jolas (Boston: Beacon Press, 1994), 222.

5. Roland Barthes, *On Racine,* trans. Richard Howard (New York: Hill and Wang, 1964), 4–5.

6. Georges Feydeau, *Five by Feydeau,* trans. J. Paul Marcoux (New York: Peter Lang, 1994), 127.

7. Trans. Eugene K. Bristow (New York: W. W. Norton, 1977).

8. Lev Manovich, *The Language of New Media* (Cambridge: MIT Press, 2000), 172.

9. Jonathan Crary, *Techniques of the Observer,* quoted in Manovich, *Language of New Media,* 173.

Technology and
Dramaturgical Development
Five Observations

In her landmark book, *The History of the Greek and Roman Theater,* the great historian Margarete Bieber stated simply and elegantly, "The development of the theater building always follows the development of dramatic literature."[1] While historians, of course, have always attempted to explain the drama in terms of known architectural, scenographic, and technological practices, the effect of one upon the other has been less fully or successfully explored. Why, for instance, is the reverse of Bieber's statement not true? And in the rapidly changing technology of the contemporary world, is it possible that technology has become a causal factor in the development of drama?

History seems to support Bieber. In almost every culture and every historical period the dramatic text and the performance have always preceded the creation of a formalized physical theater. Aeschylus preceded Epidauros; Plautus and Terence preceded the Theater of Pompey; the standardized Noh theater evolved well after the plays of Zeami; the Comédie Française (both building and company) followed in the wake of Molière; the list goes on. That a physical theater structure might be created to suit the needs of an evolving drama and mode of performance is not in itself surprising, although all too often historians—grasping for the few tangible straws available to them—try to explain the older drama in terms of the extant theater structures. But what is more striking is that the reverse is rarely if ever true: the theater building and its concomitant technologies has seldom given birth to new forms of dramatic art that have had a life or significance beyond the immediate entertainment and gratification of its contemporary audience. This suggests a deeper root cause or underlying necessity that can be

Presented at "Space—Dramaturgy—Scenography," Helsinki, August 1996; published in *Theatre Research International* (summer 1999).

found, I believe, in the relationship of the institution of theater to the society and culture that spawned it. Historically, the theater has been both a laboratory and a battlefield for emerging and evolving ideas of a growing society. But change, of course, as Plato recognized, is potentially dangerous, especially for those who depend upon the status quo for power or wealth. In those societies with dynamic theatrical cultures, the emergence of authoritarian government has frequently been accompanied by the attempt to halt the evolutionary forces of theater by literally turning living culture into monuments to the status quo.

Taking the ancient Greek theater as a case in point, one sees a process of vital evolution throughout the fifth century. But at that point in which the theatrical art was perceived to be at its peak, in which evolutionary transformations had essentially ceased and were, in fact, no longer desirable, at that point at which the theater had become not a tool for change but a tool for the validation of authority, inextricably bound up with the ruling political forces, the theater was literally set in stone by Lycurgus, thus ensuring that it would cease to evolve. It became, instead, a cultural icon. By capturing the physical theater at a particular point and concretizing it, the dramatic theater became a fixed, unchanging entity. The energy of an evolving theater in transition gave way to stagnation; the stone theater of Lycurgus was a major contributing factor to the decline of Greek theater. Likewise, following the death of Molière, Louis XIV combined the warring theater companies of Paris into the single Comédie Française, creating an institution that was quickly followed by an architectural monument of a theater. Innovation in the French theater of the time ceased almost immediately. In both these cases, and in many others, the transformation of living theaters into architectural edifices also transformed the art from a theater of the playwright into a theater of the actor. The emphasis shifted from original creation to the repetition and interpretation of existing texts.

Because of the great cost and upkeep of permanent theaters, because of the inevitable commitment that the community must make to the construction of such theaters, and, not incidentally, because of the opportunity for self-aggrandizing public monumentality on which political leaders seem to thrive (the "edifice complex"), permanent theaters were almost always created by the authorities or by the state, not the people of the theater. (The Elizabethan theater, a creation of actors and businessmen, is a notable exception, although even there, the theatrical momentum was eventually subsumed by the courts of James and Charles with the result that theater and theater architecture were prime targets of the Cromwellian revolution.)

First observation: Cultural edifices are inimical to change and unresponsive to art. Given the opportunity, the state will always erect such edifices to preserve the status quo, but this will lead to artistic decline.

There have been, of course, instances of an opposing pattern in theater history. The Teatro Olimpico, for instance, was a creation of academics combining an imperfect knowledge of classical history with Renaissance technology. It did not evolve out of existing theater practice, nor did it emerge in response to the demands of any contemporary form of drama (it opened with a spectacle production of *Oedipus*), and, significantly, it generated no new forms. If advancements in dramaturgy can lead to developments in theater architecture and technology, shouldn't the reverse also be true? But there are no new forms of drama traceable or attributable to the Teatro Olimpico. As significant as that theater is as an architectural icon, it was, dramaturgically speaking, a kind of stillbirth. It is not that the new technologies of the Renaissance generated no new forms of theater. Most obviously, the many stunning examples of technological innovation of the period led to the development of so-called spectacle theaters such as the Salle des Machines that demanded the creation of a specialized drama. But this had no long-term effect upon play development. The significance of Corneille as a playwright, for example, emanates from *Le Cid* or *Horace,* plays written for the earlier court and popular theaters that still owed something to the theater in the market square. The plays he wrote for the spectacle theaters such as *Andromède,* though fascinating in their own right, engendered no permanent developments or genres.

I am not arguing that technology, scenography, and architecture have no effects on the development of the drama; they have profound effects. Perspective painting, changeable scenery, and the proscenium arch, for example, are as inextricably bound up in the evolution of illusionistic theater as are the theories of Aristotle and neoclassical scholars. One might even argue that much of Western drama owes its existence to these technical components. But in terms of direct cause and effect, theater and stage configurations that derive purely from theory or technology engender no new forms of drama.

Spectacle theaters exist today at Disney World and its many counterparts, and at the increasingly rare world's fairs; Broadway, the West End, and Tokyo's commercial theaters produce modern-day equivalents of intermezzi. But, like their Renaissance counterparts, these performances are meant for the immediate pleasure and gratification of their audience (a perfectly legitimate use of theater that should not be condemned or dismissed, by the way) and have little direct effect upon the development of drama. No one has written a body of work for Jacques Polieri's Total Movement Theater or Disney's Haunted House. Literary drama is almost always inextricably bound up in the life of the culture, recapitulating the narrative of the society or the emotional experience of individuals within the society. One goes to such theater in order to validate experience. Even formalist avant-garde theater often uses the individual as a reference point. But spectacle theater is little more than a showcase for technical wizardry, whether to demonstrate the wonders of a chariot-and-pole system or laser light and computers. The fairs and theme parks exist in what may be called "extradaily" time—they exist outside the structures of everyday life. More often than not they are found in liminal spaces, far removed from urban centers or residential communities. They are, in the language of tourism, "destination sites"—a place to which one travels to escape the routines and experiences of the quotidian world. Thus, any theatrical entertainments found inside these spaces are relegated to this extradaily world; they have no more relevance to daily life than the roller coaster rides or souvenir stands that also comprise such experiences.

But, it may be argued, theater in general has become irrelevant in our world today. As theater loses its place of cultural centrality in modern societies—at least those of the industrialized world—and with that its audiences and financial support, theatrical producers try ever harder to make this ancient art form relevant and popular. They add rock music and video images, computer-controlled special effects, and hydraulic stages that seem to be competing for Olympic gymnastic gold medals. When done well enough or large enough, these effects elicit applause and line the pockets of producers. But while commercial mainstream theater may be in the midst of a modern era of spectacle, there is scant evidence that it is contributing in any tangible way to the development of drama. In fact, the most recent trend seems to be theatrical adaptations of movies—a sort of reversal of the trend at the start of the century, when the nascent film industry cannibalized the melodrama for form and content.

> Second observation: A theater that exists to exploit new technology may contribute to popular entertainment, but will have little immediate effect upon dramaturgy.

Despite the apparent formula of drama first, theater second, scenographic developments *have,* in fact, been deftly exploited by dramatists, even to the point of significantly altering the form and content of the drama. Perhaps the most profound such example is also the earliest: the *Oresteia* of Aeschylus. Scholars now generally agree that the *skene* or stage building of the Greek theater first appeared in the Theater of Dionysus around the middle of the fifth century. Within a brief time, probably no more than a few years at most, Aeschylus learned how to exploit this new scenographic element to the fullest, creating a play with multiple levels for actors, spectacular entrances, concealment, and sudden revelations. Almost overnight, Greek tragedy shifted from simple presentations of actors on an open space, to complex physical and psychological explorations of human behavior set in theatrical manifestations of cities and palaces. While the Greek tragic theater may have had its origins in storytelling, dithyrambic dances, and ritual, the maturation of the dramaturgy would not have been possible without the introduction of the seemingly simple *skene*. Regardless of whether the scenographic development inspired new forms of drama, or whether the poets demanded new physical structures to satisfy their creativity, this is a clear case of an essential and symbiotic relationship among the theatrical components of architecture, stage design, and dramatic writing.

A similar case might be made for Shakespeare. The Elizabethan theater (in an admittedly simplified overview) evolved out of the elemental expedient of placing a medieval trestle stage or pageant wagon inside a bear-baiting arena or inn yard. James Burbage transformed this into a purpose-built theater. Kyd and Marlowe, but most of all Shakespeare, learned how to transform this crude device into a metaphor for the cosmos, and how to exploit the shape of the stage and its relationship to the audience. Using the two or three entrance doors of the stage and the overlooking second gallery, Shakespeare created a rapidly flowing, episodic narrative of multiple plots and complex themes peopled by a vast array of the most fascinating characters the stage has ever known. This, too, was the result of a partnership of scenography, architecture, and dramaturgy. *King Lear,* or *As You Like It,* or *Henry IV* could not have worked—or perhaps even been imagined—on a simple trestle stage in a marketplace. It required the transformable and multifaceted stage of the Globe, the aptly named theater whose scenography facilitated the malleable transformations of life within a "wooden O." Interestingly, modern critics attempting to put a name to this style of theater turn to a twentieth-century technology and identify this style as cinematic.

But ultimately this second observation reinforces the first. As long as the theater is in a state of evolutionary growth the drama and the architecture transform and progress together in a complex developmental dance. As the physical theater achieves a permanent form, so does the drama. The last of

London's outdoor theaters to be built, for example, was the Hope in 1614 (the Fortune was rebuilt in 1623). While drama continued to be written at a prodigious pace until 1642 (though increasingly for initial presentation at the indoor theaters), it is arguable that significant dramaturgical evolution slowed significantly if it did not entirely cease.

> Third observation: Rarely does a single development in any one field of endeavor (technology, scenography, architecture, dramaturgy) lead to a clear or immediate transformation in another. All the factors are inextricably bound up in each other and cannot be simply or precisely delineated. That is to say, we cannot neatly extract technology, say, from dramaturgy. Most importantly, evolution in the theater, whether in dramatic literature or physical production (and we could add acting as well), is more a factor of the prevailing societal norms and worldview than any specific technical or stylistic development in the art of theater.

A key factor in dramaturgical developments has been the perception and understanding of time and space. For example, as the theological worldview of the Middle Ages—a view that was ahistorical and in which time and space obeyed the laws of God, not the laws of Newton—gave way to the humanistic and scientific worldview of the Renaissance, European theater transformed from the epic mystery cycles and morality plays in which thousands of miles and many centuries could be traversed by merely walking across a simple platform stage, to the linear, sequential pictorial drama of neoclassicism. In the modern era, technology has once again transformed notions of time and space, and this, in turn, has led to new forms of drama. The greatest manifestations of this changing view and the greatest contributions to the evolution of the drama in the past six hundred years have been the introduction of the proscenium arch and the discovery of the rules of perspective painting with the subsequent adoption of perspective for the creation of theatrical scenery. In the modern era, the abandonment of the proscenium has been of equal impact and is similarly a reflection of the prevailing worldview.

The Renaissance created a theater that was a linear unfolding of images, each obeying the physical laws of time and space. The proscenium stage, by allowing the spectators a view into another world—much as the more or less concurrent emergence of the microscope and telescope did—was crucial for the development of naturalistic drama with its narrative renderings of reality depicted illusionistically on the stage. The proscenium went hand in hand with perspective scenery that created time and space in a two-dimensional format. Through the illusionistic re-creation of a specific locale onstage, the audience could project itself into a particular place that was different from where they sat. Moreover, the realistic depiction of space implied real time. Unlike the medieval theater with its simultaneous settings, the post-Renaissance theater created discrete and singular locales; movement through time and space was now sequential, not simultaneous. The images created upon these stages were seen as extensions of the auditorium, or rather, as extensions of the world of the spectator. The subsequent development of multipoint perspective, the *scena per angolo* of the Bibienas and others, broke the continuity between the stage and auditorium. The stage world could now be of a different, much larger, scale than the world of the spectators and thus a world of fantasy. But even if the subject matter of the Renaissance theater extended beyond the bounds of the everyday, the stage nonetheless conformed to the scientific and rationalist view of the Renaissance. A performance was a series of discrete images, each bound by the rules of science. It was this combination of architecture, technology, and scenography that allowed, indeed fomented, the creation of neoclassical drama and baroque opera.

The bridging of the proscenium and the unification of the stage and auditorium beginning in the late nineteenth century were crucial for the many "isms" of the modernist era and were responsible for the end of naturalism on the stage. Illusion requires a degree of aesthetic distance that the proscenium helped foster. The unified stage and auditorium is antithetical to the naturalistic impulse. Did the disappearance of the proscenium cause drama to change, or did the changing drama force the destruction of the proscenium? Or was it, more likely, a confluence of ideas whose time had come? Regardless, these developments were in keeping with a worldview in which the apparent constructions and limits of time and space of the Renaissance were disappearing. From the beginnings of human history until the nineteenth century, travel and communication had been bound by the speed of horses, water currents, and the wind. Suddenly, human transport was constrained only by the limitations of technology, while communication could occur at the speed of light. Notions of time and space transformed accordingly. Filippo Tommaso Marinetti, in the "Manifesto of Futurism" in 1909, reveled in this new sensibility: "We say that the world's magnificence has been enriched by a new beauty; the beauty of speed," he declared.

A racing car whose hood is adorned with great pipes, like serpents of explosive breath—a roaring car that seems to ride on grapeshot—is more beautiful than the *Victory of Samothrace.* . . . We stand on the last promontory of the centuries! . . . Time and space died yesterday. We already live in the absolute, because we have created eternal, omnipresent speed.[2]

Today we exist in a singular world in which all things may exist simultaneously. The linear and sequential world of the Renaissance is anachronistic. Ours is a paradoxical world of both isolation and interconnection. Contemporary audiences are comfortable with rapidly shifting barrages of images and sounds presented in overlapping, incongruent, dissociated juxtaposition. The world of computers, VCRs, and fax machines allows unfathomable amounts of information and imagery—virtually all knowledge and culture—to be accessible almost on demand. Significantly, it is no longer necessary to go to the concert hall, the museum, the movie house, or even the library in order to consume these products of culture. They can be brought into the private realm, freed from the temporal constraints of exhibition or performance. They can be fragmented, deconstructed, juxtaposed. All this has contributed to our transformation into a society of isolated individuals, both producing and consuming all this information in the privacy of homes or offices away from the life of cities. Television has produced the anomaly of audiences of one hundred million or more individuals, each at his or her own private screen. This is the generation that has produced the neologism *cyberspace* to define a location, occupied by millions, that does not exist. We are, to quote Michel Foucault, in

> the epoch of space. We are in the epoch of simultaneity: we are in the epoch of juxtaposition, the epoch of the near and far, of side-by-side, of the dispersed. We are at a moment, I believe, when our experience of the world is less that of a long life developing through time than that of network that connects points and intersects with its own skein. One could perhaps say that certain ideological conflicts animating present-day polemics oppose the pious descendants of time and the determined inhabitants of space.[3]

Fourth observation: Theater—in fact, art in general—is shaped not by specific technological developments, but through transformations in consciousness and modes of perception that may, however, be significantly affected by technology. This is the key to understanding the relationship between theater and technology.

In our so-called information age, in which we are consumed with the technology of computers, the information superhighway, the World Wide

Web, and the like, many people tend to think that somehow this must be incorporated into the theater in order to make it modern, relevant, and economically viable and that the mere inclusion of various technologies and products on the stage will magically make the theater the equivalent of television or cyberspace. This is a false way of thinking and makes a mockery of postmodernism. Anyone attending theater or opera in the last decade has discovered that the most common prop in revivals of classics is the cellular phone. Did Shakespeare or Verdi really intend for their characters to speak or sing on cellular phones? Even in less precious endeavors, the introduction of video or computerized imagery into live theater is a misguided nod toward so-called modernism. Some artists, such as singer-composer-performer Laurie Anderson, have successfully incorporated projections and computer technology into their work, but while Anderson has had a significant impact on the world of performance art, she is more closely related to the world of rock music and performance than to dramatic theater. Her influence in that sphere has been limited at best. Nonetheless, she is at the forefront of a form of live performance that is mediated by technology. We are not talking of the simple expedient of vocal amplification—all too prevalent in theatrical production nowadays—but of the use of a wide array of technology and media by the artist to transform her image and voice into components of a techno-palette that becomes the medium of artistic creation.

One multimedia artist, George Coates, has created works that have tried to mesh the worlds of cyberspace and theater. A piece from the mid-1990s, *Twisted Pairs,* is a case in point. The plot is self-consciously absurd. It involves an Amish farm girl who stumbles across a solar-powered laptop computer and subsequently meets characters from a range of online newsgroups. The characters and the text of the play were derived from actual individuals and postings found on a variety of newsgroups on the Net. Coates then created a stage set that in some way replicated the experience of being on the Net. In his own words:

> Over the past several years we have developed a stagecraft that enables live performers to inhabit illusionary 3-dimensional stage sets. The audience wears polarized glasses allowing stereographic projected stage imagery to create illusions of volumetric space. These projected "soft" sets are scaled to fit the performers' actions and serve as a theatrical infrastructure supporting all forms of multimedia from across the arts disciplines: slides, scrolling text, data animations, film with live performers.[4]

Coates creates these so-called soft sets with polarized film, data projectors, and 35 mm slides projected on specially treated screens. The scenic illusions can thus appear to project into the audience or beyond the upstage wall. The text of the play includes actual news items, events and text inspired by online events and interchanges, and pure fantasy. In addition, there is a home page on the World Wide Web for the show. Individuals who log on can answer questions and leave messages or follow the adventures of various characters. Thus, the experience of the production, for those who wish, can begin before entering the theater or continue after leaving it. It can even be experienced by those who never see it. Coates has also created works such as *Invisible Site: A Virtual Sho* in which live performances are broadcast over the Web in real time using performers from different locations around the world.

Laurie Anderson and others have taken this idea in a slightly different direction by creating performances of sound and images that exist entirely on the Web. The "audience" can watch the evolution of a plot over a period of time and follow different threads or characters. There is a limited amount of interaction possible. These performances are all digitally created; they are not live. While the cyberplays of Coates and Anderson may be finding new audiences, and may even be creating ways for theatrical techniques and structures to infiltrate the minds of a generation unfamiliar with live theater, it is not at all clear that this will have any lasting or significant impact on the creation of drama.

George Coates's work has a certain appeal and sense of currency in its attempt to incorporate both the technology and the ideology of the Web into live performance, but as with many theatrical attempts at discourse with technology, one gets a creation that is neither one thing nor another. One may wonder what is the point of trying to re-create "virtual" imagery on an actual, three-dimensional stage? Why try to get the theater to mimic the particular physical manifestations of Net surfing? As fascinating as some of these productions are, they will, I believe, become little more than footnotes to theater history. They are reminiscent of nineteenth-century melodramas that incorporated new inventions into their plots, as in Dion Boucicault's *The Octoroon,* in which a photograph is crucial for the capture of a murderer. It is not theater created as a consequence of the new technology, it is theater *about* the new technology. It *discusses* rather than *embodies.*

One of the philosophers of postmodernism, François Lyotard, says that modernism is characterized by the presence of a metanarrative: a central, unifying concept around which the culture is based. The proscenium stage, which was born at the beginnings of modern Western society, created a visual and physical manifestation of the metanarrative—a unifying framework in which a linear story or a causally connected series of images and artifacts was presented to an audience that was itself drawn from an essentially homogeneous group and collected within a single space. (The ability to darken the auditorium reinforced this concept even further by reducing the audience to a single entity in the darkness whose very existence was predicated upon its ability to project itself onto the world of the stage.) But metanarratives do not function in the postmodern world. We are in the realm of what Frederic Jameson calls "pastiche." Instead of a language—be it literary, visual, or musical—with a clarity that is accessible to all viewers, there is a fragmentation of languages. Structures have dissolved; discrete images have evaporated. The past is no longer prelude, it is merely material to be drawn upon for present use. All images, all ideas, all thoughts, are equal. Linearity is archaic, anachronistic. The term *surfing,* once reserved for an aquatic sport, is now the term of choice for significant forms of entertainment. We channel surf as we flip from TV show to TV show with our remote controls. We Net surf as we click from icon to icon on our computer screens, jumping from topic to topic, driven as much by coincidences of homonyms or alphabetical proximity as any coherent idea. But to surf means to stay on the surface, never to plumb the depths—an admirable goal on an ocean wave, a dubious one in cultural interchange. As we glide over the surface, we observe a panoply of fascinating images and fragments whose only real connection is their juxtapositional arrangement in the mind's eye.

Fifth observation: Proximity and coincidence have replaced cause and effect (narrative) as a structural principle in postmodern theater.

Yet here is where we must look for the connections and influences between drama and technology. A new drama may be emerging out of this new sensibility. American writers such as Mac Wellman and Suzan-Lori Parks construct plays in which linearity, narrative coherence, even the stability of characters from moment to moment is irrelevant. Historical figures, fantasy, news events, and real life intermingle in works that are no longer bound by narrative structures, standardized acts and scenes, or even a socially agreed-upon duration. A play—or perhaps theatrical event is a better descriptive term—can range from a few minutes (such as some of David Ives's vignettes or the somewhat older neodada sketches of Kenneth Koch) to the multihour, even multiday creations of Peter Brook, Robert Wilson, and Ariane Mnouchkine. American playwright Paula Vogel has stated that in a postmodern play, "character, plot, language, and environment or plasticity as self-contained entities correspond fitfully, if at all, and only until the playworld fragments once again."[5]

In a world in which art, perhaps even life, is being structured and experienced by a spectator alone in a room, there is a sense of emptiness and loss, and this will be reflected scenographically. The new plays reflect that loss. The new drama often exists without the presence of tangible characters. The plays of Richard Foreman, for example, which date back to 1968, contain no psychologically based characters with emotional lives, only physical manifestations of the mind of the playwright given temporary form on the stage. The Wooster Group, a New York–based avant-garde company that creates theater pieces out of the raw material of deconstructions of classic texts, has probably been more successful than any American theater company at incorporating video into live performance. In their productions, interestingly, technology has helped to reinforce the sense of emptiness that is increasingly dominant in new American drama. In *Brace Up!* for instance, a deconstruction and contemporary response to Chekhov's *The Three Sisters,* characters in several scenes are seen on video screens in a live feed from offstage video cameras. In various productions by the group, live actors have interacted with videotaped actors who were formerly in the production but have since left. In a production entitled *L.S.D. . . . Just the High Points,* an actor engaged in dialogue and action with his own videotaped image. In the aforementioned *Brace Up!* an actor who died of AIDS continued to "perform" in the piece on tape. Excerpts from Kabuki dances and Japanese horror films of the 1950s also showed up on video. In keeping with the postmodern aesthetic, Chekhov, pop culture, exotic (to Western eyes) culture, and the daily lives of the actors were equal elements in this pastiche that becomes a play.

The staging itself was an embodiment of the emptiness suggested by modern sensibility. The stage at the Performing Garage, the home of the Wooster Group, is a faint echo of the proscenium in its frontal relationship to the audience. But the actors hover around the edges and, as noted, sometimes appear only as electronic images while their corporeal bodies remain offstage. The edges of the stage seem at times to be a barrier, and to step onto the stage is a significant act for a performer. In *Brace Up!* and other Wooster Group productions, the center of the stage is frequently an empty place.

Another example of contemporary sensibilities shaping the drama can be seen in one of the most talked about plays of recent American theater: Tony Kushner's *Angels in America.* This play consists of two parts, each about three and a half hours long, for a total of eight acts and an epilogue, totaling about sixty scenes, many of which are "split," presenting two locales simultaneously. The scenes represent variously real places, landscapes of the mind, and symbolic locales. It is tempting to classify the play structurally in the tradition of the Elizabethan theater, or perhaps medieval theater, or to call it cinematic. With its relatively old-fashioned tone of political engagement and the triumph of the individual in a corporate state, it is hard to imagine *Angels* as a product of the computer age. Yet Kushner, a relatively young man who has grown up inside recent American culture, has created a play that reflects the prevailing nonlinear, juxtapositional, hypertextual world of cyberculture. Thematically, imagistically, emotionally, this play has nothing to do with the world of computers and cyberspace; it is not about that at all. But structurally, it epitomizes the modern play in the contemporary world. It has abandoned neoclassicism, romanticism, naturalism, for a flow of images and ideas that replicates the perceptual processes of contemporary audiences who *are* shaped by the hypertextual world of electronic media.

Finally there is the work of director Anne Bogart. A postmodern director perhaps best known for her deconstructions of classic texts and her work with Japanese director Tadashi Suzuki, she has also created original pieces with her company, the Saratoga International Theatre Institute. Technically, her plays are very simple. (As a footnote to this discussion it is probably worth noting that technological innovation in live performance is driven by rock music and stadium concerts—that is, after all, where the demand is and, more importantly, the money to meet the demand. The technology of the Wooster Group, for example—lavish for the world of off-off-Broadway—is simplistic by the standards of major rock concerts.) But her pieces such as *The Medium,* based on the writings of Marshall McLuhan, *Small Lives, Big Dreams,* based on the writings of Chekhov, and *American Silents,* based on the early silent film industry, are classic examples of Jamesonian pastiche—dramatic events created out of found texts, modern dance, Suzuki technique, popular culture, and collaborative input of performers. Part of Bogart's creative process consists of making actual collages of relevant images; these collages are as much as twelve meters long and become a kind of urtext for the performance. The production values of the final product are utterly simple, yet structurally they are as far removed from the realistic dramas of the first half of this century as neoclassicism was from medieval drama. They reflect a societal worldview utterly transformed by current technological sensibility. To quote Bogart, "Physicists now say that nothing touches, nothing in the universe has contact; there is only movement and change."[6]

Her plays attempt to incorporate and convey this understanding of the world that will be instinctively understood by audiences with no understanding of quantum physics.

Final observation: In the sense that all Western drama of the last six hundred years or so has evolved out of or in response to neoclassical precepts, we might say that the neoclassic era lasted until only a few years ago. What we are entering into now might be termed "neomedievalism." But whereas the original was driven by theological ideas, this movement owes its genesis and form to technology that has refashioned the neoclassical worldview.

Notes

1. Margarete Bieber, *The History of the Greek and Roman Theater* (Princeton, N.J.: Princeton University Press, 1961), 167.

2. F. T. Marinetti, "Manifesto of Futurism," in *Selected Writings,* ed. R. W. Flint (New York: Farrar, Straus and Giroux, 1972), 41.

3. Michel Foucault, "Of Other Spaces," *Diacritics* 16 (1986): 22.

4. "George Coates Interviewed by His (Virtual) Audience," *Theatre Forum* (summer–fall 1996): 27.

5. Paula Vogel, "Anne Bogart and the New Play," in *Anne Bogart: Viewpoints,* ed. Michael Dixon and Joel A. Smith (Lime, N.H.: Smith and Kraus, 1995), 95.

6. Anne Bogart quoted in Dixon and Smith, *Anne Bogart,* 11.

(Sceno)Graphic Style

The question of national style is an intricate and politically charged issue in the culturally diverse society of the United States. Literary and performance theory is dominated by the field of cultural studies, and almost every endeavor is viewed through the narrow lens of what has come to be known as "identity politics." Especially in our two major cultural centers, New York and Los Angeles, with their richly complex and ever-changing mix of races, ethnic groups, and economic classes, to suggest that one visual or theatrical style might speak for all segments of society is deemed "politically incorrect." It suggests that the component groups have no individual identity and that a uniform style has been imposed upon them by the dominant faction within the culture. In other words, the idea of "national style" raises the specter of cultural imperialism. In the present social and political climate of the United States, this topic leads us down a treacherous road indeed. Politics aside, the presence of so many cultural and ethnic groups would suggest that a "national style" is, in fact, a vast conglomeration of styles—sometimes interacting to create something new, sometimes maintaining a distinct identity.

This is an inevitable outcome of the unique way in which American society has been built over several hundred years. It is a society composed almost entirely of people who came from somewhere else—sometimes forced, sometimes by choice. There seems to be little stability in American society; it is a nation in flux. Large numbers within the population move from one house, city, or region of the country to another with alarming frequency. Thus, any scenographic style that might emerge from the physical environment—the landscape that imprints itself on the mind from birth within a more stable community—has been replaced by an eclectic aggre-

Presented at a conference on nationality in stage design at the University of Haifa, November 1998. The conference was convened by the Israeli Center of the International Organization of Scenographers, Theatre Architects, and Technicians (OISTAT), as part of the celebration of the fiftieth anniversary of the establishment of the State of Israel.

gation of fleeting and confused images that now comprise our collective topographical consciousness.

In a sense, this is true of the very history of theater design itself in the United States. Some of the most influential designers of the American theater—Boris Aronson, Joseph Urban, Jo Mielziner, Rouben Ter Arutunian, Ming Cho Lee, Tony Walton, George Tsypin—were born abroad, while many others studied abroad. American design in the twentieth century, like American culture itself, was characterized by an eclectic confluence of international styles and influences. And interestingly, in more recent times, those designers who possess a strong signature style, from designer-director Robert Wilson to such scenographers as Robert Israel, Paul Steinberg, and Adrianne Lobel, have done much of their work not in the United States but in Europe and Asia.

Given the fragmentation of the American theater and its relatively small audiences, and the declining opportunities for establishing hallmark scenographic styles, it is increasingly difficult to say that there is a national style of scenic design in the United States today. And yet, as in almost every period, a recognizable visual motif has emerged that I will call "international chic." Its origins, I believe, are found in the art world of the 1970s—in the art photography and photorealist painting of the period, as well as in the neoformalist theater of Richard Foreman and Robert Wilson, but it is most prevalent today in graphic and commercial art and advertising. It is found on the pages of almost every magazine, on television and film, on billboards, and in the displays of stores and boutiques. Given the pervasiveness of this style, it has developed a mass audience, and as a result it has insinuated itself back into the theater. We have theater that looks like fashion advertising, and fashion ads that look like theater.

For a style to be truly "national" it must permeate all levels and aspects of society. International chic seems to do just that. It is inevitably affected by computer technology, in which use of pixels establishes the color palette and the graphic form of this style; and at the same time the ubiquitous presence of computers in our society and the increasing familiarity of the World Wide Web contribute to the rapid dissemination of this visual style. Because neither the media nor cyberspace respects national borders, cultural boundaries, nor even linguistic barriers, this is an international style that will be recognizable to everyone.

While the result may be international, I believe that its origins are in the eclectic and constantly transmogrifying nature of American society, which in turn has given rise to this postmodern mode. Like the fabric of the nation itself, it draws upon an international potpourri of styles and influences and, most important, does so almost randomly. The images of contemporary commercial art, as well as those of American scenography, can, within a single frame, span centuries, artistic movements, high and low culture, while defying any adherence to the logic of cause and effect. Philosopher Fredric Jameson identifies pastiche as a significant characteristic of postmodernism. The historical past is indiscriminately cannibalized—images, styles, and particular iconographic systems are invoked, *not* for their associative values (that is, not to remind us of a particular moment, event, or historical period), but for their "pastness." What they evoke is a vague sense of a previous time, of the old, of history—but a history devoid of any understanding or meaning. Thus, for a contemporary audience, an image from a thirty-year-old television show, the daguerreotypes of the Civil War, Renaissance paintings, and representations of ancient Rome are all vaguely equivalent. They are little-understood icons of an undifferentiated past. The result is the "simulacrum," a term that derives from Plato and more recently has been popularized by French theoretician Jean Baudrillard. A simulacrum, to quote Jameson, is an "identical copy for which no original has ever existed."[1] Historically, scenic design has either re-created an identifiable locale, or created an idealized place (think of the intermezzi designs of the Renaissance) that, though fanciful, possessed verisimilitude. Current design often presents neither the real nor the ideal; it presents collages of form and image that signify without meaning. The images evoke or provoke but defy rational explanation within the physical world. This is in part the result of current imaging technology, of course. Computers can transform images, make them lie, alter them, enhance them. The photographic image, once a symbol of verisimilitude (though it was always, at the very least, a carefully selected fragment of reality) is now an unreliable collection of images at the service of the artist.

What are the characteristics of this style? To begin with, it is typified by images—both people and objects—in isolation. The primary object becomes fetishized—it is caressed by the camera lens or by the theatrical light. On the page the object is often set in relief against an out-of-focus background (a quality of the camera lens that is, of course, difficult to achieve on the stage); on the stage it may be foregrounded by intense backlighting or side light. The image is strongly sculpted by shadow in ways that objects rarely are in the real world. Occasionally an object appears, startlingly, as if illuminated by nineteenth-century footlights. There tends to be a rich saturation of color that can take one of two forms: either warm hues that evoke a vague sense of nostalgia for an almost turn-of-the-century look, sometimes creating an aura as if the object or person was seen through

2. Robert Wilson's *Time Rocker,* 1997, music and lyrics by Lou Reed, text by Darryl Pinckney. (Photo: Hermann and Clärchen Baus.)

smoke or haze; or a saturation of cool, unnatural colors somehow echoed in skin tones or in the object's surface. In the latter case lines are often impossibly sharp and crisp, making the objects almost jump off the page or screen. This is a world vaguely reminiscent of science fiction, a world of harsh fluorescent lights, and the infrared and ultraviolet rays of the laboratory. There is a cold clinical aspect to these images that passes for a millennial vision of the future.

In the case of the nostalgic image it is a re-creation of a world vaguely recollected from film noir and sepia photographs. It creates a longing for a time that we think we remember, or a world of our parents, or of a mythological past; perhaps a time when things were simpler and happier, or perhaps a world of mystery evocative of the most mystifying or frightening fantasies of children's tales. These are seductive images that appear to provide alternatives to the reality in which we live. The images are suffused with nostalgia, but for a sensibility that we think we should have, not one we have really lost—because it never existed. These are not real worlds, now or ever.

Whether in print or on the stage, action or immanent action has been supplanted by the tableau. And even when the images imply a scenario or vaguely defined activity, they are self-referential or self-absorbed. Persons in these images, like eighteenth-century actors, stare directly at the audience or project an attitude of disinterest or even defiance. In this new world, individuals exist in isolation from each other and to some degree from the world around them. They stare at us, like defiant animals in a cage—or perhaps we are the ones in the cage, being languorously observed. We are beckoned to participate, yet held at arm's length.

What does it mean? This is a style in which any coherence that exists is that of the frame or of formal structures; there is little identifiable correspondence with the natural world. It is a style in which objects are intended to stimulate desire and longing—to make the blood flow faster—and yet, because these are unreal images, the desire leads to frustration. These are unattainable objects. So the new style is one of coldness or false warmth, alienation, fragmentation, and loss. It is, I believe, a millennial style. Unable or unwilling to see the future, we look at the past—but a past seen through the filter of casual and haphazard collections of knowledge and images that are contemplated and randomly accessed, but not explored. It is a product of fear—fear of a world whose coherence disintegrates into a million pixels of color in which each dot takes on an independent value contiguous with, but independent of its neighbor. It is sleek and beautiful, evocative and mysterious, yet ultimately shallow and unknowable and totally unenlightening. Like most styles that have come to typify particular eras, it reflects the society and the culture from whence it comes.

Note

1. Fredric Jameson, "Postmodernism; or, The Cultural Logic of Late Capitalism," *New Left Review* 146 (July–August 1984): 74.

Can Theater and Media Speak
the Same Language?

From its very beginnings in ancient Greece, theater has been fascinated with technology. From flying machines to pyrotechnics, artists and audiences alike have been determined to ignore Aristotle's warning—that spectacle is "the least artistic" aspect of theater—and instead have indulged themselves in a veritable feast of spectacle. The history of scenography is, at least in part, a history of the exploitation of new technologies for the purpose of creating scenic wonder and amazement. Yet until the twentieth century, theater technology was primarily mechanical. The technician's task was to make things move and sometimes to make actors defy the laws of gravity. The real trick was to minimize the appearance of human agency, that is, to make things appear to move of their own volition, to animate that which is normally inanimate. But since at least the work of German director Erwin Piscator in the 1920s there has been a significant new component in the scenographer's palette: projections, film, and more recently, video. As with the older technologies, these cinematic and electronic tools, especially when first introduced on the stage, sometimes functioned as little more than gimmicks meant to delight, surprise, and mystify the audience. More often, though, they are used as a form of scenery—either as a substitute for painted or constructed illusionism, or as an abstract and imagistic background, or as a scenic component within a setting.

I would like to suggest that with some notable exceptions, projected scenery, and especially film and video, does not work—does not function— on the stage. I am not proposing a rule—rules, after all, are meant to be broken—nor am I suggesting that there are no examples of successful uses of video or film in theater. In most cases, however, the use of projections and moving images is disconcerting, even confusing to spectators; and it rarely functions as its users intend. What I am suggesting is that such projections

First presented at "Scenoweather" conference, Tallinn, Estonia, November 2000.

and images draw upon a fundamentally different vocabulary from that of the stage; it is not a scenographic vocabulary. Unless the intent is specifically to create a sense of dislocation and disjunction, or to draw upon the cultural signification of film and video in our media-saturated age, the placement of such technology and imagery on the stage is tantamount to carrying on a conversation in two languages. Communication is still possible, but content is overwhelmed by form.

The reasons why projections do not work well onstage are complex; they involve physiology (how the eye sees), psychology (how the brain interprets the signals it receives), and philosophy (what vision is, and how culture informs the way in which we see). It also involves political philosophy. Modern technology is largely a product of a capitalist system, and just as the photograph is inextricably bound to the industrial revolution of the nineteenth century, electronic media are tied to late-twentieth-century modes of communication and perception that are part of the multinational economy of our time. As philosopher Martin Heidegger noted, "The essence of technology is by no means anything technological."[1] Its importance lies in its reordering of perception and is thus subject to a range of political, social, and economic influences.

Let me start with a fundamental truth about the stage: Theater is the only art form to use that which is signified as the signifier of that object. A novelist evokes an image with words, a painter replicates an image with paint, but the theater artist uses the very object itself, or else a simulacrum: A human being signifies another human being; a chair signifies a chair; and the three-dimensional space of the stage signifies the three-dimensional space of . . . a room, a palace, a forest, a garden, or even a stage. The theater, of course, sometimes engages in illusion. But unlike, say, a photorealist painting in which we may have to study the work of art up close to determine whether it is a painting or a photograph, we would never mistake the two-dimensional image for the three-dimensional world being depicted. The photograph is a re-presentation of a moment or object taken out of the ongoing spatial and temporal flow of the so-called real world. A photorealist painting is a representation of that object known as a photograph. On the stage, however, though we may be tricked into believing that painted canvas or wood is marble, brick, or wallpaper, we are nonetheless dealing with real surfaces and volumes. A floor that is treated to look like tile may in fact be made of wood, but it still functions as a floor—it may be walked upon. One cannot swim in a painting of an ocean or eat the fruit in a still life.

The key element, I believe, is space or volume, and that, in turn, implies time. As human beings we intrinsically understand that we live in time and space. When we sit in a theater, we extend that fundamental understanding to the stage. It does not matter whether the production in question is illusionistic or presentational, we sense the spatiality of the stage with its textures, volumes, and dimensions. The actors we see are like us: they have volume, they move through space, and thus they move through time. In order to cross the stage, exit through a door, sit on a sofa, eat a meal, or engage in a sword fight, they will have to move across visible and knowable distances, and we can reasonably know how much time will elapse as they do so. Although the fictional time of the play may not coincide with the real time of the theater, on some level we know that the actor exists in real time, just as the fictional character he or she creates exists in the fictive time of the narrative.

But what happens when the scenography includes a projected image? Unless the projected image is painstakingly captured in the exact proportion to the stage and performers, and in perfect alignment with the sightlines of the spectators—something nearly impossible to achieve—the audience experiences the disjunction of perceiving a different world. In the Wooster Group's production *Rumstick Road* in 1978, there was a moment in which an image of Spalding Gray's mother was projected over an actress. As the actress violently flipped her long hair back and forth, she went in and out of the frame of the projected image. At those moments when the live and projected image coincided, the effect was electrifying. Usually, however, with projected imagery there is no spatial continuity between stage and auditorium and consequently no ability to comprehend time. As in some sort of science fiction story, it is as if a parallel universe has somehow entered into our space-time continuum.

It is perhaps worth noting that illusionistic scenery works only from a particular vantage point—in the baroque era, for instance, only from the royal box—and that the stage world is often depicted in a different scale from that of the auditorium. But either we compensate psychologically, or else the disjunction is exploited. Leonardo's *Last Supper* in the Santa Maria delle Grazie in Milan is not, of course, a theatrical setting. Nonetheless, Leonardo's use of perspective is relevant to an understanding of theatrical space. The painting, at one end of the chapel, appears at first glance to extend the architecture of the space. Yet this is misleading; the height of the painting off the floor in combination with the peculiar perspective means that it can be seen as a true extension of the room only by a spectator from a particular vantage point that no spectator standing in the room can have. Much Renaissance scenery after Serlio also attempted to create an illusion of continuing the space of the auditorium onto the stage. But again, the illusion works only from an extremely limited viewing angle. So we may say that pictorial space, while possibly mimicking the exterior world, remains contained and self-referential; it is inward looking.

Part of this disjunction, in fact, comes from the way in which the audience understands the temporal referents of the image. No matter, for instance, when the scenery or the theater was built, we experience the stage in the here and now; we know it exists because we can see it in front of our eyes and we know we could go on the stage and touch it and move through it. But a projected image is different. The projection exists in the present, of course, but the image is from the past; the image was photographed, filmed, or videoed prior to presentation. The very process of developing film involves a step called "fixing"—making the image permanent. A fragment of the time-space continuum is abstracted and becomes an *object* for visual consumption. As film historian Vivian Sobchak says, "The photograph freezes and preserves the homogeneous and irreversible *momentum* of this temporal stream into the abstracted, atomized, and secured space of a *moment*."[2] The objects or people within the photographic image may no longer exist; at the very least they will have aged, however minutely. Time has transformed the subject while preserving the object. The projected image, therefore, is dead. André Bazin calls it "mummification." It captures and preserves something from the past for re-presentation in the present. The very thing that makes family photographs, historical documents, or works of art valuable—their ability to capture the past or allow us to revisit unchanging images that have given us pleasure—transforms them into fetish objects. They are, in the words of John-Louis Comolli, like gold, "the money of the 'real.'"[3] But this becomes a negative virtue on the stage that requires dynamic presence. Moreover, because photographs produce images of the world rivaled only by the human eye, the eye has lost its historically privileged place as a processor of information. On a stage that combines live images observed through normal visual processes and photographic images in which an eye observes mechanically reproduced images, the two systems inevitably clash.

There is, of course, one exception to the "mummified" image—a live video feed that projects a video image as it is captured. This addresses the question of temporal dissonance but raises the issue of spatial dislocation. If the image is "live," where is it in relation to the space of the stage? Is the real image the one on the video monitor or screen, or is it the object or person being captured by the camera?

Crucial to our understanding of the mechanics of perception in these contexts is the idea of framing. How, for instance, do spectators account for the fact that the world on the stage, though apparently sharing the same physical space, depicts a different world from that of the auditorium? When Lear stands on the heath, we see that he is blown by wind and rain, yet we, the audience, remain warm and dry; when Nora leaves Torvald in *A Doll's House,* we may intellectually know that the actress is merely going to her dressing room, but we believe that Nora is slamming the door and going out into the street from whence her possibilities are infinite. The key to our comprehension is the frame. While a proscenium-type stage may posses a very literal frame, any stage, no matter how it is configured, no matter what its architectural relation to the audience, always constitutes a frame. A frame is a form of visual organization; it creates a self-contained space carefully delineated from the world around it. As with a painting, this pictorial organization—this radical self-containedness—creates an internal logic that may differ from that of its surroundings, and yet the frame imparts a sense of order and a consistent ontology that allows us to comprehend what we see. Let us take an obvious example such as a painting of a landscape. The visual image within the frame appears to obey the visual order of an extrinsic world; that is, it "re-presents" the external world within the self-contained world inside the frame. We may see, for instance, trees, fields, animals, and the like. What is in the frame, however, will not relate directly to its immediate surroundings, which are the space and architecture of the world outside the frame. Think of the experience at a museum or gallery or even an individual home. In close juxtaposition there may be a landscape, a cityscape, a still life, an interior of a room, and an abstract image. Tall buildings or trees may be depicted as only centimeters high, while relatively small objects may fill a canvas a square meter in size. Furthermore, the frames allow us to place these unrelated images cheek-by-jowl, without any resultant visual dissonance. And of course, none of the images have anything to do with the wall on which they are hung.

In regard to framing, the theater is not unlike a painting. Because the action that unfolds before our eyes is framed by the stage, we accept its internal logic within the larger envelope—the larger frame—of the theater itself. We can view a world on a different scale that obeys different rules, and yet sit in our seat relatively undisturbed by this cosmic rupture.

For a variety of reasons projections, particularly cinematic projections, do not obey the same rules. Movies, too, are framed, of course, just like paintings and similar to the stage. If you go to the cinema, the projected image fills the wall at one end of the theater. Its size in relation to the viewer means that it virtually fills the entire field of vision. It has often been pointed out that sitting in a darkened movie theater comes close to fulfilling Richard

Wagner's vision for Bayreuth in which the individual spectators are obliterated in the darkened auditorium and become a communal audience that then projects itself into the idealized world of the stage. But what makes the movies even more attractive on some level than the theater or opera is its ability to present us with an infinite world. We can defy laws of time and space as movies take us in a blink of an eye to worlds past and future, far and near. The philosopher Edmund Husserl talked about the *Augenblick,* the timeless blink that in an instant captures "a scene of ideal objects" and presents it to the consciousness.[4] The most transformative stage is no match for the projected image that can present an almost infinite series of "blinks" as it were. One is reminded of French filmmaker Jean-Luc Godard's dictum that the movies are truth twenty-four times a second.

This, of course, suggests another quality of movies. We have come to understand them as a kind of documentary capturing of reality. Even though from the beginnings of cinema's history (think of the fantasies of Georges Méliès) through such recent movies as *The Matrix,* the image has been manipulated—a fictional world is created as surely as in any painting, sculpture, or novel—yet we persist in believing that what is on the screen must in some way be true. The cinematic image transforms even the most blatant fantasy into reality. The theater, on the other hand, though composed of real objects—wood, canvas, paint, papier-mâché, and the like—transforms a concrete reality into a kind of fantasy. Everything on the stage becomes a sign.

When movies or even still pictures are projected on a stage, at least two realities come into conflict. First, the frame has changed. A projection on a stage is contained within a frame—a projection screen, perhaps, or a wall of the stage—that is contained within the larger frame of the stage with its pictorial and architectural elements, which itself is contained within the larger frame of the theater. This changes our whole relation to it. No longer is it a Wagnerian image overwhelming our individual consciousnesses; it is one element among many. Even if it is a large projection, we see it in relation to the living actors, scenic units, and even the walls of the theater. Thus corporeal reality, imagistic reality, and symbolic reality are brought into proximity and often into direct conflict.

The projected image also raises the pictorial question of figure and ground. In a painting or even in a photograph, our mind processes visual information in such a way that we see certain objects as figures placed against a background that provides us with visual clues as to size and distance (which implies time). A simple example is provided by seeing an airplane in the sky. Our eyes, our knowledge of the world, and our experience tells us that the airplane is an object moving against the background of the sky, not the other way round. Yet in ancient times and still within certain cultures or perhaps among children, the stars of the nighttime sky are sometimes perceived not as objects against the background of the sky, but as pinpricks in a kind of canvas. In such a situation, the sky is seen as the foreground, and the stars as bits of light from the firmament beyond. This same process allows us to comprehend a framed painting hung on a wall. The painting becomes a figure against the ground of the wall on which it is hung. Thus, it is seen not as rupture within the wall, or some strange permutation of the architectural features of the wall, but simply as an object hung on the wall.

When an image, especially a cinematic or moving image, is projected on a stage, however, there is confusion and dislocation. Because the projection is framed, it becomes the object seen—the figure—against the ground of the set or the stage. In addition, because an object is more likely to move than the ground, the moving image on the stage further reinforces its function as figure. But the projected image is not a finite object. Again, our eyes and our cultural knowledge of photographic or cinematic images lead us to understand that the image seen within the frame is a mere fragment of the larger environment from which the image was produced. The framed projection implies a boundless image. A tension is thus created between the potentially unlimited expanse of the image projected and the self-containedness of the physical projection. An even greater tension is created between the unlimited bounds of the projected image and the architectural realities of the stage.

In the case of video or film, the image is further complicated by movement. Onstage we see objects in movement against the generally static ground of the stage or scene. But in the cinema, nothing is stable. The moving camera defeats the stability of the image. The movement is not simply an objective reproduction of movement in the external world; rather, the movement is specifically enhanced by the subjective intentions of the director or camera operator. To quote Sobchak again,

> Unlike the photograph, a film is semiotically engaged in experience not merely as a mechanical objectification—or material *reproduction*—that is, not merely as an object for vision. Rather, the moving picture, however mechanical and photographic its origin, is semiotically experienced as also subjective and intentional, as *presenting representation* of the objective world.[5]

In cinematic projections, figure and ground are both capable of movement and transformation. In the movies, this becomes a cinematic tool, a vocabulary understood by spectator and filmmaker alike. But on the stage it creates at least two perceptual systems. There is also the purely physiological factor of the attraction of the eye for moving images, perhaps a vestige of our prehistoric mechanism for survival. The human eye seems ineluctably drawn toward the flickering image of the movie or video, even when a living being is equally available within the line of sight, thus creating a competition for focus.

Philosopher Fredric Jameson talks about the way in which the cinematic "thickens" the photographic. By existing as both presentational and representational, as something both subjective and objective, as suggesting a past and a future (because of its re-presentation of an image from the past through forward motion), it "transforms the thin abstracted space of the photograph into a thickened and concrete *world*," to quote Sobchak.[6]

The instability of the projected image also raises the question of what might be known as "erasure." A stage set, relatively speaking, is permanent and unchanging. Though one set may be replaced by another through mechanical means, we know that the first set has not evaporated into thin air. The objects that comprise the set still exist. Although the visibility of the set may be affected by light waves, the presence of the set is not affected by immaterial projections of light and shadow. If the electricity goes out, the decor still remains. But a projection is nothing but light and shadow reflected off a surface. It has no corporeality, it has no presence, it has no permanence. A chair left on a stage will remain until the theater crumbles to dust; a projection of a chair exists only as long as the projection remains. It can be erased in the blink of an eye. The very idea that one image, the projection, is created by light, and the other, the stage set, is created by objects that are made visible by their ability to reflect light, creates two perceptual orders, two kinds of reality. The paintings of Georges Rouault provide an interesting example. His paintings bear a strong resemblance to stained glass windows, a painterly equivalent of stained glass; images in his work are created by geometric blocks of color enclosed within heavy dark lines. With his permission, at least one of his paintings was in fact re-created as a stained glass window. Not surprisingly, it did not work. The once neutral and self-contained canvas became a translucent window animated by light and informed by its relation to its architectural environment. We might look at projections on the stage in the same way. The self-contained world of the stage is suddenly perforated by a live image animated by light with different systems of reference. Two similar images are subject to vastly different interpretations because of the quality of the material and the context in which it is read.

But the example of the stained glass reminds us that historically, different

3. The Wooster Group's *Brace Up!* from 1991, directed by Elizabeth LeCompte, set design by James Clayburgh, lighting by Jennifer Tipton. Note the use of video monitors. (Photo: Bob Van Dantzig.)

media have been combined successfully. Some architecture such as cathedrals contains sculpture as part of its vocabulary, not to mention stained glass with its painterly qualities; much Moorish and Islamic architecture is transformed through decorative and painterly embellishments; collage begins to bridge the gap between painting and sculpture, and so on. The key element in all these cases is that two or more vocabularies are intentionally combined with a keen awareness for how one informs the other. And so there are, in fact, forms of theater in which media are consciously used in order to heighten the theatricality of the performance. The best example is the Wooster Group, whose work is part of an ongoing investigation of spatial reality, temporal reality, the relation of live theater to our video culture, and a questioning of the nature of "presence." While the use of video by the Wooster Group acknowledges the omnipresence of video in contemporary society and very consciously calls into question our various modes of seeing, video does not substitute for more conventional scenographic elements in their productions. Rather, it becomes a provocative challenge to the very notion of theater in our time.[7]

Although the Wooster Group has pioneered ways of incorporating

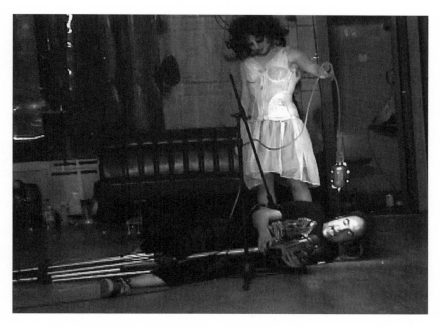

4. *Bend Your Mind Off,* by Collapsable Giraffe. Eric Dyer holds a video camera as Erin Douglass dangles light. (Photo—captured from video—courtesy Collapsable Giraffe.)

media and technology onto the stage, there is still a sense of media as fetish object; there is an almost reverential air to its presence. A younger generation of theater artists has demystified video and technology. Collapsable Giraffe and Radio Hole, two groups inspired in part by the Wooster Group, literally play with technology. Video images are created by performers in full view (there is no Oz here, hiding behind a curtain), and monitors and cameras are literally tossed about the stage. There is no fetishizing of technology; it is the raw material of this generation's world and has no more mystical quality than the cans of beer they hand out to spectators upon entering the theater. But these groups are not producing literary dramas with conventional decor, so the use of images and video could never be mistaken for a substitute for other forms of scenery.

There are other examples from the United States and around the world, but I think that the successful examples that I know of are surprisingly few. Too often the theater creators are more concerned with the technology and the momentary theatricality of the filmic or digital image than with under-

standing and exploring the way in which two vocabulary systems interact.
Or they fail to acknowledge that there are multiple visual vocabularies. At
least within Western society, our modes of perception and our modes of
thinking are undergoing a radical change for perhaps the first time in some
five hundred years. The new technologies cannot simply be placed upon
the stage without acknowledging and understanding this fact.

Notes

1. Martin Heidegger, "The Question concerning Technology," in *Basic Writings,* ed.
David Farrell Krell (New York: HarperCollins, 1977), 287.
2. Vivian Sobchak, "The Scene of the Screen: Envisioning Cinematic and Electronic 'Presence,'" in *Materialities of Communication,* ed. Hans Ulrich Gumbrecht and K.
Ludwig Pfeiffer (Stanford: Stanford University Press, 1994), 92.
3. Quoted in Sobchak, "Scene of the Screen," 91.
4. Quoted in Martin Jay, *Downcast Eyes: The Denigration of Vision in Twentieth-Century French Thought* (Berkeley and Los Angeles: University of California Press, 1994), 267.
Husserl's argument, it might be noted, was critiqued by Jacques Derrida.
5. Sobchak, "Scene of the Screen," 95.
6. Sobchak, "Scene of the Screen," 98.
7. See "The Wooster Group as Cartographers," in this volume, for a more detailed
discussion.

Looking Into the Abyss

The late French philosopher Michel Foucault devotes the first chapter of *The Order of Things: An Archaeology of the Human Sciences* to an analysis of the optical symbols and spatial relationships in the seventeenth-century painting by Velázquez known as *Las Meninas*. Much art history, of course, is based upon such formal analysis. What I find appealing about Foucault is the manner in which his probing of the image leads to an explication of social structures and hierarchical relationships of power within a particular society. *Las Meninas* and any number of other paintings share certain elements with scenography: there are characters interacting within a dynamic spatial structure comprised of symbolic scenic pieces depicted with an emblematic and emotional use of color and line. A world has been created and presented to us whose signifiers beg to be decoded, and yet these same signifiers can evoke a sensation of pleasure simply by being devoured by the eyes. Is this not also true of much theater? Could we not take a stage design—a theatrical environment—and wade into the depths of its forest of symbols, its spatial dynamics, and its existence as a site for revelation? Where are the Foucaults, Arthur Dantos, Clement Greenbergs of scenography?

Perhaps the relative lack of such scholarly analysis or critique of scenography is attributable, at least in part, to the instability of the scenographic object. First, if I were to present a stage design for consideration, what exactly would I show? A painted rendering? A model? A photograph of an empty set? (And, if that, a black-and-white or color photo?) A photo from a production with the actors?—but then, how to decide which moment of the production to show? Would the photo be only of the stage (which would emphasize the setting as an independent work of art), or would it include the auditorium as well (which would emphasize the convention of presentation)? A painting, no matter how illusionistically or cleverly it represents space, is still a fundamentally two-dimensional medium. Theater—

Presented at the University of Art and Design, Helsinki, March 2001.

and as obvious as this is, we must state it—is a spatial art; it occurs in three-dimensional space. We can analyze the space in *Las Meninas* precisely because it has been carefully structured according to the rules of perspective; only the Italianate stage designs of the Renaissance functioned somewhat in the same manner—and then, only for the king. And even so, it still included three-dimensional elements.

Theater—here is another truism—is a temporal art; it occurs in time. Other than through the normal process of aging, Velázquez's painting has not changed in 350 years. But a theatrical setting changes every minute through the movement of actors, the shifts in light, and often the physical transformations of the setting itself. It also changes because of the presence of the live audience in relation to real space. (One might argue that a painting changes depending on where it is hung—its context—and who is looking at it. This is certainly true, and in this it shares certain qualities with theater. Anyone who has first encountered a fresco in an art history book, for instance, is often shocked when experiencing the work in its actual location. But by and large, a painting remains an arrangement of paint delimited by a canvas; its formal elements will remain unchanged as long as the canvas maintains its integrity. The Infanta in *Las Meninas* cannot physically or psychologically respond to the energy of the onlookers in the Prado, nor can she alter from night to night her spatial relationship to the other figures, objects, or architecture depicted.)

Finally, Velázquez created people, space, light, clothing, furniture, and architecture through paint and canvas; nothing is "real," although we easily *read* the space and its contents because it corresponds to our understanding of the real world. It is, in Platonic terms, a shadow of a shadow. Theater, on the other hand, is the only representational art that uses the object being signified as a signifier. In other words, on a stage, a table is represented by a table; a person is represented by a person; and the space of a room is represented by the space of the stage. Thus, if I were to show you a photograph of a stage setting and attempt to analyze it as Foucault analyzes the painting, I would be forced to interpret multiple sign systems that are often at odds with each other. Although the photograph could be considered a document of reality, the object being documented—the stage set—is a three-dimensional space now rendered into a two-dimensional image and captured in a moment of time. That moment *may* reveal something about the set, but it is one fractional slice of the theatrical production that is made up of an infinite number of such temporal slices. (Again, one might argue that Velázquez's painting also captures a moment of time, but how many hours, days, or even weeks did the subjects pose, frozen in time, for this moment?

Furthermore, our analysis in this case is not of the real space or the real people but of a painting that is an object unto itself; we are not analyzing the real room depicted in the painting but the image created by Velázquez. The equivalent would be analyzing the formal elements of the photograph, not the setting it depicts.)

Nevertheless, although *Las Meninas* is a painting, it *is* theatrical and has much to tell us about theatrical space. The painting appears to focus on a young princess, but it actually depicts an artist standing in front of a large canvas (we see only the back of the canvas) and he is staring in our direction—apparently at his subjects, whom we do not see. Other members of the court are in the foreground, some of whom are also staring at the subject and thus, seemingly, at us. A painting, like the stage, is inherently confrontational and oppositional; the only way in which to apprehend it is to face it—to encounter it head on. There is something aggressive about both painting and theater: it thrusts itself in our path, imposes itself upon our space, demands a response. (A brief digression, if I may. Many forms of ritual, ceremonial theater, celebratory performance, religious festival, etc. tend to be either processional or environmental, meaning that the spectator is in some way incorporated into the context of the performance and the larger surrounding world; confrontation is replaced by integration. Even the ancient Greek theater was a fragment of a larger civic festival that was largely processional in nature, although interestingly, as the tragedy became formalized, the civic procession culminated in a confrontational experience— the spectators seated in the Theater of Dionysus facing the chorus and actors on the *skene* and orchestra. The confrontational mode of theater is largely a modern, Western form.)

In painting and most theater, spectators stare at an image or space that has been delineated, that is detached, in some way from the surrounding space. In some cases the characters of a painting or the stage seem to be unaware of an audience, thus inviting a voyeuristic response as we gaze at them with guilty pleasure. At other times the figures acknowledge us, stare at us, creating a dialectical relation to the artwork—we are watching ourselves being watched, which really means that we are watching ourselves watching. Furthermore, when figures in a painting look back at us, as they do in *Las Meninas* and in much theater, there is an implied extension of the visible space into the virtual area in front of the canvas. In perspective painting there are one or more vanishing points—points where lines of vision converge. Technically these exist in Velázquez's painting as well, but the background is murky, making the vanishing points less obvious. The very focus of the painting, a kind of virtual vanishing point, is, in fact, not visible because it exists approximately where we are standing. The vanishing point of *Las Meninas* is in our eyes. What happens when, more than three centuries later, we find ourselves implicated in the Spanish court? We can ask the same question of any piece of theater that implies our presence within the fictional world of the performance. The moment that we are acknowledged by a character on the stage (or in a painting), our own reality, our own presence, is somehow brought into question. If an actor looks at me, I, too, have become an actor in the particular, often fictional, world of the stage.

Foucault focuses on a particular element of the painting that may not be immediately apparent to the viewer. On the wall behind the painter, amid some other paintings, is a mirror, and in this mirror can be faintly seen the models for the portrait being painted. It is presumably King Philip IV and his wife, Mariana. Foucault remarks that this mirror, in apparent defiance of the laws of perspective, reflects nothing of the visible world of the painting but instead reflects the ostensible subjects of the painting within the painting. To quote Foucault,

> Its motionless gaze extends out in front of the picture, into that necessarily invisible region which forms its exterior face, to apprehend the figures arranged in that space. Instead of surrounding visible objects, this mirror cuts straight through the whole field of the representation, ignoring all it might apprehend within that field, and restores visibility to that which resides outside all view.[1]

In the illusionistic theater, the auditorium is a void beyond the front threshold of the stage. In fourth-wall realism, the theater does not exist. If this space—do we call it virtual space?—is acknowledged at all by the performers, it is under the pretense that it is an extension of their world; they see something in this space that is other than the auditorium; they respond to something that is not there. In such a configuration, where are we? What happens to us when we are replaced by a virtual landscape? If a mirror were part of the set, would we expect it to reflect us—the spectators—or the virtual world that is an implied extension of the setting? (Etymologies confound us here. *Auditorium* is from the Latin and means, of course, the place of hearing. Our word *theater,* however, comes from the Greeks, from the *theatron,* or seeing place. While the gerund *seeing* referred to the action of the spectators, it could just have logically referred to the space into which the more presentational Greek actors looked as they delivered their speeches. They looked into the seeing place or place of vision.)

It is by now a cliché that the theater is, as a character in *Don Quixote* states, "the mirror of human life, the model of manners, and the image of the truth." Similarly, Hamlet declares, "the purpose of playing . . . is to hold, as 'twere, the mirror up to nature." The characters in a play, for instance, may tell us something about ourselves, because we believe that we see ourselves in them. The pains, joys, loves, and losses that characters in a drama experience we take to be our own. We look at the stage and see our world reflected back. But this, of course, is an illusion. We are neither kings nor queens nor supernatural beings; we do not regularly swallow love potions, murder our parents, or mourn the loss of cherry orchards; we do not, at least not literally, stand by a tree at the side of the road day after day and wait for Godot. Moreover, our world appears to obey Newtonian rules of time and space; the stage world does not. In our quotidian world we cannot, as in the prologue of Shakespeare's *Henry V,* move "here and there . . . jumping o'er times, / Turning th' accomplishment of many years / Into an hour-glass." Even Einsteinian physics will not allow this. So why is it that when we view this distorted world filled with characters who are nothing like us, we still see ourselves and our world? How is the stage a mirror? What does it reflect?

The very act of looking, even voyeuristically, implies a reciprocal action, a return of the gaze, and hence an illusion of reflection. In this sense the stage may be compared to what Nietzsche, in a different context, called an abyss. "Whoever fights monsters," declared Nietzsche in *Beyond Good and Evil,* "should see to it that in the process he does not himself become a monster. When you look long into an abyss, the abyss also looks back into you." Remember that Plato banned theater (and all mimetic arts) from his republic because of his fear that it would transform both the viewer and performer into the monster being represented. We look at the stage and it returns our gaze. What better definition of a mirror? But an abyss also implies something with no bottom, something unknowable, something terrifying. To look into the stage is to look into a world of mystery, but also, I believe, a world of terror. Richard Wagner certainly understood this when he created Bayreuth. By turning off the houselights for the first time in history he obliterated not simply the individual but the audience itself. In order to survive, the audience had to project itself across what Wagner termed the "mystic chasm" onto the ideal world of the stage. To go to the theater meant risking the loss of self.

But the mirror in *Las Meninas,* as Foucault points out, does not reflect what it logically should; it does not reflect the spectator. How could it? The painting is fixed and the spectator is ever-changing. The mirror of that painting reflects an object forever absent; the virtual subject. We have all seen stage settings in which there are mirrors. In most cases the mirror is treated so as not to reflect the audience. The intrusion of an audience into the fictive (or at least formal) world of the stage would be disruptive. Moreover, the mirror, which obeys only the laws of optics, not those of the scenographer, would reflect the obverse side of set pieces and furniture, it would reflect offstage spaces, it would reflect shafts of stage light into the eyes of the audience. In other words, a functional mirror in an illusionistic set would reveal the very mechanics of the illusion, everything that is not part of the illusion, thus destroying it. So on the stage, in most cases, an actual mirror reflects nothing; it is an empty piece of décor or possibly a symbolic scenic element. (It is probably worth noting that in cinematography, the trick is to film the image in the mirror without revealing the presence of the camera. There is also graphic software that will automatically impose reflections onto appropriate surfaces at the mathematically correct angles within visual computer compositions.)

The presence of a mirror in the painting forces us to think about the act of reflection; it forces us to think about our relationship to the painting. In order to talk about the stage as a sort of mirror I want to use a term also coined by Foucault: "heterotopia." Foucault identified two particular kinds of social space: utopias and heterotopias. Utopias, he explained, were fictional, idealized, unreal spaces. "They present society itself in a perfected form," he declared, "or else society turned upside down."[2] In one sense, then, the world depicted on a stage could be considered a utopia: it is a place that does not exist and yet it bears, as Foucault would say, "a general relation of direct or inverted analogy with the real space of Society." A heterotopia, on the other hand, is more of what anthropologist Victor Turner calls liminal space: a real place but one that exists outside the boundaries of everyday society or behavior. Turner discussed this concept in regard to pilgrimages and other ritualized social events, but Foucault applies his term to such locales as cemeteries, sacred sites, vacation resorts, and formal gardens. The mirror, according to Foucault, is a special object that can be defined as both a utopia and a heterotopia. The mirror is a utopia "since it is a placeless place"—it enables the viewer to see himself where he is not; where, in fact, he is absent. But it is also a "heterotopia in so far as the mirror does exist in reality, where it exerts a kind of counteraction on the position that I occupy," says Foucault.

From the standpoint of the mirror I discover my absence from the place where I am since I see myself over there. Starting from this gaze that is, as it were, directed toward me, from the ground of this virtual space that is on the other side of the glass, I come back toward myself; I begin again to direct my eyes toward myself and to reconstitute myself there where I am. The mirror functions as a heterotopia in this respect: it makes this place that I occupy at the moment when I look at myself in the glass at once absolutely real, connected with all the space that surrounds it, and absolutely unreal, since in order to be perceived it has to pass through this virtual point which is over there.[3]

If we understand the stage as a mirror, then it, too, is a complex combination of the Foucauldian utopia and heterotopia. Like the mirror, the stage is a real place, but unlike the mirror, the space seen on the other side of the curtain or footlights (the anachronistic terms we use to define the threshold between the so-called real space of the auditorium and the fictive world of the stage) is not virtual but real. And yet, on another level, it is no more real than the image in the mirror. As an audience member I could, in theory, cross over the threshold onto the stage, but to do so would shatter that world just as certainly as an attempt to pass through the looking glass—Alice notwithstanding—would shatter the mirror. The world depicted on the stage possesses its power—its reality—only so long as I cannot touch it, cannot enter into it. It is a world of the gaze, of the voyeur; touching is forbidden. (There are, of course, forms of theater in which the threshold is purposely shattered, in which spectators are invited onto the stage or in which performers enter the auditorium. But these are purposeful and self-conscious violations of decorum. In some cases these transgressions are comic, creating laughter that is really a laughter of fear at the dissolution of boundaries and hence safety; in some cases the transgression is an attempt to dissolve the formal structures of the theater—that is to say, society—in order to create a new paradigm. This was especially popular in the political theater of the 1960s and 1970s as in many productions of the Living Theatre or Performance Group. Most such experiments have limited success at best.)

How are we able to recognize ourselves in a mirror? After all, in the normal course of events we cannot see ourselves. The mirror, however, reflects back to us a known world. The objects we see in the mirror—the elements that make up our spatial reality—are recognizable. I look into the mirror and see, let us say, a room, and it is an image of the room in which I am standing. The one unidentifiable image in the reflection is the person staring back at me. If everything else in the mirror can be identified as corresponding to the physical space around me, then the one unrecognizable figure, the one situated in the physical locale equivalent to my own, must be me. The theatrical stage, of course, does not function optically as a mirror; it does not automatically reflect back the physical space and objects facing it. Nonetheless, everything on the stage is carefully constructed or arranged to create the metaphoric illusion of a reflection. In contemplating the stage as mirror, what we seldom stop to consider is that in order for us to recognize ourselves—in order to recognize our world—we must be able to comprehend the stage both visually and spatially, just as we comprehend the world we see in our bedroom mirror. The stage, in other words, must be readable.

The stages of every society are different, and yet each of those societies saw its theaters as an reflection of its world. Take some of the most obvious examples: the orchestra and *skene* of the ancient Greek theater; the trestle stage of itinerant commedia dell'arte performers; the architectural stage of the seventeenth-century French court; the picture-frame prosceniums of the nineteenth century that enclosed illusionistic box sets; and the highly schematized structure of the Noh stage. At first glance these stages have only the most fundamental formal elements in common with each other. Yet each reflected something about its particular society's understanding of space. Each theater space was understood as a mirror of its particular world. The spectator who gazed into each version of the abyss saw him- or herself reflected back.

A complex translation occurs every time we go to the theater. First, we must recognize that a particular demarcation of space is a stage, and therefore that that space is, at least metaphorically, separate and distinct from the space we as audience occupy, even though it may be only a few feet distant from us and occupy the same architectural structure as we do. Second, we have to be able to identify the world created within that space. Such a world may be a replica, of sorts, of known or knowable spaces such as an interior of a house or a palace, a forest, a town square, a street. This illusion may be created in painstaking detail, or conjured up by a few suggestive elements. But even if it is a seemingly abstract space, we must be able to understand it as a space in which the characters or actors of a play may exist. Thus, a simple throne on an otherwise bare stage may be as evocative of a palace as an elaborate re-creation of a medieval throne room; the tables and chairs of the Beijing Opera may signify mountains just as much as the illusionistic ice ledges created by Ming Cho Lee for *K2* some twenty years ago. But just as we must recognize that a collection of marks on a page is a written language, so too must we recognize that a particular arrangement of space is a stage and that somehow, when looking at that arrangement of space, we are seeing our world.

What does space—the world in which we live—look like? More specifically, what does such space look like today? How do we see it, how do we recognize it, how do we define it? Martin Heidegger has said that we do not notice light, only what it illuminates. Artists—and by this I mean theater artists as well—might disagree; we do notice light. But only because we have been trained to do so, because we have become sensitized to it. The underlying principle, however, remains. What we see and how we see it is shaped by our culture. So, how do we recognize our world when we see it on the stage? The world as reflected on the stage at the beginning of the twentieth century looked different than it did in the middle of the nineteenth century and different than it looked at the end of the twentieth century. I can say with certainty that in one hundred years we will see the world in yet new ways.

The more-or-less simultaneous development of the camera and photographic image on the one hand, and the field of psychology on the other, led to conflicting strains within nineteenth-century art. Photography, of course, encouraged the faithful reproduction of the external aspects of reality. The increasing sophistication of scientific tools and the steadily growing body of knowledge of the workings of the world about us encouraged a scenography that attempted a faithful re-creation of the environments in which the characters lived. On the other hand, psychology and its related disciplines suggested an inner reality more ephemeral, less tied to the visible and concrete, and which was thus seen as somehow more truthful.

The photograph captures the complexities of the three-dimensional world and renders it onto the flat two-dimensional surface of the paper. The stage set did something similar, rendering the objects of the world into flat, planar images. It might be argued that this was nothing new, that the painted image had substituted for the plastic object since the Renaissance. This is true, to a degree, but a significant shift occurred in the nineteenth century. The scenographers of the Renaissance and Baroque understood that there was a difference between the human being and the painted setting. The actor resided on a forestage, sharing the same architectural space as the audience (sometimes quite literally, as in the French and English theaters that allowed spectators to sit on the stage). But in the nineteenth century, the actor was cut off from the auditorium, trapped behind the proscenium, and forced to share the two-dimensional space of the painted stage. German director Georg Fuchs at the Munich Art Theater attempted to make a virtue of this tendency with his so-called relief stage that purposely emphasized the contrast between the three-dimensional actor and the essentially two-dimensional sculptural relief of the scenery on a very shallow stage.

It was Adolphe Appia, of course, who more than anyone understood that the pictorial stage of the Romantic era was no longer an adequate mirror of our world. "Our present stage scenery is entirely the slave of painting . . . which pretends to create for us the illusion of reality," wrote Appia in 1902. "But," he continues, "this illusion is in itself an illusion, for the presence of the actor contradicts it."[4] Appia understood the fundamental contradiction between the actor who is, ipso facto, "real," and illusionistic scenery. With Appia we have a rupture in the post-Renaissance narrative of history. The scientific goal of capturing the visible world and re-presenting it could not coexist with the living actor who was not a re-presentation, not a fictive body, but an actual specimen of the knowable world. Thus, visual illusionism would continue most successfully only in two-dimensional forms: the photograph and the cinema. The stage would have to reimagine itself as an environment for the real body of the actor.

The nineteenth century, which built railroads and canals to support the economic structure of society, was a period of linear narrative. Representational scenography reinforced this narrative view. The re-creation of space implied a re-creation of time. The scenographic production of space provided the possibility of connecting a series of real-time events. As noted earlier, theater, like the novel, could leap across time and space with a few words, as could the film where the editor could achieve the equivalent effect with a jump cut. But on a moment-to-moment level, theater had to obey natural laws. A character who entered through a door had to traverse a quantifiable space in order to reach a table, say. This took the same time on the stage that an equivalent action would take in the real world. Time could be negated only by a convention such as closing the curtain or dimming the lights that implied the obliteration of space. The nineteenth-century theater, much as Western society at large at the same time, was focused on the intersection of time and space.

Appia did not eliminate time from the stage, of course. But by substituting the sculptural space of the stage for the illusionistic image of the painted surface, he was able to emphasize the durational and rhythmic qualities of time over the linear and narrative qualities. Appia's Wagnerian designs still made reference to the world outside the stage, though more symbolically than illusionistically, but his designs at Hellerau for Emile Jacques-Dalcroze broke from referential imagery altogether and created a stage world of abstract scenic elements whose power came from their relation to one another.

This is one of the major shifts in the conception of the world at the beginning of the twentieth century. The world was seen not as an arrangement of connected spaces or sites, but as an accumulation of self-sustained sites that existed in relation to one another. We went from a sequential world to a relational one. Once again Foucault provides us with at least one explanation of how sensibilities and perceptions changed:

> The great obsession of the nineteenth century was, as we know, history: with its themes of development and of suspension, of crisis and cycle, themes of the ever-accumulating past, with its great preponderance of dead men and the menacing glaciation of the world. . . . The present epoch will perhaps be above all the epoch of space. We are in the epoch of simultaneity: we are in the epoch of juxtaposition, the epoch of the near and far, of the side-by-side, of the dispersed. We are at a moment, I believe, when our experience of the world is less that of a long life developing through time than that of a network that connects points and intersects with its own skein. One could perhaps say that certain ideological conflicts animating present-day polemics oppose the pious descendants of time and the determined inhabitants of space.[5]

Part of the reason for the shift was the remarkable technological developments of the period. From approximately 1880 to the start of World War I the world witnessed the development of the telephone, X-ray, cinema, bicycle, automobile, and airplane, all of which had in common the reordering of perceptions of time and space. This perceptual shift was given an intellectual and theoretical basis with Einstein's theory of relativity, which not only transformed physics but entered popular consciousness as well. Social and artistic innovations that flowed from these accumulated developments included the stream-of-consciousness novel, psychoanalysis, and cubism. In this way, the whole conception of the world changed, and thus the stage picture had to change as well.

In a remarkably short span of time, Appia, Gordon Craig, Oskar Strnad, Robert Edmond Jones, and many other designers stripped the stage of its nineteenth-century accoutrements and began the process of re-presenting the stage as an independent physical site that emphasized its spatiality.

Two theoreticians were largely responsible for the next developments of the spatial stage: Antonin Artaud and Gertrude Stein. In *The Theatre and Its Double* Artaud declares, "We intend to base the theatre upon spectacle before everything else, and we shall introduce into the spectacle a new notion of space utilized on all possible levels and in all degrees of perspective in depth and height and within this notion a specific idea of time will be added to that of movement."[6] This declaration is often taken as the clarion call that led to Happenings, environmental theater, and the emergence of nonfrontal stages. This is true as far as it goes, but Jacques Derrida in his essay "The Theatre of Cruelty and the Closure of Representation" explicated the text in terms of the rejection of nineteenth-century notions of time and space.

> The stage will no longer operate as the repetition of a *present*, will no longer *re*-present a present that would exist elsewhere and prior to it . . . a present whose plenitude would be older than it, absent from it. . . . Nonrepresentation is, thus, original representation if representation signifies, also, the unfolding of a volume, a multidimensional milieu, and experience that produces its own space. *Spacing,* that is to say, the production of space that no speech could condense or comprehend . . . thereby appeals to a time that is no longer that of so-called phonic linearity.[7]

Gertrude Stein, searching for an alternative to narrative, commenced to explore theater "from the standpoint of sight and sound and its relation to emotion and time, rather than in relation to story and action." As a result she concluded that "anything that was not a story could be a play." The focus on the unities in neoclassical dramatic theory had been an attempt to control the relationships of time, space, and narrative within the dramatic structure. In neoclassical drama, time determined space, which, in turn, limited physical action. Stein understood that the theater is a temporal and spatial phenomenon, but she set about to divorce the two structures. The audience brings to the theater other possible perceptual mechanisms and emotional needs that do not require a narrative bound up in temporal and spatial considerations. The result was the landscape drama. The basic structure of the landscape play was one of relations and juxtapositions rather than the linear flow of conventional narrative.

> The landscape has its formation and as after all a play has to have formation and be in relation one thing to the other thing and as the story is not the thing as any one is always telling something then the landscape not moving but being always in relation, the trees to the hills the hills to the fields the trees to each other any piece of it to any sky and then any detail to any other detail, the story is only of importance if you like to tell or like to hear a story but the relation is there anyway. And of that relation I wanted to make a play and I did, a great number of plays.[8]

She elucidated the landscape drama through the metaphor of train travel versus airplane travel. In the former, a rider looking out the window sees a series of images going by in sequence as the train moves through the landscape. As the images pass by, the rider is also remembering what has passed, and is simultaneously anticipating what will come next. In contrast, a passenger on a plane looking out a window sees the entire landscape below in an instant. As in a landscape painting, the observer is then free to look at specific elements within the landscape at leisure and in any sequence. An entire image (complex of ideas) could be grasped immediately. Stein proposed a theater with the structural equivalent of a landscape where the parameters and content may be determined by the artist, but the method and organization of viewing and processing information was largely controlled by the spectator. The experience for the spectator became more contemplative or meditative than the rushing experience of linear drama; relationships replaced sequentiality.

In the twentieth century linearity and narrative evaporated from the stage because the world that was being reflected was no longer based upon sequential time structures. Spatiality was the new paradigm. (Of course, illusionism and realism continued in the theater, but these genres became either anachronistic or ironic.) Increasingly, the stage became a signifier of itself; that is, the stage represented a stage—an amorphous space that contained an infinite number of potential spaces but seldom specified any one space in detail. The stage was a place of relations and juxtapositions. Nowhere was this more evident than in the work of Robert Wilson. Acknowledging the influence of Gertrude Stein, Wilson created literal landscapes or perhaps dreamscapes. Wilson's stage became a site for surrealistic images, phantasms, and repetitive movements. Wilson, of course, became famous not only for his visual compositions (the so-called theater of images) but for his glacial pacing within productions of protracted length. Time seemingly ground to a halt in his early work, and temporal perception became disoriented and distorted. In Wilson, space and time coexist but almost in opposition.

Wilson, for me, epitomizes the Foucauldian notion of the epoch of space. The power of Wilson's theater derives from the juxtaposition of images as well as the repetition of actions that preserve what Gertrude Stein calls "the continuous present." There is seldom linear movement through a Wilson opera. Wilson has rightly been compared to the surrealists, but I would also argue that his suspension of time combined with his spatial and imagistic creations is, in fact, the theatrical equivalent of cubism: we have the luxury of contemplating an object/person/movement from multiple angles that would normally be inaccessible in a standard temporal framework.

Richard Foreman began with a similar approach to time, but his presentation of space was always more enclosed and confined. Foreman was concerned with the manipulation of space and the relationship of the spectator to the space of the stage. Whereas there was always an almost pristine and spare quality to the works of Wilson, Foreman anticipated the late-twentieth-century preoccupation with chaos. It may help to place Foreman's approach in some historical context. In the Middle Ages, for instance, theatrical locales were most often presented simultaneously, but there was still a linear structure to the narrative. Each space was discrete within the larger frame of the medieval stage. From the Renaissance through the nineteenth century, locales were presented sequentially, each image being thoroughly eradicated from view as it made way for the next locale or image—like a slate being wiped clean. But Foreman's productions are increasingly cluttered as the stage fills with the detritus of image and action. Images and ideas are not cleared away, not wiped clean, after their initial presentation; rather, one idea, one image, is heaped on top of another. It is a layered world. But these layers are as much temporal as spatial. While Foreman paved the way for postmodern theater in the United States, there is a fundamentally Romantic sensibility to his plays—they are, after all, about the mind of the artist.

Part of Foucault's definition of a heterotopia is that it contains a multiplicity of spaces. In the traditional sense a stage, of course, contains multiple locales; it is in fact a potential site of all places, real or imagined. But there is always a sense of the singularity of the stage. The stage, which by definition is a framing of space, creates an impression of itself as one unified space. Technology, however, has found a way to present multiple sites or locales simultaneously: video. The presence of video monitors onstage creates the equivalent of windows into other spaces. Video punctures the time-space continuum of the stage. Just as the mirror of Velázquez's *Las Meninas* allows the world beyond the frame into the space of the painting, so video monitors allow other spaces—and, significantly, other times—into the time-space of the stage. In the United States, the most successful exploiter of this technology has been the Wooster Group, whose particular use of video is an attempt to capture multiple times and locations within a single framework or to re-present the visible image within itself as an act of dislocation through reframing. At the same time the Group creates what I call a porous spatiality. In several of their productions the offstage and onstage spaces bleed together as actors offstage are seen on video monitors onstage. The

5. *I've Got the Shakes,* **by Richard Foreman and the Ontological-Hysteric Theatre, 1995. An example of the use of strings and the accumulation of clutter. (Photo © Paula Court.)**

stage, in fact, often becomes an empty abyss in a Wooster Group production, and it is the fringes and the unseen that are filled with action. The onstage monitors provide fragmentary glimpses of that which is otherwise absent. The question arises, is the "real" object the image that is seen on the video monitor, or is it the unseen actor whose image is being transmitted in real time? The Wooster Group acknowledges the shifting aesthetics of our age, in which image and reality are often interchangeable and reality is a phantom idea that is ultimately meaningless.

Edward W. Soja in *Postmodern Geographies* states that modernization "is a continuous process of societal restructuring that is periodically accelerated to produce a significant recomposition of space-time-being in their concrete forms."[9] Foucault's ideas of heterotopias as well as the spatialization of history (he saw the major midcentury philosophy of structuralism, for instance, as a spatial construct; it looks at the synchronic relationships of disparate social or cultural practices and in lieu of a causative view of history—i.e., linear or sequential, that is to say, timebound—it posits the spatial juxtapositions) were developed in the 1960s. That means that he was describing late modernism. But the world has changed since then. What does it look like now? If the stage is still a mirror of the world, what is it reflecting?

If the twentieth century was, indeed, the "epoch of space," the twenty-first may be the epoch of chaos and uncertainty. Heisenberg's uncertainty principle, which has come to be the metaphor of choice for the current age, replacing Einstein's relativity, posited that we cannot know of a subatomic particle both its location and its movement simultaneously. Until we observe it, there are infinite possibilities; the very process of observing something alters it, even destroys it. More important, what we observe is not the truth, but a captured state of being that eliminates all the other potentialities. The stage is somewhat like the famous conundrum of Schrödinger's cat. In his thought experiment demonstrating the principles of quantum mechanics, Schrödinger posited a cat in a box that would be killed by cyanide gas that would be released if a particular atom decayed within the hour. Until the box is opened, the cat, suggested Schrödinger, is neither alive nor dead but contains all possibilities. The theater, in essence, is Schrödinger's box. Until the curtain rises, all possibilities exist; once the play begins, the cat, as it were, is dead or alive. The raising of the curtain (even metaphorically) reveals the cat. But I think we are more comfortable in this day and age with potentialities and lack of certainty.

We in the theater, protectors of an anachronistic art, attempt to valorize its unique qualities: its liveness, its presence, its spirituality. But something has shifted in contemporary consciousness. The terms *virtual reality* and *cyberspace* suggest the changing perception of phenomenological ontology. The world is no longer knowable nor tangible. Space has given way to webs that need not have dimension, form, or even temporal continuity. The visual is no longer reliable. Jean-Luc Godard once said that film is truth twenty-four times a second. But nowadays, film is a record of digital manipulation. The truths revealed in *The Matrix* or *Crouching Tiger, Hidden Dragon* are not the truths Godard was talking about. They are not based on the correspondence between the visible world and the image captured by the lens.

It is said that certain aboriginal peoples used to be afraid to have their photographs taken by anthropologists because they thought that capturing their image meant capturing their soul as well. The Wooster Group's use of technology, I believe, was based on a similar kind of fear. They experimented with the disappearance of self on the stage and its re-presentation on video out of a fear of the loss of themselves as artists. But younger generations have no such fear. In fact, it is just the opposite. It is the mediation of the live actor that seems real. The simple, unmediated actor in three-dimensional space is not comprehendible, not readable, not knowable. The question for us, then, is how the theater—an inherently phenomenological enterprise—reflects back an iconography that is derived from the world of the nontangible and nonphysical. What looks back at us from the abyss today?

If Velázquez were alive and painting today, would the mirror be replaced by a video monitor? Would the court be staring at the monitor and not at us? Would the tangible and static image of the painting have been replaced by a video image?

Notes

1. Michel Foucault, *The Order of Things* (New York: Vintage, 1994), 7–8.
2. Foucault, "Of Other Spaces," *Diacritics* 16 (spring 1986): 24.
3. Foucault, "Of Other Spaces," 24.
4. *Adolphe Appia: Essays, Scenarios, and Designs,* trans. Walther R. Volbach, ed. Richard C. Beacham (Ann Arbor: UMI Research Press, 1989), 101.
5. Foucault, "Of Other Spaces," 22.
6. Antonin Artaud, *The Theatre and Its Double,* trans. Mary Caroline Richards (New York: Grove Press, 1958), 124.
7. Jacques Derrida, *Writing and Difference,* trans. Alan Bass (Chicago: University of Chicago Press, 1978), 237.
8. Gertrude Stein, *Lectures in America* (New York: Random House, 1935), 125.
9. Edward W. Soja, *Postmodern Geographies* (London: Verso, 1989), 27.

PART II Scenography in Context

The Scenography of Chekhov

> The stage demands a degree of artifice . . . you have no fourth wall. Besides, the
> stage is art, the stage reflects the quintessence of life and there is no need to intro-
> duce anything superfluous on to it.

These were Chekhov's words to an actor during the rehearsals for the
Moscow Art Theatre premiere of *The Seagull,* and they encapsulate the
ongoing struggles Chekhov would have with Stanislavsky's productions.
Chekhov was a symbolist playwright trapped in a naturalist theater. In his
texts the settings were described with a stark, yet poetic minimalism and
could be seen as part of the symbolist project to fuse interior and exterior
states of mind. For Chekhov, as for Maeterlinck, whom he greatly admired,
the concrete elements of the external world were manifestations of emotional states of being, what Richard Wagner called "soul states." The settings are virtual road-maps to the psyche, and so complete is the
identification of the character with the decor that if the setting were taken
away, the character would cease to exist. "I love this house," says Madame
Ranevsky in act 3 of *The Cherry Orchard.* "Without the cherry orchard my
life would lose its meaning, and if it must really be sold then go and sell me
with the orchard."

Such unity of scenography and self is unique among the playwrights of
the time. Nora, in Ibsen's *A Doll's House,* for example, must have a house
to leave, of course, but for all the specificity of Ibsen's stage descriptions, no
single item has the resonance or necessity of the bookcase in *Uncle Vanya,*
the dining table in *The Three Sisters,* or the nursery in *The Cherry Orchard.*
These are crucial emblematic and atmospheric elements, and set pieces even
function as determinants of the rhythm of his plays, such as the chair over
which Yepikhodov stumbles in *The Cherry Orchard.* Yet Chekhov was not

Published in *The Cambridge Companion to Chekhov,* ed. Vera Gottlieb and Paul Allain.

so much interested in the details of real life as in the evocation of a state of mind, of the so-called *nastroenie,* and everything on the stage was subordinated to this end. Chekhov's scenography aims at an emotional sensibility, not a documentary recording of domestic decor.

And yet, the popular conception of a Chekhovian setting is not the spare and evocative one implied by the stage directions, but one that is rich and cluttered; it is an image of painstakingly detailed houses, rooms, and old furniture, all imbued with the crushing weight of memories and unfulfilled desires, as in Michael Blakemore's production of *Uncle Vanya* (London, 1988), which was described by one critic as "choc-a-bloc with saplings, samovars, and duff furniture."[1] Chekhov has become so closely identified with this imagery that he has joined that small fraternity of playwrights who have lent their very names to the language as adjectives. But whereas *Sophoclean, Shakespearean, Brechtian,* or *Pinteresque,* for example, primarily tend to identify a style of writing, a point of view, a particular content, or, more ephemerally, a dramatic world, the term *Chekhovian,* more than any other, conjures up a landscape. It is, almost by definition, a visual style. It is so ingrained in our consciousness that when performance artist Stuart Sherman created his rarified deconstruction of Chekhov's texts entitled, simply, *Chekhov* (1985)—a twelve-minute abstraction of gestures and sounds—his stage directions called for "a realistic Chekhovian drawing-room, with large Persian rug and dining-table (on which can be seen teacups, playing cards, an ashtray containing a half-smoked cigar, and candlesticks) . . . an armchair, a samovar, and a cabinet, which hold icons, books and family photographs." Though Chekhov may never have described such a room, it was instantly recognizable to spectators as the quintessential Chekhovian landscape. (This "room," which occupied half the stage, was peopled not with actors but with two-dimensional cutouts on which were printed fragments of Chekhov's texts.)

But if such particularized scenography is not explicitly demanded in the texts, then why do we retain this impression? While the symbiotic relationship of Chekhov and the Moscow Art Theater, of course, proved beneficial for both of them, the naturalistic approach of Stanislavsky and his designer, Viktor Simov, had the unfortunate effect of encasing the plays in a highly detailed, representational, physical world that has imprinted itself on theatrical consciousness. The plays and the decor have become inextricably linked, not unlike the later designs of Caspar Neher for Bertolt Brecht, or Jo Mielziner for Tennessee Williams. From the 1950s onward, however, directors and designers have tried, with varying degrees of success, to break away from the naturalistic framework and find something more in keeping with Chekhov's symbolist tendencies.

6. *Chekhov,* by Stuart Sherman, 1986, a mixture of Chekhovian iconography
and text. (Photo: Kirk Winslow, courtesy Stuart Sherman.)

Given the theatrical practices of the day, the naturalistic approach to
scenography was probably inevitable. Neither Stanislavsky nor Chekhov
had the vocabulary for creating a new style. Moreover, Stanislavsky, for all
his influence on twentieth-century theater, was immersed in the late-nineteenth-century aesthetic. His work was a culmination of more than a century of developments toward psychological realism in acting and Romantic
realism in design. Scenographically, this meant the illusionistic practices of
fourth-wall naturalism. Chekhov, for his part, despite some knowledge of
Western European symbolist playwrights, had not, of course, seen the productions of Paul Fort's Théâtre d'Art in Paris. Even if he had, a formal
scenography was never clearly articulated by the symbolists, although playwright Pierre Quillard set forth a symbolist approach to design: "Speech
creates scenery like everything else."[2]

Chekhov was inexorably approaching the same aesthetic on his own,
something that Maxim Gorky apparently recognized in Chekhov when he
wrote: "You are a man who can create a character with a mere word, and
with a sentence tell a whole story."[3] Quillard called for a mise-en-scène that
would "emphasize the infinite multiplicity of time and space." By abolish-
ing the accretions of the naturalist stage, the symbolists hoped to free theater

from its inevitably flawed attempts to reproduce reality and instead allow theater to "be what it should be: a pretext for a dream." Though Simov and Stanislavsky neither attempted nor achieved such a visual world, Quillard's aesthetic anticipated the post-1960 approach to Chekhov.

Chekhov's minimalist set descriptions, in fact, are closest in spirit to the ideas of Appia (though with no direct influence, since most of Appia's writings came after Chekhov's death). The second act of *Uncle Vanya,* for instance, is described thus: "The dining room in Serebryakov's house. Night. The watchman can be heard tapping in the garden. Serebryakov is sitting in an armchair in front of an open window, he is dozing." That is all—no description of furnishings or decor, although there are references throughout the act that indicate the need for a table, a window, a door, a sideboard, and a few chairs. Think of Chekhov's settings as Appia declares: "We shall no longer try to give the illusion of a forest, but the illusion of a man in the atmosphere of a forest. Man is the reality, and nothing else counts. . . . Scenic illusion is the presence of the living actor."[4]

By the time of *The Cherry Orchard,* Chekhov seems clearly to be attempting a symbolist-like fusion of interior and exterior states of mind, one in which the very walls of the house seem almost transparent. The setting for act 1 of *The Cherry Orchard* is described as "a room that still goes by the name of the nursery. One of the doors leads to Anya's room. It is dawn and the sun will soon come up. It is May. The cherry trees are in flower, but in the orchard it is cold, there is morning frost. The windows in the room are closed." The locale is identified and we are told that there is a door and, significantly, where that door leads. If this were Ibsen or Shaw, there would be detailed descriptions of furniture, bric-a-brac, carpets, wall coverings, and the like. But what is important in this description is the *exterior;* there is a continuity between the nursery and the world beyond, as if the nursery can be understood only in terms of the context or environment in which it sits. Exterior scenes, in turn, have a fluidity that takes them beyond the mere confines of the stage. Act 4 of *The Three Sisters,* for instance, unfolds in "the old garden attached to the Prozorov house. A long avenue of fir trees at the end of which is seen the river. On the other side of the river—a forest. On the right is the terrace of the house." The house is almost an afterthought. What is clearly most significant for Chekhov is the vista stretching into the distance with its implication of continuity and the promised land that the sisters can never reach: a garden, a river, a forest—left unstated, of course, is Moscow, far beyond.

While the stage directions for *The Seagull* are the most detailed of the major plays, Chekhov already evinces an eye for the larger picture and the unseen world that surrounds his characters:

> Part of the park on Sorin's estate. A broad avenue leads from the view of the audience into the depths of the park toward a lake. A platform stage—pieced together and hastily built for a home performance—has been placed across the avenue in such a way that the lake cannot be seen. To the left and right of the platform stage is shrubbery. There are a few chairs and a small table. The sun has just set.

In *My Life in Art,* however, Stanislavsky describes the same setting with the pride of someone who has learned well from the duke of Saxe-Meiningen and André Antoine.

> On the very forestage, right near the footlights, in direct opposition to all the accepted laws and customs of the theatre of that time, almost all the persons in the play sat on a long swinging bench characteristic of Russian country estates, with their backs to the public. This bench, placed in a line with some tree stumps that remained from a destroyed forest, bordered an alley set with century-old trees that stood at a measured distance from each other. In the spaces between their trunks, which seemed mysterious in the darkness of night, there showed something in the form of a proscenium that was closed from sight by a large white sheet. This was the open-air theatre of the unsuccessful and unacknowledged Treplev.[5]

The problem was conflict of intentions. Chekhov, doctor that he was, observed the real world in careful detail, but then distilled it to poetic essences. Stanislavsky took the essences and fleshed them out again into three-dimensional illusions. In his correspondence with Stanislavsky regarding *The Cherry Orchard,* for example, Chekhov indicates a very specific inspiration for the environment. "It's an old manor house," he said of the Ranevsky estate. "Some time ago the people who lived there did so on a very rich scale, and this must be felt in the setting. A feeling of richness and cosiness."[6] A few weeks later he provided more details:

> The house is a large two-storied one. . . . [It] has to be large and solid: made of wood or stone, it doesn't matter which. It is very old and of enormous size of a kind which holiday makers don't rent but pull down and use the materials to build summer cottages. The furniture is old-fash-

ioned, stylish, and solid; their financial straits and debts haven't affected the furnishings.[7]

Yet Chekhov did not intend for Stanislavsky to build an actual house; after all, we never see the exterior. The point was to create the essence of such a house on the stage. Stanislavsky, nonetheless, moved toward greater and greater detail. Meyerhold described how the 1905 revival of *The Seagull,* for instance, became even more illusionistic:

> Every corner of the set was laid bare: there was a summer house with a real roof and real columns; there was a real ravine on stage. . . . In the revival the windows in the improved set faced the spectator so that the landscape was visible. Your imagination was silenced, and whatever the characters said about the landscape, you disbelieved them because it could never be as they described it; it was painted and you could see it.[8]

While Chekhov may not have had a specific symbolist vocabulary with which to describe his settings, he understood the contradiction of mingling the found objects of the real world with the careful artifice of the stage. "There's a genre painting by Kramskoy," he explained to an actor during the rehearsal of *The Seagull,* according to Meyerhold, "in which the faces are portrayed superbly. What would happen if you cut the nose out of one of the paintings and substituted a real one? The nose would be 'realistic' but the picture would be ruined."[9] A few years later, shortly before his death, Chekhov would echo this sentiment, writing of *The Cherry Orchard,* "Stanislavsky has ruined my play."[10] By mixing two-dimensional painted scenery with real furniture, not to mention a very real crying baby, Stanislavsky had, in essence, put a real nose in the artistic framework of the play.

Chekhov went in and out of favor in Russia and the Soviet Union over the following decades. Despite a move toward a more lyrical and impressionist decor, especially in the designs of Vladimir Dmitriev in the 1940s, the scenography was still solidly in the tradition of Simov with one notable exception. In 1944–45, Alexander Tairov directed a theatricalist production of *The Seagull* at the Kamerny Theater that was clearly intended as a rejection of the naturalistic style of Stanislavsky's productions and especially those of the socialist realists dominant in the Soviet Union at the time. Perhaps inspired by the demand for new forms by the character of Treplev, and with a nod to Appia and Craig, Tairov largely replaced illusionistic scenery with platforms and black velvet drapes and an almost exclusively black-and-white color scheme that led some critics to describe it as funereal. In the waning days of World War II and in the wake of Stalin's purges, the starkness of the set must have been striking. By the 1950s, in both the Soviet Union and elsewhere, the conventional "Chekhovian" set—more accurately, a "Simovian" set—began to seem dated. Moreover, the elements of Chekhov's settings that once served as a subtle and detailed semiotic guide to a complex psychosocial world became meaningless except as self-referents. Naturalistic settings, whether for Chekhov, Hauptmann, or Strindberg, became indistinguishable allusions to a previous century. And the specific props, costumes, and set pieces now associated with Chekhov no longer signified aspects of Russian society at the turn of the century but came to stand for Chekhov's plays themselves. New approaches were needed.

Directors and designers working since the 1960s have attempted to rid the stage of lingering nineteenth-century sentimentality while emphasizing the fluidity of inner and outer worlds. The pastiche approach typical of postmodernism was particularly well suited to Chekhov. Designers seemed to be following the advice of avant-garde composer and theoretician John Cage who, when asked about how to treat classics, suggested that rather than simply rejecting them, they should be "quoted" in new productions. Fragments of traditional Chekhovian scenography placed and juxtaposed within a more abstract environment became increasingly common in productions from the 1970s onward.

The first step in breaking the realistic, sentimental grip was taken in a 1960 production of *The Seagull* directed by Otomar Krejca and designed by Josef Svoboda at the Tyl Theater in Prague. Svoboda encased the stage in black drapes so that the actors were in a theatrical void. The park—indeed, the natural world—existed emblematically as leaf-filled branches hanging over the stage through all four acts. Interiors were suggested by furniture and fragmentary scenic units such as a window with drapes (but no surrounding walls). More important, the atmosphere of each scene was created through the use of changing "light curtains," one of Svoboda's technological creations, that created a scrimlike effect. Thus, the entire play occurred in a fluidly changing, but essentially unified environment. Exteriors and interiors blended, and the external world was always visibly present in the house.

The same year witnessed similar approaches for the first time in the Soviet Union. Nisson Shiffrin's decor for *The Seagull* at the Moscow Art Theater included a surround that depicted trees and the horizon as well as the sky in both exterior and interior scenes; the interiors contained no ceilings and only partial walls. At the same time, tall window drapes, taller than the rooms, hung in the exterior as well as interior scenes, creating an ever-present sense of spatial memory or anticipation. For *The Seagull* at the

Tsvilling Theater in Chelyabinsk, designer Daniil Lider used overhanging branches, remarkably similar to Svoboda's, as well as a sort of curtain hung on a clothesline. The motif of branches overhanging the stage through exterior and interior scenes proved popular in the Soviet Union and could be found in Mikhail Kurilko's design for *Uncle Vanya* in 1966 at the Kupal Theater in Minsk and in Enar Stenberg's production of *The Seagull* at the Moscow Art Theater in 1969.[11]

By 1962, the attempt to visually fuse the interior and exterior scenes appeared in England at the newly opened Chichester Festival Theatre. Sean Kenny's design for Laurence Olivier's production of *Uncle Vanya* consisted of a simple wooden back wall with two windows and a door. With the windows blacked out in the first act it became the garden; with light coming through them the stage was transformed into the interiors of acts 2–4. The great innovation, however, was the use, perhaps for the first time anywhere, of a thrust stage for Chekhov. Not only were the internal boundaries destroyed, but some of the separation between the stage and the audience seemed to disappear as well, leading a contemporary critic to note that "[Chekhov's] people had not been more closely allied to us."[12]

Olivier continued the atmospheric, nonnaturalistic approach in his famous London production of *The Three Sisters* at the National Theatre in 1967 with designs by Svoboda. Here Svoboda's light curtains were replaced by a surround of stretched cords tied from floor to grid, while window frames were placed between two layers of cords. Through the use of light, the cords could become "solid walls, delicate bars, or shimmering depths without precise limit."[13] The cords also served as a screen for Svoboda's trademark projections. Although minimal pieces of furniture were employed, this was an essentially abstract setting creating a theatrical rather than illusionistic environment.

By eliminating naturalistic approaches to scenography, the associations that go with it are likewise eliminated and the stage reasserts itself. It is no longer an *illusion of* reality, but an *allusion to* reality. Walls, doors, and especially windows become ephemeral, transformable elements that, as Svoboda noted, are at the heart of Chekhov:

> Windows are very special things in Chekhov. The thoughts and desires of the characters fly out through the windows, but life and its realities fly in the other way. The windows must be created by means of light, like that of the French Impressionists—light dispersed in air. . . . The windows lead us to all of Chekhov's atmosphere, the interiors are not bordered or limited, but diffused.[14]

Meanwhile, Soviet director Georgy Tovstonogov had expressed a similar point of view in his production of *The Three Sisters* at the Bolshoi Dramatic Theater in Moscow in 1965, designed by Sofia Yunovich. "In our production," explained Tovstonogov,

> the rooms in the Prozorov house were not delimited by walls, ceilings, windows or doors. Furniture . . . was distributed over all of our huge stage. A crystal chandelier hung over the table. Near the center of the stage stood a lonely Empire column, which supported nothing. Sunlight poured in through windows placed upstage behind a gauze which was hung along the circumference of the stage. The play of light and shadow on the column (caused by branches swaying behind the windows) and the soft twittering of birds created the atmosphere I wanted: spring, peace, and prosperity. A few minutes after the play had begun—more precisely, just before Vershinin's entrance—the light was cut on the windows behind the gauze, and they seemed to disappear. In the last three acts, in exactly the same way, there were illuminated windows in the Prozorov house, and an alley of birches (done three-dimensionally). And they disappeared in exactly the same way a few minutes after the act had begun. It seemed to me that these three-dimensional bits of scenery had served their purpose in indicating the place of action. All they could do further during the course of the play would be to distract the attention of the audience from the action itself.[15]

Tovstonogov also believed that the contemporary audience was more familiar with the experience of films than of the static theater and that Chekhov would be more comprehensible if staged in a cinematic form. By using a revolve and mobile platforms that projected toward the audience, he attempted to create the equivalent of close-ups, pan shots, reverse angles, and the like—the vocabulary of the film that constantly alters the orientation of the spectators to the scene to enhance or replace the movement of actors.

Anatoly Efros's production of *The Three Sisters* at the Malaya Bronnaya Theater in Moscow in 1967 went even further in fusing exterior and interior. The setting was reduced to nothing but a solitary, stylized tree with copper leaves, which represented the avenue of birch trees and also served as a coatrack. The influence of Samuel Beckett as the spiritual descendant of Chekhov was clearly making itself felt.

The conflation of inner and outer worlds has continued to be a strong motif in Soviet and Russian productions, as seen in the designs of Valery

Levental, Sergei Barkhin, David Borovsky, Mart Kitaev, Daniil Lider, and Eduard Kochergin. Though each of these designers has a unique style, the productions are often typified by fragmentary set pieces or furniture sitting like icons or islands in the midst of an open stage; often nature is seen not only blending with the man-made world but seemingly overpowering it. The latter is evident in Vladimir Serebrovsky's *Ivanov* in Baku (1978), in which the dining room was open to the garden and autumn leaves covered the floor, or David Borovsky's MAT production in 1976, in which branches and vines have overwhelmed the exterior of the house.

The most aggressive proponent of the fusion approach has been Romanian-born director Andrei Serban, who has worked since the early 1970s in the United States. In his *Cherry Orchard* at Lincoln Center in 1977, designed by Santo Loquasto, symbolic elements were isolated against a luminous background of barren trees, and the visual images were echoed by symbolic actions such as a plough dragged across a field by peasants. The ballroom was depicted as a structure that could be viewed as either a giant gazebo or as a cage. The white-on-white color scheme suggested both a formality and isolation or barrenness. Despite a negative response this production received from the more conservative New York critics, it spawned a host of imitations. Serban did a *Seagull* in Japan in 1980, designed by Kaoru Kanamori, that took a more romantic turn but nonetheless carried on the motif of a continuous interior and exterior. The inside was suggested by a repetitive row of window frames that, while reinforcing Svoboda's remark about the importance of windows in Chekhov, functioned almost as an abstract motif. A wood-planked stage floor unified the entire stage space.

Any hint of coldness gave way to the warm wood textures of Serban's *Uncle Vanya* (1983), also designed by Loquasto. But just as the symmetrical row of windows of the Japanese *Seagull* worked in opposition to the romanticism of the wood and trees, the romanticism of this *Vanya* was offset by the geometric pattern of the ground plan. The setting here consisted of platforms and steps with a few pieces of furniture; rooms and spatial divisions were defined by differing levels rather than actual walls. The idea for the set was generated by a reference in the play to the empty house being like a maze. The effect was, according to Loquasto, "the sweep of a Beckett landscape, but one where you also had warm wood and familiar Chekhov textures. . . . But by stretching the space, it took on the ascetic serenity of an Oriental walkway as well."[16]

Yet another approach to Chekhovian fluidity has been to create a sense of endlessness through rooms and spaces that continue beyond the spectator's view, tantalizing the audience with a maze of offstage spaces that

7. *The Cherry Orchard,* **Vivian Beaumont Theatre, 1977, directed by Andrei Serban, designed by Santo Loquasto. (Courtesy New York Shakespeare Festival.)**

remain frustratingly inaccessible. The intimation of such a world is already
present in *The Three Sisters* with the ballroom visible through columns
behind the drawing room, in *The Cherry Orchard,* where, again, the ballroom is visible beyond the archway behind the drawing room, and in the
first act of *The Seagull* with the lake hidden behind the makeshift stage.

One of the earliest productions to approach the play in this way was *The
Cherry Orchard* designed by Karl Ernst Hermann in Berlin in 1969. It
employed a classic box set with faint echoes of the Teatro Olimpico. The
two upstage doors that led to the drawing room were placed in the back
wall in such a way that it was impossible for any one person in the audience
to see the entirety of the inner room. Furthermore, these doors were
echoed in the upstage wall of the inner room. There was an implication of
infinity—if these doors were opened, the spectators would see another
room, and another, and so on.

A 1970 production of the same play, designed by Jürgen Rose in Ham-
burg, also played with neoclassical perspective, but in a more blatant and
unrelenting fashion. The eye was ineluctably drawn to a single vanishing
point through a door in a stark box set. However, the neoclassicism was

8. Model of *The Cherry Orchard*, designed by Karl Ernst Hermann, 1969. An almost infinite expanse of rooms is implied through doorways. (Photo: Arnold Aronson.)

softened by the romanticism of flimsy gauze curtains and the warm tones of the walls.

John Conklin's design for Mark Lamos's production of *The Three Sisters* for the Hartford Stage Company in 1984 continued the same basic idea—an upstage space visible beyond the main playing area, but Conklin opted for a colder formality. The upstage openings could be understood as pillars, doors, or windows; the floor of the thrust stage had a polished surface, thus abjuring the warm textures associated with Chekhov. Beyond the openings was cold, unknown space, a void that could be anything.

The elements of formality, texture, isolated iconographic pieces, and the implication of space beyond were epitomized, however, in a Cologne production of *The Cherry Orchard* in 1983, designed by Rolf Glittenberg. This was almost a parody of a box set: towering walls seemingly inspired by Gordon Craig, though textured through the use of wood, dwarfed the performers and the few scenic elements, which resembled the vestiges of some earlier Chekhovian set. But while suggesting a type of prison, the space was not impenetrable. The rear wall could split open, admitting bright light into this confined, barren world, and suggesting a paradisiacal world beyond. A thematically similar *Ivanov* was designed by Mark Thompson for Elijah

Moshinsky's London production of 1989. A critic described the room as "a bare and almost windowless cell, like some large prison space. . . . The only relief from this stifling uniformity is a square hole, a glass-less window cut high in the back wall, through which can be seen a passing vista of blue and white clouds, and where Ivanov's watchful wife appears."[17]

Chekhov's characters are often trapped in a life or philosophy that is represented by the concrete elements of a house. The freshness or freedom of the outside world is tantalizingly visible yet inaccessible. Chekhov creates an interior by describing the exterior. In the settings by Glittenberg or Thompson, however, a formidable barrier is created between the two worlds.

When Chekhov stated, in the quote that begins this essay, that "you have no fourth wall," he was expressing the need to acknowledge the theatricality of the event. But certain contemporary productions have attempted to take the breaching of the fourth wall more literally and incorporate the audience, to some degree or other, in the production or the world of the play. If this is done successfully, the spectator is implicated in the action and the play is transformed into an existential reflection of contemporary society. Needless to say, this is a risky strategy. Any production, whether Chekhov's or not, that incorporates or attempts to incorporate the audience and theater into the staging runs into the problem of the clashing worlds of audience and performance. The suspension of disbelief can extend only so far when we are surrounded and confronted with our fellow patrons and the accoutrements of the theater. Nonetheless, the environmental theater movement of the late 1960s and 1970s has inspired some attempts. Director André Gregory brought the audience into the setting for his 1974 production of *The Seagull* at New York's Public Theater, in which the set consisted of furniture and shrubs, but no walls or even clearly demarcated boundaries, placed in a bifurcated arena space. The audience sat around the outdoor setting for the first two acts, then moved to the other side of the stage for the indoor scenes of the last two acts. An alternative environmental approach was taken by iconoclastic Soviet director Yuri Lyubimov in *The Three Sisters* at the Taganka (1975). The production began with the back wall of the theater sliding open to reveal a military band on the street outside. The sheet metal wall then closed reflecting the audience back on itself.

British director Peter Brook, as he has done so often, took a wide cross-section of all these trends and put them together in his preeminent production of *The Cherry Orchard* at the Majestic Theatre in Brooklyn, New York in 1987. The Majestic was an abandoned movie palace and vaudeville house that was only partially renovated as an annex for the Brooklyn Academy of Music. Fragments of plaster remained on exposed brick walls; the once gaudy paint of this theater could be seen in faded patches on a decayed ceiling; and the proscenium arch hinted at its former glory. The theater became a perfect metaphor for the Ranevsky estate. In the rather cavernous space of the stage, made even larger by an extension over the former orchestra pit, Brook and designer Chloe Obolensky created dramatic locales through the use of a few well-chosen objects: an armchair, a bookcase, a screen, some Persian rugs, and a few pillows. The performance extended into the decrepit stage boxes and used the proscenium doors to suggest entrances to other rooms in the house. It ranged from the back wall of the theater to the very edge of the thrust. Brook and Obolensky had merged the fictional world of the characters with the very theater itself.

The general trend of the late 1980s and 1990s has been a return to romanticism—albeit tempered by the ironic eye of contemporary designers, as in the work of Greek-born French designer Yannis Kokkos, whose *Seagull* suggests a Simovian scenography filtered through an expressionist aesthetic. But a decidedly anti-Romantic postmodernism has also arisen, nowhere more so than in the startling production of *The Three Sisters* done by the Wooster Group in New York in 1991. Entitled *Brace Up!* the piece was an adaptation-deconstruction by Paul Schmidt, directed by Elizabeth LeCompte, with sets by James Clayburgh and lights by Jennifer Tipton. Performed in a converted industrial space, the Performing Garage, the feeling inside the theater was a strange mixture of stark high-tech and homemade shabbiness. The audience sat on steep bleachers facing a simple platform stage framed by light stanchions and an assortment of industrial and film lighting equipment. An invented character, a master of ceremonies, addressed the audience, interviewed characters, and called upon the translator (who also played Chebutykin) to provide dramaturgical commentary. Television monitors glided to and from the audience across the stage floor—not unlike Tovstonogov's platforms—on which could be seen live images of offstage actor/characters who were captured on video as they spoke, onstage characters creating a visual echo of the action, and interpolations from popular movies. Like the Brook production, *Brace Up!* coalesced the fictional world with the physical theater; the video fused on- and offstage worlds, as well as the world of contemporary culture with the historicity of the play. By apparently stripping away the frame of the stage, it created a new framework in which to house the play for the spectators and performers of a postmodern culture.

One hundred years after Chekhov's death, the adjective *Chekhovian* still conjures a world of samovars, drawing rooms, old bookcases, and beloved gardens. Yet the *nastroenie* or mood that Chekhov attempted to create through the implied transparency of walls, fluidity of space, juxtaposition of near and far, and symbolic use of familiar items was a harbinger of Appia and Craig, the surrealists, and even, to a degree, Brecht, whose significantly charged props and set pieces sat in the midst of a stage void. It is tempting to contemplate what the landscape of twentieth-century Western theater would have been had Chekhov lived and had Adolphe Appia turned his talents to Chekhov's drama as well as to Wagner's operas. The successes of the original Moscow Art Theater productions are a testament to the effectiveness of Chekhov's plays, in their time, in Simov's settings. But the Chekhovian landscape has not only adapted well to the qualities of modern and postmodern scenography but has thrived, as if it has found a more comfortable home. Chekhov's continued popularity on world stages suggests that not only the themes and characters remain relevant, but the visual landscape as well.

Notes

1. Steve Grant, "Uncle Vanya," *Plays and Players,* July 1988, 19.

2. Quoted in Frantisek Deak, *Symbolist Theater* (Baltimore: Johns Hopkins University Press, 1993), 144.

3. Siegfried Melchinger, *Anton Chekhov* (New York: Frederick Ungar, 1972), 65.

4. *Adolphe Appia: Essays, Scenarios, and Designs,* trans. Walther R. Volbach, ed. Richard C. Beacham (Ann Arbor: UMI Research Press, 1989), 106.

5. Constantin Stanislavski, *My Life in Art,* trans. J. J. Robbins (New York: Theatre Arts Books, 1952), 353–54.

6. Quoted in *Anton Chekhov's Plays,* trans. and ed. Eugene K. Bristow (New York: W. W. Norton, 1977), 159.

7. Nick Worrall, ed., *File on Chekhov* (London: Methuen, 1986), 70.

8. *Meyerhold on Theatre,* trans. and ed. Edward Braun (New York: Hill and Wang, 1969), 26.

9. *Meyerhold on Theatre,* 30.

10. Worrall, *File on Chekhov,* 71.

11. See Viktor Berezkin, *Khudozhnik v teatre Chekhova* (Moscow: Izobrazitelnoye iskusstvo, 1987), 84–85.

12. J. C. Trewin, *Illustrated London News,* July 28, 1962, 154.

13. Jarka Burian, *The Scenography of Josef Svoboda* (Middletown, Conn.: Wesleyan University Press, 1974), 49.

14. Burian, *Scenography of Josef Svoboda,* 49–50.

15. Georgy Tovstonogov, "Chekhov's *Three Sisters* at the Gorky Theatre," *Drama Review* 13.2 (1968):153.

16. Quoted in Arnold Aronson, *American Set Design* (New York: Theatre Communications Group, 1985), 113–14.

17. Nicholas de Jongh, "Ivanov," *Guardian,* April 4, 1989.

Architect of Dreams
The Theatrical Vision of Joseph Urban

The content of a dream is the representation of a fulfilled wish. . . . Adults . . . have also grasped the uselessness of wishing, and after long practice know how to postpone their desire until they can find satisfaction by the long and roundabout path of altering the external world.

—Sigmund Freud

The set should be a pure ornamental fiction which completes the illusion through the analogies of color and lines with the play. . . . The spectator will . . . give himself fully to the will of the poet, and will see, in accordance with his soul, terrible and charming shapes and dream worlds which nobody but he will inhabit. And theater will be what it should be: a pretext for a dream.

—Pierre Quillard

All stage design and all architecture, it might be argued, are the realizations of dreams: ideas that begin as images in the mind are transformed by artists and artisans into tangible manifestations that are made visible to the eye and, in the case of architecture and interior design, made tactile and corporeal. Yet these metaphoric dreams, when realized, do not necessarily possess the qualities we mean when we describe something as "dreamlike." Buildings and rooms have practical functions that root us in the here and now; stage designs often work best when they do not call attention to themselves or when they serve as simulacra for the recognizable, quotidian world. But Joseph Urban—architect, scenographer, illustrator, designer—rarely limited himself to mere functionality. His works—whether department stores, hotels, castles, bridges, restaurants, theaters, art pavilions, or book illustrations, or the lavish and often haunting settings for operas, musicals, pageants, and the Ziegfeld Follies—almost always seemed to be the consummation of

Published in *Architect of Dreams: The Theatrical Vision of Joseph Urban* (New York: Miriam and Ira D. Wallach Art Gallery, Columbia University, 2001).

fantastical visions and flights of fancy intended to take the spectator or occupant on a journey through the imaginary recesses of the soul.

Urban straddled two worlds: architecture and theater. On the one hand, there was an innate theatricality to Urban's architecture—theatrical in the sense of being dramatic and playful, and theatrically conceived as virtual stage settings in which real people are characters moving through carefully designed spaces. A critic for the *New Yorker* in 1928, seeking what he thought to be an appropriately derisive term to describe Hearst's International Magazine Building, condemned it as "theatric architecture."[1] On the other hand, there is an architectural quality to Urban's stage designs. Although he rarely created the sculptural environments of his scenographic contemporaries such as Adolph Appia, Edward Gordon Craig, or Robert Edmond Jones—Urban relied much more on painted and decorative elements—an underlying use of structural detail and a sense of fully constructed spaces pervaded his designs. No matter how fanciful or fantastic the imagery he devised, whether onstage or in a book illustration, there was a palpable reality to the representation—as if one could physically enter into this imaginary world. But always, the worlds of architecture and theater intertwined: Joseph Urban built dreamscapes.

Carl Maria Georg Joseph Urban, born in Vienna on May 26, 1872, was one of the most significant stage designers of the early twentieth century. The statistics alone are impressive: from 1904 to 1914 more than fifty productions for theaters and opera houses in Vienna and throughout Europe; thirty productions for the short-lived but influential Boston Opera Company, as designer and stage director from 1911 to 1914; fifty-one productions for the Metropolitan Opera of New York between 1917 and his death on July 10, 1933 (some of which remained in the repertory until the mid-1960s); all of Florenz Ziegfeld's productions (*Follies, Midnight Frolics,* and eighteen musicals) from 1915 on; twenty-six musicals and sixteen plays for other Broadway producers; plus numerous films, mostly for William Randolph Hearst's production company. All this, of course, was in addition to his continued work as an architect, interior designer, and illustrator that had begun in the early 1890s. Urban's importance lay in his virtually unprecedented use of color, his introduction to American theater of many of the techniques and principles of the New Stagecraft, and his architectural sensibility at a time when most stage designers came from a background or training in visual art.

Despite his acknowledged importance and influence, he has remained surprisingly underrated, even forgotten. I will discuss possible reasons below, but perhaps it comes down to a few simple facts: He wrote no the-

oretical essays, nor did he set down his philosophy in a book; he was a practical man of the theater, and while his ultimately more famous colleagues
published portfolios of unrealized visionary designs, he turned out actual
settings that inevitably had to fit the very real demands of production (even
his unbuilt theaters were designed for actual projects that never came to
fruition); and finally, his innovations were often in the service of popular
entertainment and spectacle (or in the case of architecture, in the lavish
homes of the rich and famous). Aesthetically, he was never willing—never
saw a reason—to fully abandon ornament or the decorative, so his architecture was out of sync with the developing International Style, and his stage
work was never as abstract as that of the most esteemed designers of the
New Stagecraft. But as composer Deems Taylor noted in a posthumous
appreciation of Urban:

> His greatest misfortune, as well as his greatest glory, is the fact that his
> contributions to his art were so fundamental that they are taken for
> granted. . . . He revolutionized the scene designer's position in the
> American theatrical world. He was the first to make clear that the design-
> ing of stage sets is an art, and that the man who designs them is an artist—
> or should be.[2]

Symbolism and Dreams

Urban came of age in the Vienna of the 1890s, the Vienna of vibrant theater and opera, a brilliant explosion of fine and decorative arts, and, of
course, Sigmund Freud. It was a city where pleasure and intellect inter-
sected, and where the exploration of the function of art and the structure of
the mind were approached with equal passion. Like the Viennese Secessionist artists who influenced him, Urban had some affinities with the symbolist poets and painters, although his work did not derive from quite the
same spiritual and aesthetic sources, nor did it necessarily have the same
ends. But clearly, some aspect of symbolism struck a chord within him, perhaps (appropriately enough) subconsciously. Artist Hermann Barr may have
been speaking for most of the young Viennese artists of the day when he
proclaimed in 1894, "Art now wants to get away from naturalism and look
for something new. What that may be, no one knows; the urge is confused
and unsatisfied. . . . Only to get away, to get away at all costs from the clear
light of reality into the dark, the unknown and the hidden."[3] The dark,
unknown, and hidden was precisely the realm of symbolism, whose driving
force was the desire to explore the human psyche and uncover inner truths

hidden beneath surface realities. The symbolist movement that emerged in Paris in the 1880s under the leadership of poet Stéphane Mallarmé was heavily influenced by the writings of composer Richard Wagner, particularly by the latter's quest for a mythological foundation for the creation of art that would then serve to unify society through a communal response to the artwork. The symbolists also drew upon the mystical and sublime elements of the poetry of Edgar Allan Poe and Charles Baudelaire. All nineteenth-century art, literature, and theater, in fact, seemed to have been moving ineluctably from the replication of observable phenomena to the revelation of dream worlds and subconscious landscapes. When Pierre Quillard, a now little-known symbolist playwright and poet, described a theater as "a pretext for a dream," he could easily have been characterizing the creations of Joseph Urban. The symbolist painters sought to move from an art of objective images, or even the suggestive work of the impressionists, to an art of subjective reality that would affect the senses directly, without the mediation of rational thought.

Whether or not Urban was directly influenced by the symbolists, he was certainly absorbing the symbolist-inflected Jugendstil art all around him. Moreover, he could not have been unaware of Freud's efforts to expose the workings of the mind through the agency of dreams. The world that Urban created on the stage—of vivid color, architectural detail, and visual fantasy—reflected these intertwined realms of art and psychology.

While the creation of dreamscapes may seem an appropriate aim of theater design, it perhaps seems less understandable with architecture. Yet architecture, too, is a surprisingly apt medium for dreams. In *The Poetics of Space,* his study of the human response to space and its relation to the subconscious, the modern French philosopher Gaston Bachelard described the house as both a locus and generator of dreams:

> The house protects the dreamer, the house allows one to dream in peace.
> . . . The places in which we have *experienced daydreaming* reconstitute
> themselves in a new daydream, and it is because our memories of former
> dwelling-places are relived as daydreams that these dwelling-places of the
> past remain in us for all time. . . . The house is one of the greatest pow-
> ers of integration for the thoughts, memories and dreams of mankind.[4]

Urban began his career as an architect, and many of his early projects were, in fact, dwellings—but not ordinary or bourgeois homes. His very first commission, received at the amazingly young age of nineteen, before he had even finished his studies, was to create a new wing for the Abdin

Palace in Cairo for the young khedive of Egypt. Later in the decade he would create the Esterhazy Castle in St. Abraham, Hungary—a pleasure palace with its white marble facade decorated with gold medallions and floral patterns and its individual rooms that were riots of color, pattern, and geometric shapes. In the 1920s, in such creations as Mar-a-Lago in Palm Beach, Florida, he was a major influence, along with many of his fellow Austrian architects, in developing the Spanish colonial revival style—with its fantastical and eclectic mix of Spanish, Venetian, and Portuguese architectural elements—which came to define the extravagant homes, clubs, and resorts of the Florida land boom. But even his more conservative homes were carefully crafted visions that integrated the practical needs of domestic architecture with the fantasies, memories, and dreams of those who would dwell within.

Gesamtkunstwerk

The notion of *Gesamtkunstwerk*—the total or unified artwork—was the guiding principle of Richard Wagner's approach to artistic creation. Simply put (something Wagner rarely did in his major theoretical writings of the mid–nineteenth century), all the elements of operatic production—music, orchestration, stage design, costume, acting, singing, and even the architectural environment that shaped the audience experience—were to be unified under the vision of a single artist so as to create a single experience for the massed spectators. The impetus for Wagner's approach came not only from the belief that theater and opera were equivalent (perhaps even superior) to the other arts, but from the mundane aspects of contemporary production practice and the inherent pitfalls of the collaborative process, which often contrived to turn the typical dramatic spectacle of the mid–nineteenth century into a near incoherent pastiche. Writers customarily sold their plays to theaters that could produce them with no authorial input; composers had limited control over the performance of their music; actors chose their own costumes according to their personal tastes, budgets, and only rarely for appropriateness to the role; settings were, more often than not, composed of stock scenic units that indicated a generic castle, interior, forest, or the like as needed; rehearsals were minimal, and performances, therefore, lacked cohesion; and the relation between the images onstage and the environment of the auditorium was never considered. If, as Wagner believed, the artwork reflected a spiritual as well as aesthetic quest, then it was crucial that all elements of production be focused on the realization of the artist's vision.

While Urban never used the term *Gesamtkunstwerk* (at least not in any interviews or in the few articles he wrote), he was clearly a proponent of the unified artwork of the stage. That approach was largely unknown in the United States in 1912 when Urban did his first work for the Boston Opera, and it clearly struck the very perceptive critic of the *Boston Evening Transcript,* H. T. Parker, in his review of *Tales of Hoffmann:* "Music, drama, and setting were wholly fused into the compassing of perfect atmosphere and illusion."[5] In an interview in 1913 Urban described *Inszenierung*—the German word for the total effect of the theatrical event, equivalent to the more prevalent French term *mise en scène*—in terms that reflect the influence of the Wagnerian *Gesamtkunstwerk:*

> The new art of the theatre is more than a matter of scenery; it concerns the entire production. The scenery is vain unless it fits the play or the playing or unless they fit it. The new art is a fusion of the pictorial with the dramatic. It demands not only new designers of scenery, but new stage managers who understand how to train actors in speech, gesture and movement, harmonizing with the scenery.[6]

While theater scholars and historians associate the idea of *Gesamtkunstwerk* solely with Wagner and his theatrical heirs, the concept actually spread to other artistic disciplines as well. Inspired by that monumental Romantic work of urban planning, the Ringstrasse—the circular boulevard around central Vienna, which was created as a unified work of civic architecture, private dwellings, and public and official space—the Viennese artists at the start of the twentieth century (particularly those of the Wiener Werkstätte) believed in "the integration of all the various design elements in a single aesthetic environment," as art historian Jane Kallir stated.[7] Large-scale public works were no longer an option by the end of the century,[8] so young artists turned their energies to private homes, which were designed as theatrical environments: the architectural space became a comprehensive milieu in which every element down to the smallest detail was designed, just as it would be in a theatrical setting. And just as the theater employed an ensemble of artisans from carpenters to electricians, so the architects employed an ensemble of craftsmen including painters, paperhangers, and plumbers, all working toward the realization of a single artistic vision.[9] Urban, too, was a proponent of the unified approach. "If a building is to reflect the efforts of artistic planning," he declared, "it must be harmonious up to the minutest detail."[10] One of the practices that frustrated Urban as he developed his architectural career in the United States was the custom of using jobbed-in contractors so that there was no unity of style nor singularity of purpose among the crafts workers. More important for Urban, however, was the need for the architecture to reflect the society and environment in which it existed.

> Architecture should be adapted to the climate, temperament, needs and the national characteristics of a people. A good architect should know his country from one end to the other, know its people and understand their ideals. Only then can he hope to build intelligently.

> Architecture should be as much a part of the time and of the place as the current news. It is about time that we outgrew ancient cultural styles and intermediate mushroom growths. To have a Colonial or a Renaissance house nestled in the heart of New York is as absurd as doing modern day jobs with Colonial or Renaissance tools.[11]

The analogy between theater and architecture, however, breaks down on at least one detail. In the theater, the actors are part of the design, as it were; their costumes and their movements are specifically integrated into the setting. But architects have no control over the look or specific movements of those who use their buildings. There is an undoubtedly apocryphal anecdote about designer Eduard Wimmer-Wisgrill, who, on a visit to the Stoclet mansion in Brussels, which had been designed by Josef Hoffmann, was horrified at the way in which Madame Stoclet's Paris fashions clashed with the Werkstätte decor. Upon his return to Vienna he established a fashion workshop for the Werkstätte, presumably so that the homeowners could be suitably costumed for their settings. Even if this were the true genesis of the costume workshop, clearly there is no way to control the total architectural environment once it is out of the architect's hands.

In all of Urban's architectural projects, the interiors were completely coordinated: tables, chairs, curtains, floor tiles, wallpaper and painted decor, lighting fixtures, utensils, and appliances were all designed for the space. Urban won numerous awards for his totally designed exhibition spaces, such as those for the Secessionist exhibit at the Paris Exposition of 1900 and the Austrian pavilion at the Louisiana Purchase Exposition in St. Louis in 1904. The space for presenting art was in itself a work of art: a fully integrated environment. That Urban saw his architectural creations as theatrical spaces, at least subconsciously, may be deduced by looking at the plan and view of a room for the Goltz Villa. Each of the two depictions is presented as if it were a traditional box set with the corner of the room forming an off-center apex. What is particularly revealing is that the perspective seems to be skewed if one compares the view to the plan. The viewer, however, is not standing on the section line as the plan indicates, but rather is looking at the room as if it were a stage setting viewed from the auditorium. The rendering and plan of the Goltz room compares interestingly with Urban's stage sets, such as that for *Apple Blossoms* (a 1919 musical in which Fred and Adele Astaire made their debuts). The room depicted onstage is more elegant and the walls certainly taller than those in the Goltz Villa, but the ground plan—and the relation of the implied audience to the space—is remarkably similar.

Of course, much of Urban's work could be described as "theatrical." The prominent place of the performing arts in Viennese society and the general aim of many of the Secessionist artists to unify all aspects of art and society inevitably led to a theatricalization of the arts. But in Urban's work, the theater became an implicit metaphor. His design for the Kaiser Bridge, for example—a structure created to join the Künstlerhaus and the Musikverein for the celebration of Franz Josef's fiftieth anniversary as emperor—creates what amounts to a proscenium arch through which the baroque Karls Kirche could be seen. And while the decor of the bridge consisted of a strong interplay of linear and geometric forms layered with art nouveau filigree, the wooden structure recalled the triumphal arches and festival stages of medieval royal entries and Renaissance pageants. It was a decidedly theatrical space. The arch-as-proscenium recurs as a separator between rooms in the Esterhazy Castle; it appears to be structural but is really a decorative element that frames the space behind it in a manner almost identical to the archway of the Kaiser Bridge. The proscenium motif was picked up in the Rathauskeller, the restaurant in the basement of the Vienna town hall. The structural arches that created the ceiling inevitably evoked the comparison, but Urban emphatically accentuated the theatrical parallel in his decorative scheme. One went down a flight of stairs through an arch as if entering into a theatrical world. Once in the restaurant, the repeated arches of the ceiling created an illusion of infinite vistas. (Again, while the repeated arches were a necessary by-product of the architecture, they could not help but recall the repeating proscenium motif of Wagner's theater at Bayreuth.) The smaller private rooms off the main dining hall of the Rathauskeller were works of total design, with every surface and every piece of furniture part of the architectural scenography.

The proscenium motif even emerges in the fireplace of the Esterhazy Castle. The fireplace opening was a curved blue oval, itself framed by a rectangular mantle topped by a massive, vaguely Egyptian chimney breast within which was yet another rectangular art nouveau relief. Two high-backed benches at right angles to the fireplace provided further framing as

9. Joseph Urban, Esterhazy Castle, Hungary, 1899. (Courtesy of the Trustees of Columbia University in the City of New York, Joseph Urban Archives, Rare Books and Manuscripts Library, Columbia University.)

well as "audience" seating, funneling all attention toward the "proscenium." The arrangement of the benches was repeated in several Urban interiors, notably in the entrance foyer to the Wiener Werkstätte shop that Urban opened on Fifth Avenue to sell the works of his Austrian colleagues in order to raise money for them following World War I. (The shop, unfortunately, was a financial failure.) Here the benches have been replaced by Urban's modernist take on Queen Anne chairs.

Theatrical Architecture

The term *theatrical*—a dismissive and pejorative term when used by Urban's architectural critics—referred to the fact that his designs tended toward the flamboyant, decorative, and illusionistic. In an era when, increasingly, the credo was "Form follows function," Urban's architecture often masked its structures; form followed fantasy. Urban believed that public space should be designed with the same sense of total environment and aesthetic pleasure with which one created a stage setting. He was creating dramatic worlds for real people. Following the metaphor to its logical end, his architectural projects could all be seen as "theaters," an impression reinforced by his frank assertion that a building facade was a form of advertising—a marquee.[12] Just as Renaissance palaces advertised the power and culture of the Medicis, he explained, so too "a beautiful building is the sandwich board of its owner."[13] This philosophy was his rationale for the billowing facade of the Ziegfeld Theatre, which opened on Sixth Avenue and 54th Street in 1927.

> The whole idea back of the Ziegfeld Theatre was the creation of an architectural design which should express in every detail the fact that here was a modern playhouse for modern musical shows. . . . The strong decorative elements of this part of the façade have nothing to do with usual architectonic proportions. They are meant as a poster for the theatre.[14]

For theater buildings in New York, wedged into narrow spots on crowded streets, Urban felt there was a particular challenge that could be met through designing the public face of the building "around the electric light sign and incidentally the fire-escape and the marquee." The proposed Max Reinhardt Theatre, intended for the productions of the innovative German director but unfortunately never built, was perhaps the epitome of this philosophy. The facade was to be covered in a skin of Vitrolite, "a gleaming black glass." Cutting horizontally across this surface was to be a pyramid of six fire escapes outlined in gold metalwork with white panels that would contain advertising signs, while the center of the facade would be bisected by a tower of gold grillwork containing the emergency stairs and topped with a delicate, perforated late-gothic spire. The result, at least on paper, was a facade of dramatic contrasts that radiated like a gleaming beacon into the New York City night. "A decorative scheme of such force," he explained, becomes a necessity when the theatre has to compete with the sheer bulk and height of surrounding skyscrapers. It is far too easy for a low facade to be crushed and lost in the confusion of metropolitan building."[15]

The facade of the Bedell Company store on 34th Street, designed in 1928, used the same gleaming black surface material. In place of the horizontal fire escapes—unnecessary for a department store—there was a massive curved grillwork over the entrance that served, in essence, as a stunning scenographic device, similar to the crowns that sat above the royal boxes in baroque theaters. Furthermore, the plate glass shop windows along the street and the show windows along an interior arcade functioned not unlike theatrical prosceniums. Significantly, architect Shepard Vogelgesang, who wrote about the design, compared the lighted columns of the arcade to Hans Poelzig's design for the Grosses Schauspielhaus, Reinhardt's monumental theater in Berlin.[16]

For sheer theatricality, however, nothing in Urban's work surpasses his schemes for a new Metropolitan Opera House. It is the embodiment of his belief that "a theatre is more than a stage and auditorium. It is a place in which to experience a heightened sense of life."[17] Otto Kahn, chairman of the Metropolitan's board of directors, began planning for a new opera house in the mid-1920s. Of the several sites under consideration, one on West 57th Street between Eighth and Ninth Avenues seemed the most feasible. Urban sought an architecture that would be as radical as Wagner's theater at Bayreuth and yet one in which the social functions and spaces—foyers, smoking rooms, restrooms, dining areas—were to be carefully considered. "The purpose back of the building of a new opera house today," declared Urban, "must be to find an architectural form so free that it can in turn set free every modern impulse which would tend to heighten and develop the form of grand opera, to make it not grandiose but grand, majestic, as large in spirit as in scale."[18] Urban's several proposals do, in fact, possess breathtaking grandeur, theatricality, and splendor. The exterior was almost fortresslike, the interior suggested a cathedral. But his plans may also be seen as excessive, even vulgar—at least one critic likened it to Albert Speer's creations for Hitler. Ultimately, it was a theatrical vision for a theatrical space. Yet, because of disagreements among board members, rivalries among architects, disputes over accommodations for patrons (Urban's plan to extend the stage the entire width of the theater would have eliminated the side boxes), and ultimately financial difficulties and the depression, the project was never realized; the Metropolitan Opera had to wait until the mid-1960s and Lincoln Center for a new building. It is unlikely, however, that funds could ever have been raised for such a structure; nor is it clear that the opera company could have survived the debt and operating costs had it been built. But the future of New York culture, not to mention Manhattan's West Side, would have been permanently changed, and it is intriguing to speculate whether Lincoln Center would then have been built.

Urban and the New Stagecraft

In 1911 Urban was commissioned to design three productions for the new Boston Opera Company's spring 1912 season: *Pelléas et Mélisande, Hänsel und Gretel,* and *Tristan und Isolde.* These productions marked a turning point in American scenographic history. Urban was subsequently appointed stage director and designer for the company, and he moved to Boston later in 1912. Scene painting in America at that time was generally a poor version of easel painting. Pictures were painted on canvas and most often were illuminated under undifferentiated white light that flattened the image, destroyed any sense of illusion, and emphasized the wrinkles and flaws in the canvas. In the words of producer and critic Kenneth Macgowan, this scenery was typified by "large-sized colored cut-outs such as ornament Christmas extravaganzas . . . [and] landscapes and elaborately paneled rooms after the manner of bad mid-century oil-paintings in spasmodic three dimensions."[19] Even the most artistically painted versions of such scenery—and there were some notable scenic studios at the time—were nonetheless a kind of semiotic code; they suggested or pointed to the particular, often generic, environment in which the audience was to imagine the play or opera unfolding but which never could be mistaken for the real thing. Urban's *Pelléas,* however, was a startling revelation to Boston audiences. As described by Macgowan, "it was made of strange, shadowed, and sun-flecked glimpses of wood and fountain, tower, grotto, and castle, vivid in varied color, full of the soft unworldliness of Debussy's music."[20] Summing up Urban's Boston work, Macgowan declared that "his scenery, costumes, and lights have given the productions of the opera-house a distinction which they could never have obtained through their singing and acting alone."[21] This is a remarkable statement. For perhaps the first time anywhere, certainly for the first time in this country, a critic was acknowledging the role of the mise-en-scène or *Inszenierung* in the theatrical event, placing it on the same artistic level as the music and singing and affirming its ability to shape audience response.

The new approach to scenography, known as the New Stagecraft, was a response to the increasingly crowded and overly detailed excesses of late-nineteenth-century stage naturalism. In place of simulation, representation, and illusion, the New Stagecraft was typified by simplicity, suggestion, and impressionism. Unnecessary details and clutter were stripped away; locale was created through the spare use of a few emblematic elements; and the scene was made to suggest "an atmosphere of reality, not reality itself; the impression of things, not crude, literal representations."[22] In 1915, for an article in *Theatre* magazine, Urban was asked to define "modern" design. "Certain painters, weary of complex combinations of form and color, have sought to return to simple lines and a palette of primary colors," he replied. "Call it modern, if you must, it is in reality Middle Age and Orient mixed. It is Albrecht Dürer, Memling, Watteau, Chardin. . . . A formula for modern art? It is this—I think—grace and simplicity."[23]

This grace and simplicity could be seen in several of his Boston productions. For Wagner's *Tristan und Isolde,* for instance, the usually detailed depiction of a ship was eliminated. In its place was Isolde's couch on a bare stage enclosed by towering, dimly lighted, yellow curtains. For Offenbach's *Les Contes d'Hoffmann* Urban eliminated footlights, created a diffused lighting that seemed to bathe the singers' faces in a natural glow, and used raised platforms to distinguish the imaginary tales from the "real" world of the prologue and epilogue. His Montmartre set for Charpentier's *Louise* may strike us today as fairly conventional and painterly, yet in contrast to the contemporary fare Macgowan saw it as "pure impressionism." Instead of the usual "impossible pretense at a city of real mortar and a sky of true azure depths," he saw "simply a picture into which fitted music and personages, all in the same new world of interpreted emotion."[24]

One of the innovations of the New Stagecraft was the use of "portals," a device that Urban essentially introduced to American stage design. Portals were proscenium-like frames set within the stage behind the actual proscenium. They had the practical effect of narrowing the sometimes massive openings of many opera house stages to more manageable proportions. Since the baroque era, designers had employed "sky borders" or foliage borders—parallel strips of canvas painted (and sometimes shaped) to resemble the sky or tree limbs—to hide the fly space and, later, lighting equipment. It was an accepted convention, but as an illusion it had long lost its effectiveness. The portal functioned to restrict sight lines without pretending to be something it was not. Like the "prosceniums" that Urban introduced into his various architectural projects, the portals had the effect of reemphasizing the theatricality of the production: they blended the architectural quality of the actual proscenium with the artifice of the setting and were thus both scenic and architectural. Most often the portals were constructed of canvas stretched on wood frames, but Urban also employed gauze. By framing a scene in graduated thicknesses of gauze he could create an aesthetic distance or a sense of unreality. This technique is particularly notable in the rainbowlike triangular arch for Jaromir Weinberger's *Schwanda* at the Metropolitan Opera in 1931 or, less obviously, in Ernst Krenek's *Jonny spielt auf* of 1929, but can even be seen in the Broadway production *Flying High.*

Urban also employed what could be described as miniprosceniums within his settings, as he had within his architecture, to frame scenic vistas. Examples abound but might be noted particularly in the garden scene of the Boston production of *Don Giovanni,* in which Turkish arches framed an art nouveau garden and a brilliant Urban-blue sky, or in Gasparo Spontini's *La Vestale* at the Metropolitan Opera in 1925, in which a Roman triumphal arch framed the Roman city beyond. These portals not only served as focusing devices but, by allowing the spectator only a limited view of a vista, suggested a much larger expanse and far greater detail. The scenes glimpsed through these arches were, like Shakespeare's poetic evocations of scenery, suggestive, thereby allowing the spectator's imagination to complete the image in far greater detail than possible with the scene painter's creation.

Urban was not merely the designer, he was also the stage director for many of the operas that he worked on, something that may surprise us. The rising prominence of the director and increasing specialization of the designer through the twentieth century has encouraged a separation of these roles. Contemporary audiences now associate the combined director-designer either with avant-garde artists, such as Robert Wilson, or the creators of spectacle, such as Franco Zeffirelli. But early in the twentieth century, Urban was exercising a significant artistic control, and as such he was able to bring innovations to the staging and acting while fusing the visual and performative elements of the opera into a unified whole. Boston critic H. T. Parker, an early advocate of the New Stagecraft, was rapturous in his praise, writing that in *The Tales of Hoffmann,* Urban "freed the singing-players from the outworn conventions of operatic acting, persuaded them to sink themselves into their parts and to adjust their parts to the play."[25] Parker went on to prophesy that "some day, the records may say that a revolution in the setting and lighting of the American stage dates from the innovations at the Boston Opera House."[26]

Two of the primary sources for the New Stagecraft were Swiss designer Adolphe Appia (ten years older than Urban) and English designer and director Edward Gordon Craig (born the same year as Urban). Appia set out to resolve the false dichotomy between two-dimensional scenery and the three-dimensional plasticity of the actor. He abandoned illusionistic decor for the sculptural space of the stage and took advantage of the new technology of electric light to revolutionize stage illumination, literally sculpting space with light. He did not reject decor altogether, and particularly in his designs for Wagnerian opera he created a suggestive and impressionistic style of scenery that evoked mood more than specific locale. Craig similarly rejected the trompe l'oeil stage of the nineteenth century. His signature contribution was a system of moving screens that could constantly transform the space of the stage. His designs often involved towering pillars and walls that gave his settings a sense of grandeur.

Craig and Appia clearly had an impact on Urban. As early as 1908 a Craig-like massing of strong vertical, angular columns and steps can be seen in Urban's design for Wagner's *Die Meistersinger* at the Vienna Opera. But unlike the soaring, almost gravity-defying semigothic creations of Craig,

Urban's early attempt seems earthbound and heavy. A few years later, a similar approach was used in his Boston *Parsifal*. In a striking contrast, though, Urban the colorist comes through even amidst the shadowy gray tones inspired by Craig and Appia—a fiery orange sky is visible through two angular gray columns. His sacred forest for *Parsifal* at the Metropolitan Opera, however, shows more than influence; it seems to be a virtual copy of Appia's 1896 rendering of the same scene. This Appian approach to the forest makes a telling contrast with the forest from act 5 of Liszt's *St. Elizabeth* from 1918. The treatment of the individual trees in both settings is similar, but the arrangement of them and the use of color in the latter created something more akin to Urban's fairy-tale illustrations.

Several members of the new generation of American designers at the start of the twentieth century studied with Appia, Craig, and others in Europe. Notable among the young Americans were Robert Edmond Jones and Lee Simonson. According to the now accepted history, the first example of the New stagecraft to be produced in America was Jones's design for Anatole France's *The Man Who Married a Dumb Wife* at New York's Wallack Theatre in 1915. The play served as a curtain-raiser for the English director Harley Granville-Barker's production of George Bernard Shaw's *Androcles and the Lion*. Jones's setting, done in shades of black, white, and gray—like much of the work of Appia and Craig—used simple geometric shapes, creating the impression of a wood-block print, vaguely Japanese in feeling, but also medieval. Because it was done on Broadway and was unlike the standard Broadway fare, the set received significant press (both positive and negative), which helped to establish the apparently new movement and lent credence to the appealing story of a single production giving birth to a new aesthetic. The fact is that more than six months earlier, designer Samuel J. Hume had mounted a highly touted exhibition of new European stage design at his studio in Cambridge, Massachusetts, which was subsequently mounted in a Fifth Avenue gallery in New York City. More important, of course, were the three seasons of Urban's Boston Opera productions. His setting for act 2 of Puccini's *Madama Butterfly*, in particular, is remarkably similar to Robert Edmond Jones's supposedly groundbreaking design three years later.

Urban's *Madama Butterfly* was composed almost entirely of rectangles surrounded by a decorative geometrical frame. The arrangement of shapes was, in essence, a blueprint for Jones's later version. Urban was strongly influenced by the Wiener Werkstätte—the Viennese arts and crafts movement with its reliance on geometric detail and decorative line—and this

10. Joseph Urban, *Madama Butterfly,* Boston Opera, 1912, detail of Butterfly's house. (Courtesy of the Trustees of Columbia University in the City of New York, Joseph Urban Archives, Rare Books and Manuscripts Library, Columbia University.)

production and many others reflect that aesthetic. Werkstätte-like decor also informs many of Urban's Broadway interiors. It is instructive to compare the *Madama Butterfly* to his fundamentally similar elevation for the Werkstätte-inspired bedroom in the Redlich Villa in Vienna with its surface carved into rectangular blocks offset by geometric decorative motifs. The pattern can be seen again in the 1913 design for Bizet's *Djamileh* in Boston. One significant difference between the Urban and Jones designs is the use of color. The bold black-and-white checkerboard patterns of the stage-left window unit of *Butterfly* are surrounded by a palette drawn from the blue-violet end of the spectrum, with exclamatory red highlights along the bottom. Jones, by contrast, introduced color to his setting only through the costumes.

But in 1915, any theater or art done outside of New York City remained essentially invisible (and in theater, at least, the situation has not changed all that much). Urban attracted the attention of the cognoscenti, but the real recognition ultimately went to Jones because he was the first to be seen in New York.

Color and Art Nouveau

Joseph Urban, first and foremost, was a colorist. All of his innovations—on the stage, in architecture, and in decoration—can be tied to his unprecedented use of color, which was virtually unmatched in the twentieth century. His appreciation of color was heightened by his eight-month stay in Egypt when he was nineteen.

> My arrival in the harbor of Alexandria was really my first big color impression. The strange deep blue of the Mediterranean; the white city, the flaming sails of the boats, the riot of color in the costumes and over all a purple sky. This enormous impression followed me my whole life and dominated for years my color schemes. I think the indescribable blue of the Egyptian sky created my life long love of BLUE.[27]

Indeed, a deep, rich, shimmering blue is his trademark, and to this day there are both a scene paint and a lighting gel known as "Urban blue." This blue showed up in one of his early New York theater productions, *Riviera Girl* (1917), evocatively described by *New York Times* theater critic John Corbin.

> The Mediterranean is not seen, nor any detail of villa or foliage, of ledge or shore. Only the sky is visible, and it is without cloud or star. But the coloring, the lighting, of this sky has exhausted the resources of the modern theatre. It is a deep and magic blue; velvety in texture, yet suggesting limitless regions of heaven. It is a symbol, if you wish, of the Mediterranean—the very breath and spirit of the Côte d'Azur. And it dominates the successive scenes with a sense of imaginative unity only less persuasive and compelling, than that of the music. The architectural features of the foreground are similarly broad and harmonious-monumental in line and spacing, richly simple in color. Avoiding every detail that may distract the eye, or weary it, they strike a note of beauty, stimulate the imagination in full accord with the mood of the composer.[28]

Only in the work of Russian designers Alexander Benois and Léon Bakst for the Ballets Russes—at roughly the same time Urban was creating his first stage designs—could one find such a brilliant use of color. Bakst, in particular, articulated a theoretical foundation for his use of color, citing the correspondences between particular tones or juxtapositions of colors and the emotions that they induced in the spectators. Although astute critics would later note the emotional impact of Urban's palette, Urban himself said little on this matter. Because the Ballets Russes toured throughout Europe, and because Bakst and Benois articulated a color theory in relation to their designs, and perhaps because the Ballets Russes was seen as avant-garde and thus more serious than the Ziegfeld Follies or even opera, Bakst and Benois had a more immediate and far-reaching impact in revolutionizing design than did Urban.

Symbolism may have played some role in Urban's use of color. Paul Gauguin and Émile Bernard in particular, whose paintings in the late 1880s were part of a style known as synthetism, believed in the equivalence or correspondence of particular colors and emotions. Drawing in part upon medieval techniques, Bernard employed bold color patterns, while Gauguin moved toward nonnaturalistic uses of color and flattened planes. The Nabis group who followed in their footsteps (Denis, Bonnard, Sérusier, Vuillard, Maillol, and others) valorized color as a tool for emotional communication. "We can no longer *reproduce* nature and life by more or less improvised trompe-l'oeil," declared Maurice Denis, "but on the contrary, must reproduce our emotions and our dreams by *representing* them, using forms and harmonious colors."[29] The bold, expressive use of color came to dominate a wide range of arts across Europe at the turn of the century. It is especially evident in the work of two artists who had a strong influence on Viennese developments, Edward Burne-Jones and Ferdinand Hodler. In Vienna, the symbolist approach to color was most pronounced in the paintings and decor of Gustav Klimt, whose use of line, form, and color seems to anticipate or parallel Urban's scenic style.

But the artist whose work most clearly correlates to Urban's in its use of color and technique is Georges Seurat. The shimmering colors that Urban achieved on the stage were created through a variation of Seurat's pointillist technique, which broke up color into its component parts and juxtaposed complementary colors in a seemingly abstract mosaic pattern that, when seen in toto, created a unified image. Urban can be seen using this technique early on, in one of his book illustrations in which the "points" of color are quite pronounced. Urban painted scenery not as an illusionist imitation of nature but, as one writer put it, "as a medium for the reception of colored light."[30] Urban understood that color on the stage (as opposed to on an artist's canvas) is a result of the particular combination of paint pigments and stage lighting—red pigment, for instance, becomes visible only under red light or the red part of the spectrum within "white" light. Thus, instead of covering a canvas with flat expanses of paint as had been the practice of most scene painters, Urban took a semidry brush and spattered it. For his skies, for example, he used several shades of blue spattered over each other, then further spattered the canvas with red, green, and silver.[31] In the scene shop, under work lights, the resultant painting looked gray; but under stage light employed with subtlety the differing flecks of color were picked up and reflected—Urban could create anything from dawn to moonlight. The effect was "as suggestive of reality," claimed Macgowan, "as is any painting by Monet."[32] The fragmented palette created a luminous, shimmering effect that repeatedly evoked the word "magical" from critics and observers.[33]

Urban's palette was not limited to blue, nor was his technique limited to pointillage. As with his Jugendstil or art nouveau colleagues, he drew upon the brilliant colors and undulating forms of exotic flowers and foliage, the mysteriously patterned world seen through the microscope, and other enigmatic examples of nature; there was also a distinct influence of Japanese prints and other Asian forms. This variety of color could be seen over and over in his repeated use of dripping foliage, as in the garden viewed through the portals of Verdi's *Otello* at Boston in 1914; the ultimately unused garden for the Met's *Parsifal* in 1920; countless *Follies* designs; as well as the murals of the Ziegfeld Theatre and the murals and ceilings of many restaurants and hotels, such as the St. Regis Hotel roof garden, the Central Park Casino, or the elevators of Bedell's Department Store. These designs used a dizzying array of pastels and drew heavily from the red and violet end of the spectrum. Such a palette was alien to the turn-of-the-century naturalists and literalists and was seemingly anathema to the Jones-Simonson school of new stagecraft with its monochrome palette.

Related to Urban's use of color was his sensuous treatment of line. With precedents in the arts and crafts movement and symbolism, and with a conscious nod toward medieval art and orientalism, art nouveau was typified by a provocative and decorative use of line—"line determinative, line emphatic, line delicate, line expressive, line controlling and uniting" as Walter Crane, an artist influenced by William Morris, put it in 1889[34]— which functioned visually much as sound had in symbolist poetry. Line, as art historian Peter Selz explained, "became melodious, agitated, undulating, flowing, flaming."[35] Such adjectives well describe the sinuous lines of many of Urban's illustrations from the 1890s, most done in collaboration with his brother-in-law Heinrich Lefler, as in the underwater castle image in *Chronika der drei Schwestern* (Chronicle of the three sisters) from 1899. This use of line is a crucial element in his drooping foliage patterns and murals, recurs constantly in various *Follies* productions, and emerges rather startlingly in the Aubrey Beardsley–like tableau curtain of "Tinturel's Vision" for the Met's *Parsifal* or the Erté-like curtain for *Lohengrin*. With the exception of some Ballets Russes designs, such use of line was rare on the stage throughout this period except in the work of Urban. It was particularly striking when juxtaposed, as it sometimes was, against the geometric forms of the Werkstätte-inspired designs.

The complete marriage of line and color, not surprisingly, found its most triumphant form in Urban's architecture; and in architecture nowhere was this more brilliantly demonstrated than in the Ziegfeld Theatre. As Urban himself characterized it, it was to be a place where "people coming out of crowded hours and through crowded streets, may find life carefree, bright and leisured."[36] The interior was designed with no moldings so that everything would flow together smoothly, "like the inside of an egg," and the decor was envisioned as a single, unifying, encompassing mural. "The carpet and seats," explained Urban, "are in tones of gold, continued up the walls to form the base of the mural decoration where heroes of old romance form the detail in flowering masses of color interspersed with gold." For Urban this design was not merely decoration, however, but a carefully thought-out scheme for enhancing the experience of the spectators—focusing them on the stage during the performance and bathing them in warmth during intermissions. "The aim . . . was to create a covering that would be a warm texture surrounding the audience during the performance. In the intermission this design serves to maintain an atmosphere of colorful gaiety and furnish the diversion of following the incidents of an unobtrusive pattern." This design scheme was as much an example of architectural *Gesamtkunstwerk* as Wagner's opera house at Bayreuth, perhaps even more so. Because it was now employed in the service of popular entertainment, however, it was never accorded the same status or respect. (Interestingly, just as Wagner hid the orchestra from view so as not to detract from the idealist vision created on the stage, Urban hid his equivalent of the orchestra: the lighting equipment. Light was crucial in bringing his creations to life and in giving movement to the architectural forms, but in both interiors and exteriors, the sources of illumination remained hidden so as not to seem like afterthoughts or to interfere with the desired effects.)

By contrast, Urban's Paramount Theatre, a movie house in Palm Beach, Florida, was simple in its lines and employed a subdued palette of silver and green, "cool and comfortable." The rationale was simple: the rhythms of Palm Beach were "leisured and sunny," as opposed to those of New York City. "The theatre," explained Urban, "is not an escape from the life around, but a part of it, fitting into the rhythm of the community. The architecture of the Paramount Theatre . . . is accordingly simple, spacious, Southern."

Urban was a forceful advocate for the use of color in architecture—to shape the mood and enhance the functions of interiors, and to transform entire cities through the application of color to exterior surfaces. Urban, in fact, saw cities as virtual stage settings, which needed color to bring them to life. "When the morning sun gilds the city and casts blue shadows," Urban wrote in 1927,

> even the buildings of neutral coloring are often very beautiful, but there are many hours when these effects are not seen and there are gray days. Then our buildings need positive colors to enliven them. When we look at the city at night, we see light in many tones. Some are dazzling white, others are soft and warm. A building can have the same distinctiveness in the daytime. Its color can express its personality. These colorful structures will have charm on gloomy days as well as when the sunlight tints them, and at night all degrees of the lights and shadows of artificial illumination will have their part in modifying and enhancing them.[37]

The Atlantic Beach Club (1929–31) on Long Island was an example of this approach. The walls and decks were composed of surfaces of red, yellow, blue, and white stucco, which served as a background for brilliantly colored awnings and umbrellas. By the 1930s Urban was moving into bolder experiments with architectural color. The interior of the New School for Social Research's new home on West 12th Street in New York City, which opened in 1930, provided a particular challenge—a large number of rooms and auditoriums in a relatively small space with each room having a specific function. Urban used large masses of bright color on plaster surfaces to establish relationships among the spaces while distinguishing them as necessary. "The color is in fact the form, the volume," observed the architect Otto Teegen. "One does not feel that certain architectural surfaces have been painted, but that these architectural planes and volumes are actually color planes and color volumes which have been composed to make a room or a library, as the case may be."[38] According to Urban, warm colors were located

> where they receive the most light, cold where there is most shadow, a change of plane is generally emphasized by a change of color, thus the walls have one set of colors, the ceiling another. By thus modeling the

wall surfaces of a room the boxlike property of four walls is given an expression of contrasting filled spaces and void space; the monotony of the enclosing areas is transformed to an imaginative statement of the space enclosed and given a character by the emotional statement of color.[39]

It was the critic Edmund Wilson who this time criticized the building for its theatricality. "When he tries to produce a functional lecture building," complained Wilson, "he merely turns out a set of fancy Ziegfeld settings which charmingly mimic offices and factories where we keep expecting to see pretty girls in blue, yellow and cinnamon dresses to match the gaiety of the ceilings and walls."[40]

Building on the New School experience, Urban saved his boldest architectural color work for what was to become the last project of his life: the 1933 Century of Progress International Exposition in Chicago for which he was appointed director of exterior color and consultant on lighting. His plan seemingly amalgamated the Nabis approach of saturated, emotion-charged colors with Bauhaus-like surfaces of geometric planes. The plan was to create a unified approach to color for the entire fair—color as an architectural medium, not decoration. He set out six guiding principles

1. Color to be used in an entirely new way.
2. Color used to co-ordinate and bring together all these vastly different buildings.
3. Color to unify and give vitality.
4. Color to give brightness and life to material not beautiful in itself.
5. Color to give the spirit of carnival and gaiety—to supply atmosphere lacking in our daily life.
6. Color that should transport you from your everyday life when you enter the fairgrounds.[41]

He created a palette of twenty-four colors, all of the "brightest intensity": one green, two blue-greens, six blues, two yellows, three reds, four oranges, two grays, white, black, silver, and gold. The plan was for approximately 20 percent of all surfaces to be white, 20 percent blue, 20 percent orange, 15 percent black, and the remaining 25 percent to be spread among the yellows, grays, greens, and silver.[42] It is one thing, of course, to create such a bright and vibrant color scheme for a world's fair, quite another to transform a functioning city.

Ziegfeld Follies

Despite his numerous brilliant productions for the Metropolitan and Boston
Operas, and despite his major architectural works, Urban became—and
remains—best known for his work with Florenz Ziegfeld.

Following the closing of the Boston Opera, Urban returned to Paris in
July 1914 to direct Wagner's *Tristan und Isolde,* the first German opera pre-
sented there in thirty years, but the outbreak of the war stranded him in
Europe. Producer George Tyler, however, managed to bring him back to
New York to design a production of Edward Sheldon's *Garden of Paradise,*
Urban's first Broadway show. The production itself was a failure, but
Urban's sets and new aesthetic attracted attention. The nine fantastical
scenes included a castle, a storm at sea, a fairy bower, and a sequence under
the ocean. In a contemporary article on the production, the writer Louis
DeFoe seemed to understand that the New Stagecraft had arrived:

> A glance at the flat, dark blue of an Urban seascape brings with it a sense
> of limitless distance. And all the mechanical contrivances and details of
> the *mise-en-scène* are so coordinated that they contribute to the unity of
> each effect. So in Mr. Urban's method of adorning the stage the old,
> unsightly and unillusory "borders," wrinkled and unstable "back cloths,"
> and obvious, clumsy "cut-outs" of conventional theatrical scenery have
> entirely disappeared. Illusion through suggestion takes the place of pic-
> tured actuality.[43]

But the scene changes were unwieldy and necessitated nearly an hour's
worth of intermissions, which contributed to the demise of the show. With
the *Follies,* at least, Urban would never make that mistake again. He learned
how to make scenery move as if it were music.

Among the few people who saw *The Garden of Paradise* was Florenz
Ziegfeld, who was looking for a designer to give the annual *Follies* (which
had premiered in 1907) a more sophisticated look. He hired Urban, who
had never seen the *Follies,* and took him out to Indianapolis to catch up with
the 1914 edition on tour. Urban's first—and accurate—impression was that
the show was little more than a series of disconnected sketches that were
equivalent, in his words, to "advertising posters." He was going to bring his
Gesamtkunstwerk approach to Ziegfeld. "I hope most of all to unify the
impression of all these short scenes, to give the entire evening a kind of
keynote," he declared.[44] The *Ziegfeld Follies of 1915,* Urban's first, astounded
audiences, in part because of the lavish settings for its twenty-one scenes,

but just as important for the way in which those scenes flowed from one to the next so that the entire revue seemed to be a single, unified entity. One of the techniques that Urban had to master was the basic vaudeville device of the "in one" scene—an interlude played in front of a downstage drop curtain that allowed large set changes to occur behind it. Some critics bemoaned the fact that a great opera designer was descending into the lower depths of crass commercial and mass entertainment, forgetting that opera had evolved in large part from baroque intermezzi—the lavish, allegorical spectacles created by leading architects and painters of the seventeenth century using fundamentally the same staging techniques as modern revues and extravaganzas. History had merely come full circle. (One wonders about the potential effect on twentieth-century theater if Appia, Jones, or Bakst had been forced to master and absorb the ancient crafts and techniques of popular scenography.)

The 1915 *Follies* included one of the most spectacular Ziegfeld scenes to that time—the bath scene, in which two smiling, golden elephants spouted water from their raised trunks into a pool of water surrounded by Jugendstil-like shrubbery. Kay Laurell as Aphrodite rose out of the pool to signal the start of a mermaid ballet. The staircase behind the pool was also the first hint of the soon-to-be-famous staircase that would showcase the chorus of Ziegfeld girls. The staircase became a central element in *The Century Girl,* produced by Ziegfeld and Charles Dillingham and designed by Urban at the Century Theatre the next year, and then appeared regularly in the *Follies* thereafter. The 1915 *Follies* was also to contain the stunning drop of a zeppelin hovering over London (seemingly, though impossibly, viewed from St. Paul's Cathedral) for a skit with comedians Bert Williams and Leon Errol. The skit was originally to be in a submarine, but after more than a dozen rewrites, which was typical of the Ziegfeld process, the setting was changed to a zeppelin, and finally the whole scene was cut during out-of-town tryouts.[45]

Although Urban provided the *Follies* with a sense of visual style and lavishness that was unsurpassed, as well as an all-important artistic unity, his designs were capable of overwhelming the whole production, even with its enormous star power. A review of the 1917 *Follies* praises Urban's sumptuous settings and notes that in his "Oriental setting, [he] has outdone himself in his employment of colors and seemingly massive structures," but goes on to protest that

> while in richness of tone and in suggestion of distance the setting is superb, it, nevertheless, obtrudes upon the players in the foreground.

11. Joseph Urban, zeppelin over London, designed for Ziegfeld Follies of 1915. (Courtesy of the Trustees of Columbia University in the City of New York, Joseph Urban Archives, Rare Books and Manuscripts Library, Columbia University.)

There is no personality definite and dominant enough to stand against it successfully, and therefore most of the fun and satire that had been contrived for the scene went for naught.[46]

The significance of Urban's work with Ziegfeld was in bringing artistic excellence, visual wit, and a sense of opulence to popular entertainments. Moreover—and quite astonishingly—he introduced the aesthetics of Wagnerian *Gesamtkunstwerk* and the scenic innovations of the New Stagecraft to Broadway. The New Stagecraft as presented by Robert Edmond Jones, Lee Simonson, Sam Hume, and others was spare, dark, serious, and pregnant with meaning and import; Urban presented scenographic inspiration as frothy dessert for audience consumption, perhaps never fully realizing its significance. But it laid the groundwork for Broadway musicals for the rest of the century and for the Hollywood musicals of the 1930s and the extravaganzas of Busby Berkeley. Urban created, in other words, a new scenic and visual vocabulary that permeated popular consciousness.

Urban, as an outsider in American culture, saw the puritan streak that ran through the culture, particularly its attempt to separate high and low art. But he also understood that the two were not necessarily separate.

> I believe you can make your fun and your pleasure and your diversion artistic as well as your more serious plays. In America you have seemed to feel that you must do serious things seriously, but that you can do things meant for pastime very carelessly. That ought not to be so. You ought to take just as much care in providing your fun as you do your education.[47]

Conclusion

Urban made a very conscious decision to stay in the United States, and he became a naturalized citizen in 1917. Unabashedly pragmatic, he declared that the economic situation in the United States was far more conducive to the development of the scenic art than it was in war-torn Europe, and he believed that New York was about to become the center of the design world.[48] While his American colleagues looked to Europe for inspiration and artistic leadership, Urban absorbed the democratic American spirit that valorized popular culture and freely mixed so-called high and low art. At least one historian has wondered if Urban's place in history might have been greater had he remained in Europe.

Urban's pragmatism included his belief that the theater could be an arbiter of taste, that like architecture, interior design, and crafts, it could shape the cultural sensibility of the spectators. "If only one person each night sees something in my stage settings which quickens his or her interest in beauty, I shall be supremely happy."[49] But this Werkstätte-inspired aestheticism was not in keeping with seriousness of the "art theater." The cutting edge was to be found in the so-called little or art theaters of the day, such as the Provincetown Playhouse, where the plays of Eugene O'Neill were first produced. The monochromatic, sculptural, expressionist settings created by Jones, Simonson, Cleon Throckmorton, Sam Hume, Norman Bel Geddes, and others were more appropriate for the neosymbolist, quasi-expressionist plays emerging from the hands of the new American playwrights of the teens and twenties—with their probings of the psyche and the dark inner workings of the soul—than were the colorful and often decorative creations of Joseph Urban. The dark, suggestive scenographic creations of Jones and his colleagues also lent themselves to the new psychological stagings of Shakespeare and other classics being mounted by Arthur Hopkins and later by Margaret Webster and Eva Le Gallienne. Again,

Urban's often colorful fantasies seemed out of place. (His rather sunny 1916 *Macbeth,* for instance, provides a vivid contrast to the somber tone of most contemporary Shakespearean productions.) As a result, the work of designers such as Jones, Simonson, and Bel Geddes was seen as art, while that of Urban was categorized as decoration. And the *Follies,* providing a bourgeois and upper-class clientele with spectacle and pulchritude (tasteful and sophisticated though it may have been), was either ignored or denigrated by literary and art critics.

Ironically, Urban may also have been harmed by his prodigious creations in such a wide area of endeavor. In 1930 an article on the designer drew a fanciful but theoretically feasible picture of Urban's range and interaction with his audience.

> It is possible for a person to walk out of a house designed by Urban, to pack one's clothes in a trunk he designed, to go for a ride in an automobile of his design, to drive to a theatre of his creation to see a show for which he did the sets, then to go to any one of a number of restaurants or nightclubs he decorated, and after dining to spend the night in a hotel, the furnishings and decorations of which again reflect Urban.[50]

As much as we might admire the range of this seemingly Renaissance individual, it made him, to some degree, suspect. Many of the leading theater practitioners at the beginning of the twentieth century were attempting to establish theater as an art, as opposed to an entertainment. Edward Gordon Craig entitled the major collection of his essays *On the Art of the Theatre;* Stanislavsky called his autobiography *My Life in Art,* and his company was the Moscow Art Theater (just as Georg Fuchs had founded the Munich Art Theater). A person who designed furniture, interiors, industrial products, restaurants, and nightclubs, however, was at best an artisan or a craftsman. Adolphe Appia, after all, did not design kitchenware, Robert Edmond Jones did not design luggage. (Norman Bel Geddes, it is true, actually made his mark as an industrial designer—he was largely responsible for the "streamlined" look—but had less impact as a stage designer.)

Joseph Urban's legacy is still felt on Broadway in the musical theater designs of Robin Wagner (and before him, in the work of his mentor Donald Oenslager) and in the Andrew Lloyd Webber extravaganzas. Echoes of Urban, if not his direct influence, can be discerned in the rich blue tones of Robert Wilson productions, not to mention Wilson's mixing of modernist design and crafts with scenography. The theatricality of much postmodern architecture, notably that of Frank Gehry, has precedents in Urban's work.

Urban's influence could be explicitly seen in the New York World's Fairs of 1939 and 1965 and of other similar expositions. It is seen in the developments of the new Times Square with its unabashed use of color and advertising marquees and in much contemporary theater in which art and entertainment dissolve into one another. And it exists wherever bold colors and undulating lines create a world of wonder and fantasy. Joseph Urban should hold a place as one of the most significant figures in twentieth-century design and architecture. Perhaps the twenty-first century will correct the oversight.

Notes

1. Quoted in Randolph Carter and Robert Reed Cole, *Joseph Urban: Architecture, Theatre, Opera, Film* (New York: Abbeville Press, 1992), 183.

2. Deems Taylor, "The Scenic Art of Joseph Urban: His Protean Work in the Theatre," *Architecture*, May 1934, 290.

3. Quoted in Hans Bisanz, "The Visual Arts in Vienna from 1890 to 1920," in *Vienna, 1890–1920,* ed. Robert Waissenberger (New York: Tabard Press, 1984), 116.

4. Gaston Bachelard, *The Poetics of Space,* trans. Maria Jolas (Boston: Beacon Press, 1994), 6.

5. H. T. Parker, "The Opera Outdoes Itself . . . 'The Tales of Hoffmann' Produced as Never Before in America," *Boston Evening Transcript,* November 26, 1912.

6. From the *Sunday Leader.* Typed manuscript in the Joseph Urban Collection, Rare Book and Manuscript Library, Columbia University (hereafter JUC), box 34, file 5.

7. Jane Kallir, *Viennese Design and the Wiener Werkstätte* (New York: Gallerie St. Etienne/George Braziller, 1986), 22.

8. See Carl Schorske's introduction to Kallir's *Viennese Design,* especially p. 8; for a far more extensive investigation, see his book *Fin-de-Siècle Vienna: Politics and Culture* (New York: Vintage Books, 1981).

9. Kallir, *Viennese Design,* 49.

10. Frank Cadie, "Excels Because He Does Not Specialize," *Brooklyn Eagle Magazine,* March 30, 1930.

11. Cadie, "Excels."

12. Joseph Urban, "Wedding Theater Beauty to Ballyhoo," *American Architect,* September 20, 1928, 361.

13. Urban, "Wedding Theater Beauty," 361.

14. Joseph Urban, *Theatres* (New York: Theatre Arts Press, 1929).

15. Urban, *Theatres.*

16. Shepard Vogelgesang, "Architecture and Trade Marks," *Architectural Forum* (1929): 900.

17. Urban, *Theatres.*

18. Urban, *Theatres.*

19. Kenneth Macgowan, "The New Stage-Craft in America," *Century Magazine,* January 1914, 418.

20. Macgowan, "New Stage-Craft," 416.

21. Macgowan, "New Stage-Craft," 416.

22. Macgowan, "New Stage-Craft," 418.

23. Typescript, JUC, box 34, file 5.

24. Macgowan, "New Stage-Craft," 418.

25. Parker, "Opera Outdoes Itself."

26. Parker, "Opera Outdoes Itself."

27. Manuscript, JUC, box 34, file 5. See also Otto Teegen, "Joseph Urban's Philosophy of Color," *Architecture,* May 1934, 257.

28. John Corbin, "The Urban Scenery and Some Other Matters," *New York Times,* September 30, 1917, III.8.

29. Maurice Denis, "From Gauguin and van Gogh to Neo-classicism," in *Art and Theory, 1900–1990,* ed. Charles Harrison and Paul Woods (Malden, Mass.: Blackwell, 1993), 51.

30. Taylor, "Scenic Art," 276.

31. Taylor, "Scenic Art," 279.

32. Macgowan, "New Stage-Craft," 421.

33. See, for example, Hiram Kelly Moderwell, *The Theatre of To-day* (New York: John Lane, 1914), 103.

34. Quoted in Peter Selz, introduction to *Art Nouveau: Art and Design at the Turn of the Century,* ed. Peter Selz and Mildred Constantine (New York: Museum of Modern Art, 1959), 10.

35. Selz, introduction, 10.

36. Urban, *Theatres.* All subsequent quotes relating to the theaters are from this source.

37. Quoted in Teegen, "Urban's Philosophy of Color," 262, 265.

38. Teegen, "Urban's Philosophy of Color," 261.

39. Quoted in Carter and Cole, *Joseph Urban,* 204.

40. Carter and Cole, *Joseph Urban,* 204. Though generally well received, Urban's architectural design was particularly criticized by the architect Philip Johnson for the way in which it mimicked the International Style while failing to have form rigorously adhere to function—the design remained far too decorative for Johnson's taste.

41. JUC, box 34, file 5.

42. JUC, box 34, file 5.

43. Louis DeFoe, "A New Experiment with the Fairy Play," *Greenbook Magazine,* February 1915, 277.

44. Oliver M. Sayler, "Urban of the Opera, the Follies, and the Films," *Shadowland,* typescript, JUC, box 34, file 3.

45. See Richard Ziegfeld and Paulette Ziegfeld, *The Ziegfeld Touch: The Life and Times of Florenz Ziegfeld, Jr.* (New York: Harry N. Abrams, 1993), 73.

46. Review of *Ziegfeld Follies,* in *Dramatic Mirror,* June 23, 1917.

47. Sayler, "Urban of the Opera."

48. Joseph Urban, "Our Scenic Art Leads the World," *Sunday World,* January 18, 1920.

49. Urban, "Our Scenic Art."

50. Arthur Strawn, "Joseph Urban," *Outlook and Independent,* June 18, 1930, 275.

Richard Foreman as Scenographer

The visual world of Richard Foreman is unique and unmistakable. It is like no other design work of the American theater, now or in the past. This goes beyond mere questions of style (leading scenographers of the American stage such as John Conklin and Ming Cho Lee, for example, have recognizable and identifiable styles). It is a matter of aesthetics, even *écriture,* since Foreman's scenography is a visual construct that emerges from the same place as the text and carries with it an equivalent weight. Text, character, language, sound, space, thought, decor are, in a sense, all aspects of a single entity in Foreman's world; inextricably bound up with each other and each functioning essentially in the play.

This is not to say that these plays contain only one immutable visual form. Though rare, there have been productions of Foreman plays by other directors who brought their own mise-en-scène to the event. But these stagings became something else—an improvisation or variation on a text by Richard Foreman, as it were. But within the context of Foreman's own productions the traditional elements of presentation are not mere components of a polyphonic enterprise: they constitute, as Guy Scarpetta has said, "scenic writing."[1]

Foreman's sets are capable of evoking a sense of wonder and exhilaration in their nearly overwhelming detail and riotous juxtaposition of images and objects. One seems to have stumbled into an attic crammed with the belongings of eccentric and long-forgotten inhabitants of a house from the last century; or perhaps we are at a surreal flea market. One critic aptly described the settings as a "vaudevillian dreamscape."[2] If one approaches a Foreman production with expectations of conventional hierarchies, then it often appears as if the decor, at times, upstages the actors and the text. But in his negation of hierarchical structures no one component necessarily takes precedence. Unlike conventional decor in which "unnecessary" detail

From *Theatre Forum* (winter–spring 1997).

might be stripped away and the space designed to guide the spectator's eye—almost always to the primary actor or central action—Foreman sees the stage as a landscape in which all details are significant and in which the audience's perceptual flow may not be uniformly or singularly focused. "I like to assume that the spectator is watching the entire stage at all moments of the play," he explains, "so I try to make a stage picture in which every inch of the stage dynamically participates in the moment-by-moment composition of the piece."[3] While aspects of the decor have inevitably changed over the years—as a result of performing in different spaces as well as slowly shifting aesthetic priorities—certain stylistic tendencies have permeated almost all his settings for over twenty-five years to create the by now familiar "Foremanesque" look.

This style, if we may call it that, includes an almost aggressive frontality, regardless of the theater in which it is performed. In an age in which the thrust stage is ubiquitous and environmental performance not uncommon, Foreman's productions engage the audience head-on in a dialectic between stage and auditorium. (Foreman admits that when he directs on a thrust stage, as he has done several times at Hartford Stage or in his famous production of *The Threepenny Opera* at the Vivian Beaumont Theatre, he still tends to direct frontally. He joked that anyone planning to see *Pearls for Pigs* at Hartford should buy tickets in the center section.) This discourse between spaces and between performer and spectator is achieved in part through the employment of multiple framing devices, thereby setting the stage off from the audience as well as differentiating objects and performers from each other within the stage space. The framing consists of a wide array of seemingly naive deictics ranging from literal pointing and the use of the ubiquitous strings to literal frames such as the miniature theatrical curtain held in front of an actor's face in *Eddie Goes to Poetry City* (1991), which is then parted to mark the beginning of a new sequence in the action.

There is a determinedly homemade quality to the sets, even when Foreman is directing in relatively well funded and technically well supported institutions from regional theaters to opera houses. It is not merely the presence of props gleaned from secondhand shops; set pieces and especially the scenic painting purposely subvert the slick, polished look of commercial theater in which even dirt and decay is carefully, even beautifully, designed. Though he no longer constructs his sets himself, even in his own theater, this roughness is assiduously maintained. Part of this can be traced back to Foreman's Brechtian roots and Brecht's desire to "show that you are showing." The set reveals its own process of construction, and the objects within the set constantly reemphasize their quality of constructed theatricality.

Though Foreman would no longer accept a purely Brechtian rationale for this scenographic approach, he maintains his desire to constantly thwart the seductive nature of theater on all levels, a seduction that interferes with the spectator's active process of engaged and self-conscious perception.

> I've always been interested in showing some other energy, wiping out the normal level of interaction at which we human beings usually live— that level of daily chatter. So all those techniques including the sound and the lights and the interfering, complexifying techniques in the decor, are to show that some other energy is, at every moment, bleeding through— threatening, supporting, changing the belief in the normal social life. I never meant them [the techniques] to be alienating. I just meant them to suggest that other, generally ignored energies are around us, bleeding through us at every moment. Those are the things that are interesting.[4]

The overwhelming impression and lingering memory of many of his sets is of a somber, monochromatic color scheme, though the reality, especially in more recent productions, is often quite different. Shades of brown, black, and gray are common. When he uses bright colors, such as the red wall in *I've Got the Shakes,* or the red Oriental carpet and red flowers in *Samuel's Major Problems* (1993) they are muted and flat. "I don't know the distinction between somberness and brightness," he states, pointing out that amid somber settings there can be streamers, balloons, and bright colors. The somber quality is reinforced by strange and eerie lighting that does not always seek to illuminate the dark recesses of the stage and is sometimes turned on the audience, rendering normal perception difficult. Incandescent light in the form of bare bulbs hanging over the stage or on unshaded lamps is common, but the glare seems swallowed up in the overwhelming darkness of the stage.

Typically there are elements of Victoriana—lamps, overstuffed furniture, fringe, and the like—that create haunting echoes of a bygone era. Yet we are not in a nineteenth-century parlor or any other real space. The Victoriana creates a vaguely nostalgic aura and, as Foreman has noted, a vaguely sexual aura as well. "The overstuffed-ness is a kind of comfort, but also a kind of tumescence almost . . . a kind of erotic aspect."

Props play a crucial role in the productions, and it is often individual props that will linger in the spectator's mind long after seeing a play. Though rarely unusual in and of themselves, these objects are striking in their odd juxtapositions. *I've Got the Shakes* included dolls' heads, skulls, legal pads on clipboards, an armoire, a globe with a bowler hat, candy wrappers, and books.

Eddie Goes to Poetry City included clocks (a mainstay of Foreman's decor) and bicycle wheels. Apples, baguettes, yellow golf balls, and salvers appeared in *My Head Was a Sledgehammer* (1994), glasses of milk and bowls of cereal in *The Universe* (1996). The very familiarity and almost pedestrian quality of these objects creates a momentary comfort—we recognize these items, we may have even handled their real-life counterparts that very day—but pulled out of their familiar contexts, they create a sense of foreboding or even terror akin to that of nightmares in which the everyday world becomes alien. Though terror, per se, is not Foreman's goal, making the familiar strange lies at the root of his theater. "Only by being a tourist. . . . can you experience a place," announces a placard in *Rhoda in Potatoland*.

And, of course, there is the element that has become most identified as Foremanesque, almost to the point of cliché: string. Strings crisscross the space of the stage and even the auditorium, sometimes connecting objects and points within the space, sometimes seemingly random in their placement. The strings may be white, black, or both, creating the sense of a dotted line. They frame, they focus, they function as lines of force or energy, and, inevitably, they disrupt the field of vision. The vectorlike strings section the plane of the stage. Instead of the traditional upstage, downstage, left and right, the stage is divided into a variety of geometric shapes, slightly different for each member of the audience, depending on sight lines. And even this process is subverted by the dotted strings that may seem to disappear in midair. It is not unusual for the strings to become fascinating objects in themselves. On the other hand, for audiences familiar with Foreman's productions, the strings have become so commonplace that they are ignored—they become a kind of background noise whose presence is no longer consciously felt.

> I've long felt that theatrical space is not clearly enough defined; it never seems to have the density of something you can touch or taste, and I miss that. I found I could add compositional tension to the stage by crisscrossing it with lines of string, which lent the space a shimmering, hovering quality. That was intensified when I began to place dots of black paint on the strings, creating dotted black lines that floated in front of the audience's eyes, mixing with the objects seen onstage. It seemed to make the stage dense with its own empty space—something like the scratched lines in a Giacometti drawing.[5]

In almost all historic and cultural contexts, design has functioned symbolically and metonymically: a door or throne, say, represents a palace that

12. *Permanent Brain Damage,* **by Richard Foreman and the Ontological-Hysteric Theatre, 1997. (Photo © Paula Court.)**

in turn stands for the state and thus the world of the characters; or a door or a window may represent a room in a house, which is the most common locale of modern drama. The objects on the stage and the very space of the stage itself constantly refer to the world of the spectator either through a process of identification (the stage as extension of the auditorium) or opposition (the stage as an analogous yet inaccessible world). Even the architectural stage, in which the architectonics of the theater form a permanent emblematic decor, implies another world in opposition to the world of the spectator. But Richard Foreman's designs rarely function that way. The sets are hermetic units whose meanings reside entirely within themselves. Any reference to an external world is the by-product of the intertextuality that results from our own associations.

Foreman's playing space is psychic space. Since his plays are not illusionistic narratives but monodramas derived from the very process of thought and creation, the stage becomes an embodiment of the author's mind. It is a concretization of the nooks and crannies of the mind and a map of the flow of ideas. "The playing space," Foreman has written, "is an environ-

ment for the text to explore, a gymnasium for a psychic, spiritual, and physical workout."[6] Modern Western drama has tended to locate the psychic
space in the house or its equivalent, such as a bar. (Think of Chekhov,
Ibsen, much of Strindberg, Shaw, and virtually any American play you can
name.) Scenographically these may be naturalistic, symbolic, abstracted, or
fragmented, but they nonetheless refer to a recognizable and identifiable
entity. Ironically, Foreman, too, derives his environment from the house,
but, as with all his work, it is a highly personal and peculiarly structured
view of the home. His ideal set is his living room. "More and more," he
sighs, "I wish I could just get it [the stage] to feel, visually, like this room
where I'm sitting. This is where I write, and when I'm concentrating on the
page and writing I have this vibratory aura of the room around me and the
light around me, and I wish that could be the same experience in the theater. I want to get rid of beautiful scenic effects, but I don't know how to
do it. That is my obsession." He could be describing the house as Gaston
Bachelard did: "the house shelters daydreaming, the house protects the
dreamer, the house allows one to dream in peace."[7] In fact, Foreman's sets
bear a striking resemblance to his living room in his Soho loft, which is
painted in dark shades and has comfortable secondhand furniture and thousands of books on homemade shelves that divide the loft into semidiscrete
spaces. Little if anything within the space seems symmetrical or at right
angles.

Foreman's scenographic aim, of course, is not identity; the audience is
not intended to relax into a comfortable recognition of itself in a homey
surrounding. This is not fourth-wall realism in which we are privileged
onlookers into another world. It is what Foreman calls a "reverberation
chamber." "Whatever happens onstage," he explains, "bounces off the walls
of the set, and is reflected back and forth between the objects that are posi-
tioned inside that space."[8] The reverberations on the stage have a counter-
part in the minds of the spectators. The sights and images of this scenographic dreamscape trigger memories, associations, emotions, and even
kinetic responses, but differ from the response to more conventional forms
of design, in that these responses are not guided or prescribed.

The mysterious quality of many of the settings seem to imply an equally
mysterious world offstage, but that is not Foreman's intent. His settings have
been compared to Joseph Cornell boxes, which are self-contained fantasies,
and it is useful to think of the stage as such a sealed container. Foreman
remarks that this view of the stage has always been part of his experience of
theater. "Even when I was a teenager and went in [to New York] every Sat-
urday with a friend to see a Broadway show, I never thought of that, ever.

There was a set on the stage. It never occurred to me that there was any reality outside of that set."

For Foreman, all the energy of the performance comes from within the space of the stage and remains within that space. "Composition is always a question of the tension between a container and the contained energy that wants to break out of that container and flow forth."[9] Thus, the designs establish two forms of energy, two tensions. There are the reverberating ideas and images that bounce around the contained space of the stage, and there is the energy that flows between the contained stage and the audience—a kind of energy that permeates the fourth wall to intersect with and interact with the audience. This should not suggest that Foreman begins with a preconceived notion of space or any sort of scenic template. It begins with the space of the room. In the mid-1970s his productions were done in a long, narrow loft on Broadway in Soho that was eighty feet deep; now, at the theater at St. Mark's Church in the Bowery in the East Village section of Manhattan, he has an essentially shallow space with pillars. This inevitably informs the creation of stage space. Despite being a "frontalist," Foreman wishes on some level to envelop the audience, a desire that goes back to the idea of creating a set that is like his living room. Strings, pictures, and other scenic elements often project around the sides of the auditorium or over the audience so that, as he says, the fourth wall is actually behind the last row.

> I'm very concerned as a designer with the sides of the auditorium and what the audience has, unnoticed, in their peripheral vision as they're watching the play. Ideally I would design a four-walled room, totally designed—seating and set—and in one corner of that room would be the play. I still don't want to involve the audience, to make them think they're in the play, so within that space I would still have [barriers] like a Plexiglas wall between the audience and the play.

He is striving for the state of involved observation, like being at a party and yet not being involved in the festivities—just standing to the side and watching. Thus, Foreman is always finding ways to thwart the process of viewing—actually to thwart the process of involvement and identification.

In the productions from the 1970s and early 1980s the devices for rupturing the smooth and seductive habits of viewing included lights shining in the spectators' eyes, harsh noises, railings, and of course string. More recently the device of choice has been sheets of Plexiglas hung in front of the stage. Though clear, so that vision is essentially unimpeded, its presence cannot be ignored, and it creates both a psychological and physical impediment to the viewing process; it is like viewing the play through a window, but a window with no wall around it. Depending on the lighting, the audience may find itself reflected, ghostlike, in the glass as it looks at the stage. Images of oneself and other spectators are layered over the stage, adding texture, a reminder of the process of viewing, and disrupting, however slightly, the clear apprehension of the characters and setting. The St. Mark's space is wide, and there are usually two or three sheets of glass hanging. Foreman is careful to leave a small space between each one. If you happen to sit opposite one of the gaps in this transparent but literal fourth wall, there is a very real disruption of the viewing process as characters are seen primarily through Plexiglas but occasionally unmediated.[10]

Foreman claims not to think in visual terms as he writes. The design process happens at a later stage and continues through rehearsal. Much of this process is an attempt to create the rich textures necessary for the multivalent way of seeing. The creation of this texture, however, is an instinctual process of layering that is done in an almost painterly manner:

> I start out every year saying this design is going to be simple for this play. Then as I'm in rehearsal the words just don't have enough things to bounce off of. The words don't have enough things interfering with them or altering them. And I end up just putting more stuff on the walls, layering it with more pictures, more fringe, more strings, more stuff hanging from the ceiling. That's not really to achieve any particular visual effect, that's just to make the whole environment as dense, in a good sense, as I hope the text is. I mean, by density, as many layers, as many associations as possible operating at once.

He is reluctant to apply too much intent or meaning to particular visual choices, attributing a great deal to accident almost in the manner of John Cage describing imitating nature in its method of operation. Asked about what determined the color of a particular object, he replied,

> I feel that there's got to be a total kind of bricolage where you just make do with what's at hand, and one thing will do as well as anything else if you apply it the right way. Maybe I've only got red left, so I paint the couch red. If it's too bright, you put it in the corner. I think it's important. I do that because I think that is the way everything happens in the world, and I want my plays to reflect on every level the way things happen in the world.

Foreman's cultural knowledge is prodigious, especially his familiarity with the art movements and traditions of the twentieth century. One seeks specific influences and traces in his work. But just as he himself refers to Giacometti, the influences are there, but he denies any specific or intentional copying. One can say that there are strong suggestions of symbolism, surrealism, and expressionism in his designs, possibly elements of dada and futurism, and the occasional oblique reference to Meyerhold, but to trace any individual influence or presence would be fruitless. It is even possible to apply Lacanian analysis to the settings with Jacques Lacan's concepts of the mirror, *méconnaissance,* and the abrupt disruption of the analytic session. But again, even if such ideas lurk behind Foreman's creative process, they are not used consciously to create the mise-en-scène.

The actual process of designing is similar to the process of writing. Just as the texts emerge from pages of his notebooks, the scenographic environment evolves through thumbnail sketches until the point at which work must commence, at which time he makes a rough model, often making several models until he achieves something with which he is satisfied. When he is working for an institutional theater, an assistant will make a "neat" model based on drawings, "but for my own theater I make very rough models and ludicrously sloppy drawing instructions for whatever has to be built." When he was working in the deep loft space on Broadway in the 1970s, there were a lot of heavy and complex set pieces and moving elements, so relatively little changed from initial model to finished work. Now he tends to use unit sets with fairly simple scenic elements, so he is more open to playing with the set through the rehearsal period. "All things being equal, I would prefer to start rehearsing without any set and then decide what the set would be. But I can't do that because of the time. Every year, in my own theater, I [start out] trying to use the whole stage, and somewhere toward the end of rehearsal I just think it looks too empty, and I end up madly moving all the walls in back way down front. It's pretty much normal procedure."

The theater of fifteen years ago employed many moving elements and distorted perspective, engaging in a constant hiding and revealing of space that echoed the flow of Foreman's consciousness as well as the process of creating the plays, which he says "were really unredeemed stuff from my notebook. I would take pages out of my notebook, and it was really a movie in which everything was always changing with the feeling of where it happened. These days, though I still write by collaging a lot of material, to get that complexity that I'm talking about I look for a place in which everything can happen." Now, partly because of a shallower space, partly because economics restrict construction as well as cast size (larger casts were needed to move scenery), and partly because of different interests, this is no longer the case. In addition, as Foreman admits, he is a "closet Romantic."

A lot of this thickness of detail, a lot of this interfering of string, Plexiglas, and so forth, is probably connected to this symbolist, Romantic aura. I was very against that in the early days. That was a polemical stand that I forced upon myself and that I believed in, but as I say, I'm a closet Romantic. That means that I want something to have the richness and texture of great painting, or the nostalgia of early photographs, that have grain and that funny kind of light that's just ravishing. Now it's there, but still it's a battle. It means wanting to create a genuine aura and then continue to say, "Wait a minute, auras don't count. Or are corrupt, or whatever."

Foreman says with only a slight smile, "I've gotten sick of scenery." It is hard to imagine a Richard Foreman production on a bare stage, and it is unlikely to happen anytime soon. His stage is not an "empty space" since it is an embodiment of a rich and densely textured mind. But for someone whose life is the life of the mind, the encumbrances of the physical stage can provoke a longing for a freedom from such material concerns—for the elusive simplicity of the mind as reverberation chamber.

Notes

1. Guy Scarpetta, "Richard Foreman's Scenography: Examples from His Work in France," *Drama Review* 28.2 (1984): 23.
2. Ben Brantley, review of *I've Got the Shakes, New York Times,* January 13, 1995.
3. Richard Foreman, *Unbalancing Acts: Foundations for a Theater* (New York: Pantheon, 1992), 55.
4. This and all subsequent quotations not otherwise attributed are from the author's interview with Richard Foreman, July 3, 1996.
5. Foreman, *Unbalancing Acts,* 59–61.
6. Foreman, *Unbalancing Acts,* 54.
7. Gaston Bachelard, *The Poetics of Space,* trans. Maria Jolas (Boston: Beacon Press, 1994), 6.
8. Foreman, *Unbalancing Acts,* 57.
9. Foreman, *Unbalancing Acts,* 58.
10. Since this article was written, Foreman has ceased using Plexiglas, and though framing devices remain, there is no longer a visual barrier between performer and spectator.

The Wooster Group as Cartographers

In June 1975, a workshop of actors from Richard Schechner's Performance Group and some of their friends created an evening of three plays at the Performing Garage. The final piece of the evening was *Sakonnet Point,* created by Spalding Gray and Elizabeth LeCompte together with Leeny Sack, Ellen LeCompte, Alexandra Ivanoff, and Erik Moskowitz, an eight-year-old boy. The piece was performed again later that summer in Westerly, Rhode Island, and again at the Garage in the fall of 1975 with Sack and Ivanoff replaced by Libby Howes and Joan MacIntosh. The physicality of some moments of the production (not to mention the venue and the actors) inevitably recalled the neoexpressionism of the Performance Group, while the languid pacing suggested Robert Wilson; the tape marks on the floor and the use of objects seemed inspired by Happenings (with a pinch of Meredith Monk), and through it all, the ethereal and contemplative evocations of a time past conjured visions of the Noh drama of Japan. And then there was a mysterious red tent perched above the space from which emanated strains of Tchaikovsky and Mary Baker Eddy. The totality of the production, of course, was something different from any of the particular sources it seemed to draw upon. Here was, yet again, something new.

I say yet again, because the previous ten years or so had been a remarkable period in American theater. The period saw the emergence and development of off-off-Broadway, the return from exile of the Living Theatre, the mature work of the Open Theater, the founding of the Performance Group and its notorious production of *Dionysus in 69,* the founding of Richard Foreman's Ontological-Hysteric Theatre and Robert Wilson's Byrd Hoffman School of Byrds, the *Fragments of a Greek Trilogy* by Andrei Serban, the origins of Mabou Mines, and the development of postmodern dance. With all these came new explorations of text, performance, and the-

Presented as keynote speech at the conference "The Wooster Group and Its Traditions," Brussels, May 2002.

atrical space. With such a foundation, the "new," on some level, became the norm—one expected to be surprised at each performance. Yet even in such an environment, *Sakonnet Point* was clearly forging in new territory. The seven-minute fade at the end of the production, in which the performers lay on blankets on the floor as if at the beach, was a kind of Wagnerian mystic chasm. For the audience willing to project itself through that gulf into the realm created by Gray and LeCompte, a new world of theater awaited. But it was a challenge; it asked the spectators for both faith and a kind of rigor—a kind of Artaudian cruelty that is, as Artaud says, "lucid, a kind of rigid control and submission to necessity."[1] As the performers lay on the floor of the Performing Garage, unmoving in the fading light, one could not help but think of Artaud's further explication of cruelty as "a kind of higher determinism, to which the executioner-tormenter himself is subjected and which he must be *determined* to endure when the time comes."

Over the next decades the Wooster Group would continue to push the limits of audience expectations as well as its own sense of boundaries. Their work, if nothing else, continuously placed—and still places—pressure on the sensibilities of both spectator and performer. Through some eighteen theater and dance productions the Group appropriated blackface, pornography, fetishism, and intellectual property rights into rigorously aesthetic but seemingly apolitical contexts, thereby confounding audiences who—especially in the wake of the politically engaged theater from which Gray and LeCompte emerged—expected, if anything, the reverse. The Wooster Group reframed dramatic texts and reconfigured the stage, moving technology to the center and the live performer to the periphery. Theirs was, and is, a theater in which bodily functions mingle with neoclassicism, Godzilla with Chekhov, and pornographic film with Thornton Wilder and Gertrude Stein. It is, in short, a theater in which nothing is alien except the mundane and, perhaps, theatrical illusionism. (In *To You the Birdie (Phèdre)*, the actress Kate Valk appears to defecate onstage. While I found myself unwilling to believe that this was *not* simulated—would even the Wooster Group transgress such a taboo? Could Kate Valk, great actress that she is, defecate on cue and so neatly?—I was actually offended by the thought that this might be illusion.) But part of the Wooster Group's strategy throughout its existence has been to deflect audience focus away from analytical engagement with the text onto a hermeneutic dialogue with the performance.

To You the Birdie (Phèdre) immediately confronts the audience with this bifurcation of focus and intent. At the start of the piece two actors sit on a bench downstage center. In front of them, obscuring their bodies below the waist, is a video screen on which we see the legs of the performers. It sug-

13. *Sakonnet Point,* **composed and directed by Elizabeth LeCompte and Spalding Gray, 1975. This was the first production of what would become the Wooster Group. (Photo: Ken Kobland, courtesy the Wooster Group.)**

gests an X-ray monitor, only this is an X-ray machine that reveals surfaces rather than interior structures. Instead of allowing us to delve beneath the skin, it re-presents superficial realities in a mediated form. Although the legs seem to be those of the actors—the size, shape, costumes, and, in particular, the movements, are congruent with those of the two individuals seated before us—the image doesn't quite mesh. The representation does not precisely align with the bodies, the movements are not exactly coordinated. Moreover, if we allow ourselves to start thinking of the technical requirements, it becomes obvious that the screen allows no vantage point for a video camera; it would be impossible to capture the actual lower torsos of the actors in the way we see them presented. Either we are seeing a prerecorded image projected on top of the live, corporeal presence of the performers, or conceivably we are seeing the legs of two other performers being videoed offstage and projected over the onstage actors. The Group has used both strategies in the past; either is plausible. It is this very uncertainty, however, that floods our minds; I would be hard pressed to tell you

14. *To You the Birdie (Phèdre),* **the Wooster Group, 2002. (Photo: Mary Gearhart, courtesy the Wooster Group.)**

precisely what the two characters were discussing. Rather, the technologi-cal prowess of the Group, their layering of images, and their disruption of the conventional and predictable time-space continuum of the stage engen-ders a phenomenological investigation that erupts in the minds of the spec-tators and which, importantly, overlays the text of Racine and adapter Paul Schmidt. There is a disruption of visual, spatial, and textual continuity that draws attention to the disjuncture.

It is, of course, this very focusing on the interstices between actor and character, between two- and three-dimensional space, between real time and dramatic time, between text and performance, between process and product, between spectator and creator, that has typified the work of the Wooster Group from the very start. All theater, of course, does this to a degree; the great actors have always played upon the tension (a kind of cen-trifugal force) that exists between themselves as individuals and their char-acters as artistic constructs; theatrical space often vibrates between architec-tural presence and illusionistic evocation. Yet the Wooster Group revels in the gaps and spaces and the contradictions these fissures engender. What is the boundary between Spalding Gray the actor and Spalding Gray the character whom we see in his monologues? Between Kate Valk the actor and Kate Valk the "persona" who welcomes you to the performance? Between Willem Dafoe movie star and Willem Dafoe Wooster Group member? Between Paul Schmidt translator-adapter and Paul Schmidt actor in *Brace Up!?* Between Elizabeth LeCompte director and Elizabeth LeCompte the shadow who lurks behind the audience at performances? Between a dramatic text in the collective unconscious of the audience and the performance rendered on the stage by the Group? In Richard Foreman's *Rhoda in Potatoland* a voice says, "Certain spaces suddenly appear in the center of the audience. Find them. Find them." In Elizabeth LeCompte's creations, the spaces appear on the stage as well, and in a sense an opposite admonition seems apt: Find the boundaries that contain the spaces.

Most theater, perhaps most art, functions through the establishment of boundaries, through the creation of containers. An event, say, unfolds in a room that fits neatly within the confines of the stage; a character comfortably inhabits the body of an actor. But in the Wooster Group work, boundaries are porous at best. Events derive as much from rehearsals as from formal texts, spectators are rigorously excluded from the stage yet are addressed by performers, actors exist equally in the flesh and on video (and even on video their presence may be live or recorded, in real time or mediated; a prerecorded image may have been shot in the exact location it is being played, while a live actor on video may exist in some indeterminate offstage locale). Wooster Group performances derive at least part of their dynamic from a constant tension between pairs of objects with opposite energies. It is not unlike string theory, which posits a unified theory of physics based upon pairings of sub-subatomic particles that vibrate against each other at differing rates, thus creating different forms of matter and energy. A Wooster Group production is made up of such vibrations derived from the gaps between expectation and execution.

Tension and energy is greatest when the gap is at its smallest, in other words, when the difference between the reality and the perceived is of minimal proportions. There is a fragmentary story by Jorge Luis Borges, a mere paragraph long, called "On Exactitude in Science." It begins thus:

In that Empire, the Art of Cartography attained such Perfection that the map of a single Province occupied the entirety of a City, and the map of the Empire, the entirety of a Province. In time, those Unconscionable Maps no longer satisfied, and the Cartographers Guilds struck a Map of the Empire whose size was that of the Empire, and which coincided point for point with it.[2]

What Borges does not say, though it must be implied, is that no matter how well the map fits over the natural topography, a gap—microscopic as it might be—inevitably exists between the original and its simulacrum.

I see the Wooster Group as Borgesian cartographers, creating maps of a performative and cultural landscape, maps that fit over the landscape almost point for point, yet maps that leave a fissure that sets up a vibratory energy. From its very origins the Group mapped the landscape they inhabited, creating both alternative terrains and simulacra that seduced unwary travelers into new territories. For its first five years, of course, the Group was an entity at once indistinguishable yet totally different from the Performance Group. From its first experiments in 1975 until its incorporation in 1980, the Wooster Group and the Performance Group were one and the same: the same actors (for the most part) in the same space. Their work was identified as that of the Performance Group. (Interestingly, the official corporate name of the Performance Group—the company founded by Schechner—was the Wooster Group. Thus, the new organization, placed like Borges's map over the original, served to make visible what had hitherto been immanent.) And, it should be noted, once the Group was formally constituted, it retroactively applied its name to the pre-1980 work created by LeCompte. An analogy might be made to cartographers in postcolonial nations or in places where territory is disputed: one needs to know who is designating borders and names. The first four pieces created by the nascent Wooster Group were the *Rhode Island Trilogy,* followed by an epilogue, *Point Judith.* All of these productions centered around Spalding Gray. But while the raw material for the pieces was taken from autobiographical matter and literal samplings of dialogue, images, and events from Gray's life, the persona that the audience encountered was a theatrical construct—a simulacrum—placed carefully over the actor Spalding Gray. From here (even my choice of words, implying movement through space rather than progression through time, suggests the functionality of a map) the Group moved from mapping the psyche of Spalding Gray to an idiosyncratic road map through modernist classics: *The Cocktail Party, Long Day's Journey into Night, Our Town, The Crucible, The Three Sisters, The Emperor Jones, The Hairy Ape, Doctor Faustus Lights the Lights,* even a nod to *South Pacific.* And now they have turned, at least momentarily, to neoclassicism with *Phèdre.* As a character in Richard Foreman's *Pandering to the Masses* implores, "Find the connections."

Even the manner in which the Group's productions are created has often suggested a similar Borgesian process. In *L.S.D. (. . . Just the High Points . . .),* for example, one scene was rehearsed while the performers were high on LSD. The rehearsal was videotaped, and the tape became the new text that was re-created in performance. What the audience experienced was not so much an interpretation of a text—the most common understanding of the theatrical process—but a map of a rehearsal. In the same production, one actor, Michael Kirby, was unavailable for an out-of-town tour, so his part was videotaped and he appeared on a television monitor; a map of a performance was substituted for the "real," which, of course, was a map of process. When the piece was next performed in New York, the live Kirby returned and interacted with his video self: overlay upon overlay, map upon map.

Maps tend to be used for two purposes: they are visual representations of a place or space, and they function as tools to get from one location to another. As representations they are not confused for that which they represent. Despite the color-coded depictions of the British Empire on old globes and maps, the actual earth of these lands was not pink. Even when relief maps present terrain as three-dimensional bumps, we see it as a charming representation—but the mountain tops are not covered with actual snow nor buffeted by gales. Yet Borges's map is closer to the experience of theater in which signifiers and signified are often identical or at least of the same class of objects. Onstage, chairs may signify chairs, doors may signify doors, and people signify people. It is the latter aspect in particular that contributes to the difficulties that some spectators have had with the Wooster Group's productions. Spalding Gray the actor, together with LeCompte and other members of the company, created and then presented a fictional construct known as Spalding Gray. This construction, this map, used the body it signified as the signifier, just as it used the voice, the mannerisms, and the autobiography. Yet, like Borges's map, it was not the landscape itself. But just as we might postulate a traveler in the cartographers' empire who was unaware that he or she was traversing a fine map laid over the actual landscape, and for whom such a distinction was immaterial because the experience was identical, so too, spectators at the *Rhode Island Trilogy* or Gray's subsequent monologues may have mistaken the character for the actor. But in the context of those performances such misattribution will have only minimal impact.

Of greater consequence was the confusion of signifier and signified in *Route 1&9*. Here, white actors applied blackface and spoke in exaggerated dialect and otherwise seemed to embrace African-American stereotypes. The difference between signifier and signified became glaringly obvious, strained, politically charged, and ultimately offensive to many. It was an ill-fitting map that drew attention to the differing topographies of the theatrical world and the social world it seemed to reference. Borges never describes the material from which the cartographers' map is made, but presumably it not only fits the terrain, it simulates the textures. This was certainly the case with Spalding Gray. But with *Route 1&9,* the simulation and the apparent original grated against one another harshly, possibly because the simulation was of a caricature that by definition is itself a kind of map— a crude, distorted representation of an original, showing selected landmarks with little nuance or context. Part of what disturbed audiences was the lack of clarity surrounding these depictions. Absent a clearly defined sociopolitical viewpoint, reading the use of blackface and apparent caricature became difficult and thus disturbing. At the risk of overextending the metaphor, it was a map without orientation and thus a map that provided no direction. Interestingly, at one point in the production characters launched into a routine by black vaudevillian Pigmeat Markham. Though there were still political and aesthetic issues raised by white actors in blackface attempting such an act so completely out of context, nonetheless tensions eased slightly. At least there was a relatively familiar landmark—an actual person and existing text. The representation was rooted in a definable actuality, not gross parody. The space between map and landscape diminished. The audience as travelers, momentarily at least, were back on track.

One more example might be mentioned here. *L.S.D.* incorporated a shortened and idiosyncratic presentation of Arthur Miller's *The Crucible.* As is well known, Miller, seeing the production as a parody of his play, or at the very least an attack upon authorial control, demanded that it be cut from the production. At first a gibberish version was substituted and when that failed to appease, a structurally identical new play, "The Hearing," by Michael Kirby, was inserted, but to no avail. A lawsuit was threatened. The first attempt, the nonsense version, was a map of the terrain of *The Crucible* with the landmarks removed. The landscape was familiar yet alien. The second version could be likened to a map that preserved the terrain precisely while building a whole new empire on top. Imagine taking the street grid of a city and the building plots and preserving them exactly, but then on the plots constructing different buildings, though buildings whose doors were in the exact same locations as the originals. This was "The Hearing." Miller, rightly or wrongly, believed that the "map" was his creation and thus anything placed (built) on it was a violation of that representation.

Jean Baudrillard, in his essay "Simulacra and Simulations" (which also uses the Borges story as a point of departure), notes that "representation starts from the principle that the sign and the real are equivalent (even if this equivalence is Utopian, it is a fundamental axiom). Conversely, simulation starts from the Utopia of this principle of equivalence, *from the radical negation of the sign as value,* from the sign as reversion and death sentence of every reference."³ He then notes four stages of an image as it moves from representation to simulacrum.

1. It is the reflection of a basic reality.
2. It masks and perverts a basic reality.
3. It masks the *absence* of a basic reality.
4. It bears no relation to any reality whatever: it is its own pure simulacrum.⁴

Most theater can be included in category 1. Miller presumably thinks of *The Crucible* as representing a certain reality, and he expects any production to reflect his understanding of that reality as written. He accused the Wooster Group of number 2: masking and perverting. But LeCompte believed the third proposition: that Miller's play in fact suggested an absence, and thus her staging was intended to revert to some basic reality. "I want to use irony and distancing techniques to cut through to the intellectual and political heart of *The Crucible*," she wrote to Miller.⁵ Yet ultimately, the Wooster Group's work might be seen as Baudrillard's simulacra: something that, while containing the signifying elements of stage representation, remains its own construction whose points of reference are only itself.

Although the earliest Group productions made reference to outside material, they quickly began to reference themselves. Props, ground plans, images, actions, and motifs reappeared from production to production. What emerged might be seen as a continuous mapping of a group consciousness or artistic sensibility, but since the very aesthetic of the Group was in part a kind of Borgesian mapping, the work created was a map based upon previous maps that in turn were based on earlier maps. These were maps of maps based on original landscapes virtually unknowable to an audience, and now, perhaps, forgotten even by those who drew the original maps.

If one purpose of maps is to get travelers from point to point, it is reasonable to ask where the Wooster Group is taking us. First of all, they are taking us into a new understanding of theatrical space. I don't simply mean, of course, the physical space of the stage or the virtual space of the dramatic text. Rather, I see the Group's work as a mapping of interconnections of time and space as it shapes our experience—a sensibility described by both Gaston Bachelard and Michel Foucault. Bachelard's phenomenological perspective analyzed dream and experience through the lens of the house and the psychological, emotional, and spatial memories it engendered. For years, each production of the Wooster Group was an excavation of memories contained within their literal house, the Performing Garage (and, in the early days, the Red Tent), and the metaphoric structure of their evolving oeuvre.

Foucault has discussed the evolution of the understanding and experience of space in the Western tradition and sees it today a network of interconnectivity or, in his words, "relations of proximity between points or elements; formally we can describe these relations as series, trees, or grids."[6] He goes on to contrast utopias ("sites with no real place,"[7] something like Baudrillard's simulacra) with heterotopias, liminal spaces within society that are "capable of juxtaposing in a single real place several spaces, several sites that are in themselves incompatible."[8] What better definition of the stage? The Wooster Group is providing a road map within a real space, the theater, for a landscape of imagination, memory, and experience.

Much of the work that the Group created through 1990 bears a relationship to Bachelard's notion of space. Their texts—both those of modern drama and the performance texts created through the performative process—were derived from the basements, kitchens, parlors, and attics of their collective consciousness. As such, it was almost pointless to read their disquisitions on Eliot, O'Neill, or Wilder as textual exegesis; it was ultimately understandable only in the context of the unknowable inner lives of the performers and the formal structures created by LeCompte for purely aesthetic reasons. (And because LeCompte retained a certain degree of ensemble creation from the Performance Group days, the texts, in the end, represented multiple consciousnesses, further muddying any attempt at interpretation.) But beginning with *Brace Up!* in 1991, their adaptation of Paul Schmidt's translation of Chekhov's *Three Sisters,* the literary text became increasingly privileged. It was still situated within a Wooster Group context—they created a framework, a narrator, and an onstage translator-commentator—but the larger performance container that had overwhelmed the earlier plays-within-plays was greatly diminished. This was no eleven-minute version of an author's text; this was a production, albeit unique, of Chekhov. By the time of O'Neill's *Hairy Ape,* extraneous elements and self-referential contexts were nearly gone. In a strange way, however, this brought us back to the Spalding Gray conundrum. Were we seeing *Hairy Ape* or *Emperor Jones* or *Doctor Faustus Lights the Lights,* or were we seeing a Wooster Group construct or map placed over the apparently familiar?

Borges' story concludes thus:

The following Generations, who were not so fond of the Study of Cartography as their Forebears had been, saw that that vast Map was Useless, and not without some Pitilessness was it, that they delivered it up to the Inclemencies of Sun and Winters. In the Deserts of the West, still today, there are Tattered Ruins of that Map, inhabited by Animals and Beggars; in all the Land there is no other Relic of the Disciplines of Geography.

I wonder if the Wooster Group is abandoning its study of cartography. Although it has performed in theaters around the world, in New York City it has always created and performed in the Performing Garage. (*The Hairy Ape* was performed in a Broadway district theater, but after it had premiered at the Garage.) Although *To You the Birdie (Phèdre)* was developed at the Garage, its New York premiere was at St. Ann's Warehouse, a rather cavernous theater space in Brooklyn. The more recent revival of *Brace Up!* was also presented at St. Ann's. The ostensible reasons were a wider stage and a greater seating capacity. These may have been the true reasons, but I cannot help thinking of the Garage now as a "tattered ruin," "a relic." Borges does not tell us what happened to the empire itself. If the Wooster Group, though, is leaving its previous methods of creation and its inspirational home to the "inclemencies of sun and winter," what does the future hold for them?

Notes

1. Antonin Artaud, *The Theatre and Its Double,* trans. Mary Caroline Richards (New York: Grove Press, 1958), 102.

2. Jorge Luis Borges, *Collected Fictions,* trans. Andrew Hurley (New York: Penguin, 1998), 325.

3. Jean Baudrillard, "Simulacra and Simulations," in *Selected Writings,* ed. Mark Poster (Stanford: Stanford University Press, 1988), 170.

4. Ibid.

5. David Savran, "The Wooster Group, Arthur Miller, and *The Crucible,*" *Drama Review* 29.2 (1985): 102.

6. Michel Foucault, "Of Other Spaces," *Diacritics* 16 (spring 1986): 23.

7. Foucault, "Of Other Spaces," 24.

8. Foucault, "Of Other Spaces," 25.

Design for *Angels in America*
Envisioning the Millennium

There are two essential questions to be answered in considering the scenography of *Angels in America*. One is a fundamental scenographic question for any play: Where are we? (and how do we, as an audience, know where we are?). The other is a practical one: how can the sheer magnitude of the play be dealt with? *Angels in America* unfolds through two parts, eight acts and an epilogue, consisting of some sixty scenes, a significant number of which are "split"—presenting two locales simultaneously. Some, such as the Brooklyn apartment of Joe and Harper, Prior's bedroom, or the hospital room of Roy Cohn are recurring, but many are seen only once, resulting in a dizzying array of settings through which the spectators must be led on their theatrical journey. The practical question is a daunting one because the visual landscape must have a unity that provides an overall structure for the production while at the same time providing enough specificity to allow the audience to locate itself within the ever-changing geography of the play. Yet, from a practical point of view, the sixty scene changes must not be allowed to become time consuming or disruptive to the emotional and narrative progression of the play—they must flow with the ineluctable logic and fluidity of a dream.

The solution to the practical problems will ultimately be determined by the approach to the more philosophical question of location. If we begin with "where," the answer is, on the surface, relatively simple: We are in America. More precisely, we are in various specified locations in New York City in the latter half of the 1980s, as well as in apparently hallucinatory images and fantasies of various characters. It is from these simple observations that the visual environment—the world—of *Angels* must be drawn.

Published in *Approaching the Millennium: Essays on Tony Kushner's "Angels in America,"* ed. Deborah R. Geis and Steven F. Kruger (Ann Arbor: University of Michigan Press, 1997).

How does one present the idea of "America"? Is there an obvious imagistic or emblematic representation? Is there a single icon, perhaps, that will
provide the audience with a sense of time, place, tone, and point of view?
The British production, for example, directed by Declan Donellan and
designed by Nick Ormerod at the Royal National Theatre in London,
attempted to do so by transforming the stage into a "stars and stripes" background against which the play unfolded quite simply. But it is much easier
to convey the concept of a foreign nation to an audience than to confront
spectators with their own culture and heritage. For a British audience
(indeed, for any non-American audience) the mere sight of the emblem of
the United States is sufficient to evoke a vast array of associations—the simple environment suggested that all the characters and their actions were
enmeshed in "America," whatever that might mean for each individual
spectator. Tony Kushner, himself, plays with that sort of iconography when
he calls for a "great red flag" behind Prelapsarionov at the start of *Perestroika*.
But in the United States, the subtleties, contradictions, and even violently
opposing concepts of America make such simple emblematic scenography
problematic if not impossible.

In fact, at least part of the play's theme is wrapped up in the epic struggle
to come to terms with what America means as the millennium approaches.
Just as Prior wrestles with the angel, so must the scenographer contend with
the landscape of the play. At the start of part 1 the rabbi, talking to the
mourners of Sarah Ironson (though addressing the audience in the theater)
states, "You do not live in America. No such place exists."[1] America is a
fantasy, a chimera, made up of the individual perceptions, expectations, and
projections of hundreds of millions of individuals whose true roots are elsewhere. How remarkable to be told in the first moments of the play that the
very location identified in the title is nonexistent—a state of mind. It is, perhaps, not unlike Alfred Jarry's siting of *Ubu Roi* in Poland, "that is to say,"
as his stage directions explain, "nowhere."[2] Jarry's Poland was "nowhere"
because it was a country that, historically, existed more often as a concept of
nationhood in the souls of its people than as a political entity. America, on
the other hand, has been a political entity for over two centuries, yet it consists of such a commingling of disparate peoples that its identity as a nation
has always been a subject of debate, never more so than now. Kushner's
dramatis personae contains a veritable catalog of individuals who fly in the
face of the Reaganite image of America. It is not that Kushner's image has
more truth than any other—it simply emphasizes the difficulty of arriving at
a unified coherent image. There is no landscape that easily will provide the
world of Kushner's vision.

15. *Angels in America, Part I: Perestroika,* by Tony Kushner, at the Mark Taper Forum, Los Angeles, 1992, directed by Oskar Eustis with Tony Taccone; design by John Conklin. (Photo: Jay Thompson.)

In the production at the Mark Taper Forum in Los Angeles, director Oskar Eustis and set designer John Conklin nonetheless sought a unifying image that would evoke Americana without overly specifying or imposing a narrow view. The back wall of Conklin's set was the facade of a house that combined elements of a New England meeting house with Jeffersonian classicism. The meeting house was evoked largely by a geometrically square floor of natural wood planks set on gray boulders suggestive of a Maine or California coast. The image suggested simplicity, sturdiness, and a connection with the continent itself—all elements of American mythology. The facade was a pastiche of windows, doors, and cornices based on the designs of Thomas Jefferson, the towering intellect of the American Revolution. The total effect, though obviously a theatricalized amalgamation, was of distinctly American architecture. It created, according to Conklin, a "civilized public space."[3]

The choice was inspired—the American home, as developed over the last three centuries, has been considered the country's most original contribution to architecture. Jefferson's classicism, of course, was based on European Renaissance models that, in turn, were drawn from ancient Roman and Greek sources. So the visual imagery echoed the Eurocentric foundation of America that is depicted in the play. Here was a visual iconography that evoked the idea of America without being overly symbolic or trite.

But Conklin took the concept of the house as metaphor one step further by creating a large jagged split down the center of the facade to create, as he noted, "an ideal that was cracked."[4] The angel flew in through this crack in the wall, rather than through the ceiling, which did not exist in this production.

The Broadway production, directed by George C. Wolfe and designed by Robin Wagner, opted for neutrality rather than visual metaphor. Unity was achieved by the proscenium arch itself and ever-changing configurations of black velour flats in chrome frames. Perhaps the production's very presence in New York City, the center of the American theater world, the place where Kushner developed as a playwright, a center of gay culture and consciousness, and a place where much of the audience would know firsthand the sites referred to in the text, mitigated the need for some other visual element as a unifying image.

Interestingly, the Los Angeles production never sought to suggest New York City as a locale nor to use images of the city in an iconographic way. It would not be unreasonable for a designer to use the visual iconography of New York City as a unifying framework, but other than, perhaps, Bethesda Fountain in Central Park, Kushner sets none of the play in a recognizable locale. (There are many specific locations, such as the Mormon Visitor's Center, but they are not instantly recognizable landmarks, as is, say, the Empire State Building, which was the locale for the conclusion of *Perestroika* in an early draft of the script.) The play ranges through unremarkable apartments, offices, and streetscapes that carry no particular resonance except what is bestowed upon them by their occupants. And that is as it should be. New York City is vital to the play because it is the historical point of entry to America for immigrants on their journey to a new land, and it is still the destination for those from within the country who seek refuge from their own bleak landscape—it is a place for those who do not fit elsewhere. It is a city of the displaced, the outsiders, the adventurers, the seekers and searchers. In its diversity and lack of apparent cohesion, in its gaudy excess as well as decay, it seems to defy the standard images of America. It is the place of the "other," and thus it serves as America's "other." But as the home for everyone and a repository of history, it embodies all that is America and makes it the quintessential emblem of America at the millennium. This is an "everytown," which is to say "our town."

If *Angels in America* has a precedent in American theater history it is surely Thornton Wilder's *Our Town,* and a comparison of the two is instructive. Wilder combined aspects of Italian futurism, German expressionism, other European vanguard movements, and the ideas of Gertrude Stein with American sensibilities, especially emotional realism, to create not only innovative forms of drama but also a new way of physical presentation. Though Wilder did not invent the bare stage or emblematic scenery, he popularized them as a means of economic staging while inviting a wider audience imagination—a kind of radio for the eyes. Wilder's play is a reading of the geography of America in the first third of the American century, as well as a teleological explication of human existence. At the end of act 1 of Wilder's play, Rebecca Gibbs remarks on a letter her friend had received that was addressed to "Jane Crofut; The Crofut Farm; Grover's Corners; Sutton County; New Hampshire; United States of America . . . Continent of North America; Western Hemisphere; the Earth; the Solar System; the Universe; the Mind of God."[5] Just as Wilder provides a few scenic items "for those who think they have to have scenery,"[6] he also provides this simple explanation of the microcosm within the macrocosm for those who might need an explanation. Tony Kushner's version of "our town" is not as idyllic as Wilder's world, and God, we are told, has been missing since the San Francisco earthquake of 1906, but the play unfolds, nonetheless, in Heaven as well as on earth, and in the minds of the characters who—given the Judeo-Christian matrix of the play—were created in God's image. And if anyone doubts the connection to *Our Town,* it is made at the very end of the play, in the epilogue, as several of the characters sit around Bethesda Fountain. Prior, like a latter-day stage manager, approaches the audience and says,

> They'll be at it for hours. It's not that what they're saying isn't important, it's just . . .
>
> This is my favorite place in New York City. No, in the whole universe. The parts of it I have seen.
>
> On a day like today. A sunny winter's day, warm and cold at once. The sky's a little hazy, so the sunlight has a physical presence, a character. In autumn, those trees across the lake are yellow, and the sun strikes those most brilliantly. Against the blue of the sky, that sad fall blue, those trees are more light than vegetation, They are Yankee trees, New England transplants. They're barren now. It's January 1990. I've been living with AIDS for five years.[7]

Just as Wilder realized that the best setting for his play was the bare signifying stage, so Kushner places his play on an essentially empty stage with minimal emblematic elements to guide us. A reading of the stage directions reveals almost no description. The first time we see the Pitt apartment in Brooklyn the stage directions read only: "Harper at home, alone. She is listening to the radio and talking to herself, as she often does. She speaks to the audience" (1:16). No description of ground plan, furniture, light, atmosphere, bric-a-brac; no adjectives. Somewhat like the captured soldier's recitation of name, rank, and serial number, Kushner gives us only place, character, and basic action. In the case of Joe and Harper Pitt, we discover all we need to know about them through dialogue, action, response to other characters, and, in the case of Harper, her hallucinations and fantasies. The style of furniture, the color of the walls, the decorations, and the relative tidiness of the apartment—the sort of information often vital to our understanding of characters in O'Neill, Odets, Williams, Miller, or even Shepard or Mamet—is irrelevant here and would be distracting and limiting even if it were practical to provide such complete and illusionistic settings. Kushner's landscape, like Wilder's, is the stage, which takes us directly from the individual characters to the "mind of God" with only a bench, a chair, a bed, or "an impressive desk, bare except for a very elaborate phone system" (1:11). It is worth noting, though, that Wilder provides one of the most evocative elements possible in his settings—sound. His scenes are enhanced by specific aural effects that, to paraphrase *Hamlet,* allow us to see with the mind's ear. Kushner rarely indicates sound.

But there are, nonetheless, clues as to the look of this landscape to be found in his text. When settings *are* described or when characters talk of locales, they tend to describe barren and bleak sites. Most obvious is Harper's recurring hallucination of Antarctica, though a confused Antarctica with Eskimos. Mr. Lies describes it as "a retreat, a vacuum, its virtue is that it lacks everything; deep-freeze for feelings" (1:102). Harper is a person at odds with the given landscape of New York City. An agoraphobic, she remains in her apartment envisioning her own private Antarctica. When she does venture outside, she rarely remains in perceived reality; she interacts with the inanimate diorama of Mormon history, and even in Prospect Park she fights the surroundings to maintain her vision of Antarctica:

For a moment, the magical Antarctic light begins to dim, replaced by the glare of sodium park lights; the sea sounds and wind are drowned out by the sound of traffic as heard from the middle of a city park at night; Harper looks about, and as she does, Antarctica is restored a bit, though the city lights and sounds do not retreat entirely. (2:19)

The arrival of Hannah Pitt occurs in the South Bronx, and it is one of the few scenes with any sort of physical description of location: "An abandoned lot in the South Bronx. A homeless Woman is standing near an oil drum in which a fire is burning. Snowfall. Trash around" (1:103). It is a scene of desolation and urban blight—a vision of Hell. This vision is echoed in part 2 when Belize describes Heaven to Roy Cohn:

> Big city, overgrown with weeds, but flowering weeds. On every corner a wrecking crew and something new and crooked going up catty-corner to that. Windows missing in every edifice like broken teeth, fierce gusts of gritty wind, and a gray, high sky full of ravens. . . . Piles of trash, but lapidary like rubies and obsidian, and diamond-colored cowspit streamers in the wind. (2:77)

This diction elevates aspects of *Angels* to the poetic, but it would be a mistake to use these tonal clues as a guide for literal scenography. The magic of the scene with Harper in the park is created through sound and light, and is made possible by the essentially neutral canvas of the stage. As appropriate as any overriding image may be metaphorically, it becomes an inflexible and immutable landscape that, when realized onstage, can never fulfill the grand canvas of the text. Stages have the remarkable power to transform any object that is placed upon them—they acquire, said Russian folklorist Petr Bogatyrev, "special features, qualities and attributes that they do not have in real life."[8] The moment anything specific is placed on the stage, be it a bed, a living room, or a trash heap, its details begin to acquire special significance that starts a process, however subconscious, of interpretation on the part of the spectator. This is a play in which light, sound, and suggestion become crucial.

Ultimately, any production is faced with the overwhelming question of practicality. How are transitions made from one scene to the next? The answer will be informed in part by the way in which the director and designer interpret the structure of the play. Is the structure seen in terms of a Shakespearean or possibly Brechtian model? Is it perhaps seen as an example of the episodic structure of medieval or expressionist drama? Or is it conceived of as cinematic—that is, a series of cross-fades, jump cuts, and montage among related but disparate scenes. Since the 1930s, many critics have seen the inevitable influence of movies upon the theater and have designated almost any play that moves through multiple scenes as cinematic. Though *Angels* clearly has affinities to all these forms and undoubtedly draws from them, consciously or not, I would suggest that the play's organization and scenic movement derive from something else. Its structure is inevitably informed by contemporary sensibilities and perceptions of the world, and film is no longer the defining mode of perception. Neither, needless to say, is a medieval or Renaissance or early-twentieth-century perspective. Unless Kushner were to say that his play was based upon one of these theatrical forms, to attempt to solve the scenographic problems posed by the play by utilizing historical models will result in a clash of sensibilities.

Ours is a paradoxical world of isolation and interconnection. Certainly the audiences of Tony Kushner's generation are comfortable with rapidly shifting barrages of images and sounds presented in overlapping, incongruent, dissociated juxtaposition. The world of computers, VCRs, and fax machines allows unfathomable amounts of information and imagery—virtually all knowledge and culture—to be accessible almost on demand. Significantly, it is no longer necessary to go to the concert hall, the museum, the movie house, or even the library in order to consume these products of culture. They can be brought into the private realm, freed from the temporal constraints of exhibition or performance. They can be fragmented, deconstructed, juxtaposed. All this has contributed to our transformation into a society of isolated individuals, both producing and consuming all this information in the privacy of homes or offices away from the life of cities. Television has produced the anomaly of audiences of one hundred million or more, each at his or her own private screen. This is the generation that has produced the neologism *cyberspace* to define a location, occupied by millions, which does not exist. We are, to quote Michel Foucault, in

the epoch of space. We are in the epoch of simultaneity: we are in the epoch of juxtaposition, the epoch of the near and far, of side-by-side, of the dispersed. We are at a moment, I believe, when our experience of the world is less that of a long life developing through time than that of network that connects points and intersects with its own skein. One could perhaps say that certain ideological conflicts animating present-day polemics oppose the pious descendants of time and the determined inhabitants of space.[9]

It would be absurd to suggest that *Angels in America* is some sort of cybertech futuristic play or a theatrical analogue to the Internet. Far from it. Spiritually the play and its characters are closer to the sociopolitical dramas of the 1930s than to the avant-garde, and it remains a piece of theater abiding by relatively well established conventions of theatrical presentation. But it is in its *structure* and *spatial sensibility* that it reflects most definitely the dominant forces of our time. The philosopher Henri Lefebvre, in his major work *The Production of Space,* points out that "every society . . . produces a space, its own space. The city of the ancient world cannot be understood [merely] as a collection of people and things in space. . . . For the ancient city had its own spatial practice: it forged its own . . . space. . . . Each society offers up its own peculiar space, as it were, as an object for analysis and overall theoretical explication."[10]

Our space is, as Foucault suggests, nonlinear, nongeometric, disjointed, juxtapositional; one moves not from one contiguous space to another but across disparate spatial and temporal boundaries. Ours is the space of hypertext. In the age of computers and fiber-optic technology it seems unexceptional to be able to connect any two or more points regardless of their seeming disparity; in cyberspace, the laws of geometry do not prevail. With the click of a button, words, symbols, and images can be connected in an almost infinite string of associations. In hypertext, just as in dreams and imagination, key words or images can transport us from one locale to another, from one world to another. This is the driving logic of *Angels in America.* It is way of thinking, seeing, and conceptualizing the world that has surreptitiously entered the consciousness of contemporary culture and utterly transformed the society.

A pervasive computer culture is a recent phenomenon. But before hypertext was a familiar concept, Foucault described what he called "heterotopias." Describing them, he wrote, "We do not live inside a void that could be colored with diverse shades of light, we live inside a set of relations that delineates sites which are irreducible to one another and absolutely not superimposable on one another. . . . The heterotopia is capable of juxtaposing in a single real place several spaces, several sites that are in themselves incompatible."[11] While Foucault was using the heterotopia to analyze such varied societal institutions such as churches, vacation villages, fairgrounds, and brothels, the term works superbly as a description of theater. The stage, after all, is a single real space that can hold a multitude of places.

This heterotopic-hypertextual idea is not a recent phenomenon in theater. The simultaneous stage of the Middle Ages, the split scenes and vision scenes of melodrama, the flashback (credited to playwright Elmer Rice), and Sergei Eisenstein's idea of montage all predate in practice what Foucault described in theory. As a result, *Angels* can seem part of an old theatrical tradition, but Kushner pushes it further. As act 3, scene 5 of *Perestroika,* for instance, begins on the Brooklyn Heights Promenade with Harper talking to the Mormon mother seen earlier as part of the diorama of the Mormon Visitors Center. But the characters from the previous two scenes remain onstage. This means that Joe and Louis are at Jones Beach, while Roy Cohn and Belize are in Cohn's hospital room. During this scene Prior becomes visible in his bedroom; Louis leaves Joe and is suddenly at a pay phone in Manhattan calling Prior. This layering of scenes and transpositions of characters resemble "windows" on a computer screen—multiple locations, some hidden behind others, but any one available to foreground at any moment and in any sequence. Kushner has interwoven seven characters (one a hallucination) and five locations and has collapsed time. Another slightly different example of this hypertextual space can be found in the interconnection of Harper's Valium-induced hallucination with Prior's dream in part 1, one of the wonderful conceits of this play. In this scene, not only are the conventions of theatrical fantasy transcended, but mental space is bridged as well. The scene suggests the reconciliation between conceptual space and social space discussed by Lefebvre. The scene is an initially comic reconciliation, with echoes of the narrative and structural logic of Buster Keaton films. But again, there is a more contemporary resonance in this strange dislocation.

But the practical considerations still haunt the designer. There is, after all, no button to click that will take the viewer from screen to screen, leaping through cyberspace in milliseconds. The stage is still bound by the laws of physics, Euclidean geometry, linear time, and the limitations of human actors. And even if it were possible to somehow re-create the speed and spatiality of hypertext, to do so would subvert the spirit of the play, which is based on fundamental human relationships. Kushner is fairly clear about the type of production he desires in his note on staging, and it sounds very much like the *Our Town* school of theater:

> The play benefits from a pared-down style of presentation with minimal scenery and scene shifts done rapidly (no blackouts!), employing the cast as well as stagehands—which makes an actor-driven event, as this must be. The moments of magic . . . are to be fully realized, as bits of wonderful *theatrical* illusion—which means it's OK if the wires show. (1:5)

One reads Kushner's injunction with vigorous agreement, but it is not as easy to achieve as it may seem. There are a limited number of ways to achieve Kushner's goal, and all of them have certain drawbacks. If one were to make a list of the minimum set pieces required to produce the play (as some scholars have done for Shakespeare) the list would be fairly short—an amazingly iconographic collection of elements: a bed, a park bench, a hospital bed, a chair, a desk. Other than the unique scenes such as the diorama in the Mormon Visitor's Center, very little else is needed. Does Prior's bed need to be different from Louis's? Does his hospital bed need to be different from Cohn's? Does one park bench need to be different from another? If there is a willingness to use emblematic furniture and stick to the bare minimum, it could be possible to set at least the recurrent scenes more or less permanently on the stage so that scene shifts might be achieved largely through lighting changes and actor movement. This, indeed, was the original intent of Conklin and Eustis at the Taper: to place essential scenic pieces against the cracked facade of the background. During the development process, more specific scenery was added, and the final product was, as so many theater pieces are, a compromise among several visions. The more elements that need to move on and off the stage, the more one is dependent on actors or stagehands to do the moving. In a play with so many changes, this parade of furniture-toting figures ultimately adds not simply an encumbrance or distraction, but another level of text—a secondary play about furniture moving that exists in the interstices of the primary text.

The Broadway production had the resources—and perhaps the temptation—to employ technology for fluidity. The relatively small stage of the Walter Kerr Theatre was fitted with an elaborate winch system that allowed wagons (movable stage platforms) to glide on and off the stage with seeming ease as other units flew in or out. This is a different kind of magic, though. It is the slickness and trickery of Broadway musicals that "wows" an audience with scenery that is as choreographed as the dancers. Nevertheless, there is no question that once the decision had been made to depict each room, park, hospital room, and office with individualized scenic units, then Wagner's solution to the problem of scene shifts was the most efficient one possible. Action or dialogue could start as one wagon rolled on while another rolled off; scenes could overlap, intersect, and recombine. The proscenium stage, however, imposes a limitation on movement: wagons can roll on from stage right or stage left, and there is only so much variety possible. A certain repetitive monotony was inevitable with such a scheme. *Village Voice* critic Michael Feingold may have summed it up best when he noted that the set, "too elaborate for the pared-down version Kushner's notes request, yet too sparing of its effects to drown the play in glitz . . . gets the many scenes on and off with a flat, neat efficiency."[12]

Since the play's New York staging, productions of *Angels* have proliferated. The approaches to design have used some variant or combination of the approaches described above: unifying, metaphorical environment or neutral space; multiple scene changes or some sort of simultaneous setting. Most have sought some way to visually encapsulate the idea of "America."

Interestingly, discussions with several individuals who had seen more than one production suggested that the most emotionally powerful ones were those that, because of necessity or choice, were utterly simple and even had a "rough theater" quality to them. Notable were the production by graduate acting students at New York University and a reading of *Millennium Approaches* at the Taper as a prelude to the theater's first production of *Perestroika*. Some of the response, of course, may have to do with audience expectations and production context. We neither want nor expect production values in a reading—we come to focus on the text. But it does suggest that Kushner is right in asking for a pared-down production, and perhaps the play, somewhat like Marc Blitzstein's opera *The Cradle Will Rock,* benefits from a dramatic equivalent of a concert performance. It also suggests that the play's depth and power is such that, like most good theater, it not only tolerates, but demands scenographic exploration and experimentation. There is no one correct way to design *Angels.*

Notes

1. Tony Kushner, *Angels in America: A Gay Fantasia on National Themes. Part One: Millennium Approaches* (New York: Theatre Communications Group, 1993), 10. All subsequent references to part 1 will be indicated in parentheses in the text.

2. Alfred Jarry, "Preliminary Address at the First Performance of *Ubu Roi,* December 10, 1896," in *Selected Works of Alfred Jarry,* ed. Roger Shattuck and Simon Watson Taylor (New York: Grove Press, 1980), 78.

3. John Conklin, personal interview, January 2, 1996.

4. Conklin, interview.

5. Thornton Wilder, *Our Town,* act 1, in *Three Plays* (New York: Avon, 1976), 28.

6. Wilder, *Our Town,* 6.

7. Tony Kushner, *Angels in America: A Gay Fantasia on National Themes. Part Two: Perestroika* (New York: Theatre Communications Group, 1993), 146. All subsequent references to part 2 will be indicated in parentheses in the text.

8. Quoted in Keir Elam, *The Semiotics of Theatre and Drama* (New York: Methuen, 1983), 7.

9. Michel Foucault, "Of Other Spaces," *Diacritics* 16 (spring 1986): 22.

10. Henri Lefebvre, *The Production of Space,* trans. Donald Nicholson-Smith (Oxford: Blackwell, 1991), 31.

11. Foucault, "Of Other Spaces," 25.

12. Michael Feingold, "Building the Monolith," review of *Angels in America, Village Voice,* May 18, 1993, 218–19.

The Art of Transition
David Rockwell and Theater

Many of Rockwell Group's projects, particularly their restaurants, are often described in terms of theater, or sometimes film (the decor of Pod in Philadelphia, for instance, is reminiscent of *2001: A Space Odyssey*). To some degree the theatrical label is inspired by interiors whose colors, light, textures, eclectic "props," and ground plans seem more like stage settings than interior design. But ultimately, the theatricality refers to an emotionalism and narrative quality that had been largely eradicated from the twentieth-century architectural vocabulary by modernist aesthetics. David Rockwell welcomes the association with theater because to him it implies "emotion, narrative, the ability to tell stories—that which can profoundly move you."[1] These are the elements he wishes to bring to his architectural endeavors. Rockwell's early influences were, in fact, from the theater; he cites productions of *Fiddler on the Roof* and *Cabaret* as formative experiences. But what he gleaned from these performances was the way in which the scenic elements, particularly the movement of light and the shifting of sets, manipulated the emotions of the spectators and the dynamics of the shows. His fascination with the stage was such that he even took a semester off from his architectural studies to work with lighting designer and theater consultant Roger Morgan.

It is therefore not surprising that many of the architectural influences Rockwell acknowledges tend to come from the Italian Renaissance and baroque eras, particularly works by Michelangelo and Borromini. These artists, especially in their churches, piazzas, and public sculptures, drew people (read audiences) into each space and carefully led them through an unfolding narrative, all the while delivering the dramatic qualities of surprise, astonishment, and awe. Among the specific works Rockwell cites,

Published in *Pleasure: The Architecture and Design of Rockwell Group*, by Janet Abrams et al. (New York: Universe Publishing, 2002).

one in particular stands out: Michelangelo's mannerist design of the ante-room of the Laurentian Library in Florence. In this enclosed vestibule Michelangelo disrupted the prevailing neoclassical tenets, and in the process made the entryway more famous and significant than the library itself. The pediment over the main door is broken; pilasters taper unexpectedly toward the ground; structural columns are recessed into the walls, seemingly negating their function; the staircase itself ("nightmarish" says art historian H. W. Janson) seems to flow lavalike downward from the doorway, almost defying anyone to ascend; and of course there are the haunting blank niches whose dark frames draw attention to their emptiness. Almost every element of the room seems to defy logic and expectations. In other words, here is an architectural space totally irrelevant to the purpose of the building (a library) that nonetheless has a profound emotional effect upon anyone entering the space. Within this enclosure, form and function are completely subverted to an expressive—that is to say, theatrical—vocabulary. Michelangelo created a terrifying stage space, a kind of architectural drama of transition, through which patrons of the collection must pass as they move from the public world of the city to the private world of the Medici books and manuscripts. While David Rockwell may not aim for such disconcerting emotions in his architecture (restaurants, hotels, and ballparks do not want to evoke terror), he nonetheless seeks an equally profound impact upon those who move through the spaces he designs. "I'm not interested in static, monumental architecture," he explains. "What interests me are transitions." To achieve his goals his work draws upon the emblematic, iconographic, and environmental vocabulary of stage settings as well as the radical, often startling juxtapositions and rhythms of contemporary media.

On a certain level, architecture and theater design are fundamentally the same. They both involve the transformation of space, the control of movement through that space, and—through the use of color, line, texture, volume, and iconography—the communication of information while manipulating the emotional response of spectator-occupants. In *The Poetics* Aristotle employs the term *skenographia* (scenography)—scenic writing—to refer to the visual aspect of theatrical production. While scholars still debate what, specifically, Aristotle may have meant by this word—since there was almost certainly no use of the illusionistic or play-specific scenery we now associate with theater—the term nonetheless has a particular resonance today. Ours is an increasingly visually oriented society, and the visual is something to be *read,* to be interpreted, just as literature and language were in the past. In the case of theater, the spatio-imagistic or scenographic world of the play provides a narrative that is equivalent to that of the dramatic text. Similarly, once the architect's work moves beyond the merely functional and into the world of the symbolic and emblematic in which the visual and spatial aspects are intended to convey ideas and create emotion, it, too, is a form of *skenographia*. Architects are inscribing a text—a dramatic text or narrative— upon the landscape. Any architectural creation, from a room to a building to a cityscape, tells a story through sign and symbol; it shapes the movement of the "characters" within the environment through definition of space and thus defines relationships among these characters.

The arts of stage design and architecture have always been intertwined. In some of the most productive periods of theater history—classical Greece and Rome, ancient India (Sanskrit theater), medieval Japan (Noh), and Elizabethan England, for example—design and architecture were one and the same; the permanent architectural features of the stage and theater building served as the scenic environment and there was little or no separately created scenery. When stage design emerged as an art—indeed, as a profession—in the Italian Renaissance, most of the stage designers were, first and foremost, architects. Architecture, after all, was intended to provide a symbolic and emblematic space in which the business of state, church, or domestic life could unfold. Similarly, the designer of a stage setting was creating an ensemble of visual images that would convey the symbolic and metaphoric aspects of a fictional story through means that were intended to inspire wonder, awe, and delight.

One of the first scenographers was the fifteenth- to sixteenth-century architect Sebastiano Serlio, who created plans for some of the first modern theater buildings and devised three standard stage settings that were intended to serve all genres of drama. Using forced perspective painting—a relatively new technology at the time—on angled wings known as flats, he created an urban setting of formal buildings for tragedy, an urban setting of shops, taverns, and bourgeois houses for comedy, and a bucolic setting for satyric plays or pastorals. In other words, Serlio created a total architectural environment or landscape, and presented it through scenographic means on the stage as a background for dramatic action. Among the most stunning theatrical creations of the Renaissance and baroque eras were the court festivals of the Medici, of the Hapsburgs, and of Louis XIV at Versailles. Often staged as parts of larger celebrations of weddings, coronations, birthdays, and the like, these performances were mostly allegorical spectacles in which the dramatic text played an almost secondary role. Therefore, the designer was, for all intents and purposes, the playwright as well. The architect-scenographer created both the packaging and the content, as it were: the stage and the spectacle. The stage, in the most elaborate cases, involved the creation of gardens, fountains, and buildings, blending aspects of scenography with elements of landscape architecture, structural engineering, and even urban planning to create the baroque equivalent of multimedia spectacles. Spectacle and architecture seemed to merge.

By the eighteenth century such architectural-scenic spectacles had largely disappeared, along with the absolute monarchs, but the process, in a sense, would be reversed. Cities and parks began to be conceived as theater; architects would transform both nature and metropolis into virtual stages, in real time and space, for the unfolding of human dramas. Think of the gardens of Versailles or Kew Gardens in England or the urban plans of Pierre Charles L'Enfant for Washington, D.C., Karl Friedrich Schinkel's designs for Berlin (Schinkel was also a significant scenographer and architect of theater buildings), Baron Haussmann's redesign of Paris, or the creation of the Ringstrasse in Vienna. All of these schemes were intended to effect total control over a vast urban or natural landscape—just as a director controls the space of the stage—creating a symbolic and emblematic environment that would determine the movements of the "players" within the space, while simultaneously telling a story about that particular society.

Despite this long and respectable association of theater and architecture, the modernist architectural dictum of "form follows function" allowed no room for the implicit superficiality of theater. Thus, through much of the twentieth century one of the most negative epithets a critic could hurl at a work of architecture was to deride it as "theatrical." This was the charge, for instance, leveled against the early-twentieth-century scenic designer and architect Joseph Urban, who is an acknowledged inspiration for David Rockwell.[2] In the 1950s, the exuberant Miami Beach hotels of Morris Lapidus suffered a similar fate at the hands of critics; their gaudy populism flew in the face of officially sanctioned high-culture architecture. These and other similar approaches to architecture seemed to evoke the most negative connotations of theater.

In Western society in particular, theater is more often associated with entertainment than with the civic, social, and religious roles it has occupied in other cultures or periods. It is thus seen as nonessential, as frivolous, as self-indulgent; it is redolent of excess and flamboyance. In short, theater is classed with popular rather than serious culture, and in the modern era, the popular—except perhaps as something to be quoted by the avant-garde— was suspect. Moreover, theater tends toward self-referentiality ("All the world's a stage," said Shakespeare). But as a minimalist and essentialist modernism came to dominate the arts of the early twentieth century, as functionalism replaced aestheticism, anything decorative (i.e., nonfunctional) was to be avoided. The decorative element was, in fact, the primary issue with Urban's creations. The champions of the increasingly dominant International Style saw the International Magazine Building as a pastiche of classical references. And while the New School mimicked and exploited the International Style, Urban could not resist incorporating decorative elements within the design. Urban was making artistic decisions based upon a visual aesthetic that had little to do with the particular and necessary usage of the structure. In the late 1920s, such an approach to architecture was anathema.

Finally, theatricality also suggests a lack of stability. Theater, after all, is an ephemeral art that evaporates into thin air with the final curtain, leaving behind only fragmentary traces. Architecture, on the other hand, embodies a certain sense of permanence, even a hint of eternity. To label a work of architecture as theatrical is to imply that it is impermanent, even disposable, which seems to fly in the face of accepted wisdom. (It is perhaps worth noting that the ancient Greeks, whose architecture is living proof of the enduring potential of architecture, also created drama that, despite its incorporeality, is still performed twenty-five hundred years later.)

But the antitheatrical prejudice of modernist architecture has been giving way in recent times to a new theatricalism. Whether in the museums, office buildings, and homes designed by such architects as Frank Gehry or Rem Koolhaas, or in the restaurants, hotels, and entertainment complexes of David Rockwell, theatricality has come to be not merely acceptable but almost the dominant form—the new lingua franca of architecture. Ironically, this return to the theatrical comes at a time when traditional theater itself has lost much of its cultural importance within contemporary society. Despite the attenuation of theater as a locus for moral debate, social investigation, and simple storytelling, the culture as a whole has become increasingly theatricalized thanks largely to the impact of electronic and visual media. The reference points of the contemporary world are television, film, video, computer graphics, and various permutations of pop music and their related venues (stadium concerts, clubs, MTV, personal stereos, online videos, etc.). Rapid movement, intense color and light, continuous visual stimulation, and high-decibel sound make up the palette from which this new architecture is drawn. We are in a world of sudden and jarring transitions that often results in bold and unexpected juxtapositions and contrasts. The impact of media has had an obvious effect on traditional theater itself; plays with linear narratives, little physical action, and an emphasis on dialogue appeal to a rapidly diminishing audience. Most dramas now employ more lighting instruments than the standard musical of, say, thirty years ago because audiences' threshold of visibility has increased; almost all professional productions are now acoustically enhanced or amplified; standard narratives have largely given way to associative and juxtapositional images more closely associated with the hypertextual world of cyberspace than with storytelling. Similarly, such virtues as simplicity, elegance, and even romance are quickly evaporating in restaurants and hotels to be replaced with the idea of event or performance.

If a room, a restaurant, or a ballpark is understood as a kind of performance, then it must, on some level, be designed as a stage set. The Czech semiotician Jiri Veltrusky in 1940 offered the crucial insight that everything on the stage is a sign; any object, however mundane, is transmuted into a charged signifier by the power of the stage frame. Rockwell uses his architectural space as a stagelike frame and places within it a range of related symbols whose total effect may be greater than their individual meanings. The Japanese restaurant Nobu in New York City, for example, includes birch trunks (which enclose lights) out of which spread squared wooden poles that simultaneously suggest stylized branches as well as structural supports for the ceiling. Birch branches also form screens for private dining alcoves; stylized chopsticks form the legs of the bar stools; cherry blossoms are stenciled onto the wood floor; one wall is covered with embedded river stones. The sushi bar was conceived as a metaphoric stage set within the context of the restaurant, and the mosaic wall behind it brings the sushi chefs into dramatic relief. While the overall effect evokes the Japanese countryside, it is not a simulacrum (not a realistic set, to use theater terms) but a suggestive pastiche. The Mohegan Sun Casino in Connecticut was similarly approached. Evocative of Adirondack hunting lodges and Native American villages, the casino is a thematic environment of icons and emblems drawn from Mohegan culture and history interwoven into a multifaceted entertainment complex. Visitors to the casino or the restaurants are entering a forest of symbols (to borrow Baudelaire's phrase). But the theatrical framing creates a gestalt that allows the spectator to meld the images into a coherent whole.

David Rockwell, like the artists of the Wiener Werkstätte, Joseph Urban, and Frank Lloyd Wright before him, understands the need to design all the elements contained in a given space. He designs or supervises the furniture, wallpaper, decor, and all else within the visual and spatial environment. It is an architectural equivalent of the Wagnerian *Gesamtkunstwerk*— the total artwork in which a single visionary artist controls all the component performative elements within the ensemble. In this, his spaces are clearly analogous to stage settings; Rockwell embraces theatricality, and

**16. Nobu Restaurant, New York: Japanese restaurant as theatrical design.
(Photo: Paul Warchol, courtesy Rockwell Group.)**

each of his projects can be seen as a performance or self-contained drama. Each of his projects implies a spectator. The spaces are designed to engage the viewers from the moment they enter (or first have visual contact with the structure), to their passage and movement through the space, to their interaction with the total environment. Rockwell Group is interested in particular effects that are normally associated with theater: the initial impact through revelation of space, seduction through the combination of visual iconography and spatial manipulation, and emotional transition or transformation.

Every performance has an "entrance," that is, a moment and place where the activity and rhythm of the quotidian world ends and the fictive or festive world of the theater begins. Traditionally this event has been marked by the revelatory opening of the front curtain, through a change in lighting, or it has simply a vocal, musical, or percussive "announcement" that the show is about to begin. For the Rockwell Group, entrance, which implies transition, is one of the most powerful aspects of theater. Perhaps this is why the entrance to the Laurentian Library is so appealing to them. In a sense, the grand entrance harks back to the nineteenth-century opera houses, which extended the concept of transition and transformation to the theater building itself. Nowhere was this sense of celebratory entrance more evident than at the Paris Opéra ("one of the great theatrical spaces," says Rockwell), whose foyer and grand staircase announced a spectacular transformation from the prosaic to the dramatic and which enveloped spectators as it almost literally swept them into the dazzling world of the theater.

Because theater implies a dichotomous relationship between spectator and stage—generally there is a static viewer observing the action that unfolds within a carefully delineated space—transitions occur in front of the spectator through the movement of scenery, light, and the performers themselves. Although architecture sometimes creates passive spectators, as with facades that advertise the function and content of a building or the grandeur of certain interior spaces meant to inspire awe, more often it creates an environment in which the spectator and performer are one and the same. The "spectator" in a work of architecture generally does not observe the work from outside the frame but occupies the designed space—the stage, as it were. Transitions in architecture are generally achieved by movement of the performer-spectator through the space. (Of course, in many folk, festival, and religious performances throughout the world, as well as various performative and paratheatrical activities—parades, sporting events, political rallies, etc.—boundaries between performer and spectator dissolve, as do distinctions between performance and spectator space. In such paratheatrical events, as in architecture, linearity or sequentiality is often replaced by simultaneity.)

Nowhere is this more evident than in the Kodak Theatre. As the new home for the Academy Awards, this space that celebrates transition is seen by several hundred million people. The Oscars, in many respects, are remarkably like the late medieval performative event known as the royal entry. On these occasions, a monarch and his or her entourage would enter into a town with great pomp and be received by the populace with scenic spectacle and performative activities. A key element in these events was the phenomenon of the dual spectator/dual performer. The nobility functioned as prime performers but also as prime spectators, while the residents of the town also functioned in both capacities. At the Oscars, the Hollywood celebrities function in the role of nobility; they are at once the show and the audience, arriving to be seen, but also to observe. The Kodak Theatre must

17. Kodak Theatre, home of the Academy Awards. (Photo: Timothy Street Porter, courtesy Rockwell Group.)

provide at least two transitional spaces—from exterior to interior and from auditorium to stage. The exterior serves as an arrival stage. The "nobility" disembark, pose for the assembled spectators (both physically and electronically present), and then move from the public space of the street into the private space of the theater. Here Rockwell has provided an extra transition, important for the participants but mostly invisible to the television audience: a grand staircase, reminiscent of both early-twentieth-century movie palaces and the Paris Opéra, that sweeps the audience from the public space of the street to the mediated public space of the auditorium. Inside the auditorium there is a less well defined transition space from the seats to the stage. Normally, the only transgression of the invisible stage wall is through the senses of sight and sound, but on Oscar night, at least, certain spectators await with great anticipation the opportunity to move from the seats to the stage, a transition that is reinscribed by the camera for the audience that exists beyond the walls of the theater. Because the official audience inside the theater is also the object of viewing for the television audience, the interior of the theater must also function as scenic decor. Rockwell has created a giant "mouth" of a proscenium evocative of Radio City Music Hall and the greatest of old movie palaces (and a plush color scheme also evocative of that era), but included tiers of boxes along the side walls that evoke eighteenth-century opera houses (albeit with a more modernist line). In place of a solid dome over the auditorium is an open latticework of arches and ovals, some patterns inspired by Busby Berkeley choreography, that, at least on the theater's first Oscar night, provided an aerial stage for Cirque du Soleil. The arches spanning the auditorium reflected the shape of the proscenium so that the auditorium viewed from the stage—as is frequent in the televised performance—becomes a reverse stage with spectators as performers. Thus, not only does the theater mediate between interior and exterior, but between live and televised, between stage and auditorium, between floor and ceiling. It is a space in constant transition, with a fluid separation between the space of the performer and the space of the spectator.

Stairs are obvious representations of transition; they transcend space, allow vertical movement, and connect disparate locales. Their shape dictates the flow of vision and the movement of bodies. Together with doors they are the oldest scenographic elements, having existed on the classic Greek stage by the midst of the fifth century B.C.E. Not surprisingly, stairs form an integral part of Rockwell's vocabulary. While a necessary element in many of his projects (in New York City in particular, vertical space is often more available than horizontal space), he has turned stairs into focal point of design. In the W Hotel on Union Square the curving staircase—reminiscent of the one in the film *Sunset Boulevard*—dominates the relatively narrow lobby as it sweeps from the upper ballroom, transforming the otherwise unassuming space into a piece of heightened drama. Along with transition, another appealing aspect of theater for Rockwell is the element of surprise; each opening of the curtain or each change of scene brings the unexpected. The surprising element in the W Hotel lobby is not the staircase per se, but a rectangular patch of wheat grass at the edge of each step. It is a touch of postmodern hyperrealism, incorporating natural elements within a constructed, artificial world. The juxtaposition of the organic and artificial has been a common scenographic ploy in much contemporary stage design, which creates jarring contrasts calling into question ideas of reality and illusion. Just as everything on a stage, by virtue of being framed, is a sign—a kind of quotation from the world outside the frame—so too the elements in Rockwell Group's designs are quotations of a sort. The patches of grass refer, on some level, to Union Square Park across the street, but amid the concrete and glass of New York City, parks themselves are a kind of stage or frame in which nature is quoted.

Other grand staircases can be found in Rockwell Group's restaurants Rosa Mexicano and Ruby Foo's (whose staircase evoked images of *Auntie*

Mame for former *New York Times* food critic Ruth Reichl). Both ascend past what can only be described as scenic backdrops. In Rosa Mexicano the stairs climb past a blue tile wall on which are mounted one hundred plaster stat-uettes of divers and over which water gently cascades (a postmodern tribute to Busby Berkeley, perhaps?); in Ruby Foo's the staircase ascends along a wall of oversized red lacquer boxes containing a pastiche of Asian icons and images. The staircases are focal points of the restaurants, and anyone on the stairs automatically becomes a performer silhouetted against a decorative, theatrical background. At the same time, the stairways provide a vantage point for spectators to view the drama of dining above and below. The patron on the stair is both performer and spectator, just as the diners at the tables can function in both capacities.

Illusion, of course, is a key element in much theater design, and it, too, plays a role in Rockwell Group's creations. For the Walt Disney World home of Cirque du Soleil, Rockwell Group created what appears to be an idealized circus tent. In reality, the main housing is a solid structure con-taining stage and auditorium, but a tentlike "skirt" is stretched around the building, anchored by steel cables, and a "crown" tops the structure—all evocative of the grand three-ring tents of Ringling Brothers and Barnum and Bailey, especially at night when dramatically placed light glows through the "tent" and picks out the distinctive curves of the crown. It doesn't mat-ter that the interior has nothing to do with a tent (patrons are probably just as happy not to have to sit on uncomfortable wooden bleachers); the audi-ence has been given the illusion of entering a tent, which is still the symbol most closely identified with the circus. Illusion also plays a part in the Rock-well-designed dining room of Disney Cruise Lines. The walls of the cruise ship's dining room are covered with black-and-white drawings of Disney cartoon characters. During the course of the meal, the images transform into full color. The gradual transition is almost imperceptible and calls into ques-tion the reliability of perception. (It may also, in a most ironic way, echo the scene in Michelangelo Antonioni's film *Red Desert,* in which, as the camera pans a room in a continuous circular motion, the colors of the walls of a room are different each time.)

Over the past three centuries or so, theater has come to be associated with a narrow form of literary art: the play. But historically, theater has encompassed a wide range of spectacle and entertainment in which con-ventional drama makes up only a small percentage of the whole. The study of Renaissance theater, for instance, tends to focus more on tournaments, royal entries, aquatic spectacles, fireworks, and royal wedding festivals than on drama per se. Such events often blurred distinctions between performer and spectator, performance space and audience space. Similarly, when the history of contemporary theater is studied in the future, it will no doubt encompass sporting events, rock concerts, discos, fashion shows, parades and fireworks, and perhaps even shopping malls. Entertainment architecture can thus be seen in the larger context of performance.

One of the historical functions of theater has been to reinforce the social structure by inscribing history as well as contemporary moral and aesthetic codes on the civic consciousness. Just as Renaissance spectacles were better suited to that role in their time than the conventional drama, so too today that function is fulfilled more by media and entertainment than by traditional theater forms and institutions. But this shift from theater to media has resulted in a concurrent shift of focus or emphasis from the content to the structure. All societies have liminal spaces: locales that provide a transition from one segment of society or one part of the cityscape to another; places where the standard rules and behavior do not apply because they exist outside the spatial or temporal boundaries of official society. But in the postmodern world of cyberspace and instant communication or even the banality of channel surfing, it is the transition itself that has come to dominate. Continuous transformation has become the norm and content has become the liminal. Rockwell Group's architecture, aside from helping to emphasize the centrality of entertainment as an almost religious force within our society, places a premium on the structures of transition.

An admirer of Joseph Urban once observed that it was theoretically possible to travel from an Urban-designed home in an Urban-designed car to a restaurant, then theater, and finally hotel—all designed by Urban. Rockwell Group has yet to design an automobile, but it is otherwise theoretically possible to journey similarly amid an entertainment and domestic world of Rockwell Group's design. But whereas Urban's structures and designs tended toward the monumental, Rockwell Group tends toward creations that are at once as transitory and pervasive as the media images of current society.

Notes

1. All quotations are from the author's interview with David Rockwell February 2002.

2. See "Architect of Dreams: The Theatrical Vision of Joseph Urban," in this volume.

The Stage Is a Dangerous Machine
The Designs of George Tsypin

Among the American designers most closely associated with postmodernism are Robert Israel, Adrianne Lobel, and Michael Yeargan. But because of his prodigious talent, certainly aided by his association with controversial directors Peter Sellars and JoAnne Akalaitis, and perhaps because of his exotic background as a Russian émigré, George Tsypin has emerged as the primary designer of this new movement, becoming in the process one of the most publicized designers in recent memory, even rating a brief profile in a 1990 issue of the *New Yorker*. The range of Tsypin's work is astonishing. In 1990 alone he designed a film, *The Cabinet of Dr. Ramirez,* which is based on the famous expressionist film *The Cabinet of Dr. Caligari; Henry IV, Parts 1 and 2* at the New York Shakespeare Festival; John Adams's opera *The Death of Klinghoffer* (loosely based on the terrorist attack on the cruise ship Achille Lauro) that opened in Brussels and played in San Francisco and at the Brooklyn Academy of Music; and *Mr. Jelly Lord,* a musical about Jelly Roll Morton at the Mark Taper Forum in Los Angeles. In addition, he created an environment for a one-man show of his design-inspired sculptures at the Twining Gallery in New York, and a large audience got to see his 1989 set—or at least a portion of it—for Peter Sellars's production of Mozart's *Don Giovanni* when it was broadcast on PBS. In the same year Tsypin was awarded an Obie for his design work, including the JoAnne Akalaitis production of *Cymbeline* at the Public Theater.

Clearly Tsypin has tapped a nerve in the American theater—finding a visual vocabulary that is in sync with the contemporary mood—much as Ming Cho Lee did in the 1960s and Jo Mielziner did in the 1940s. There is a raw energy in his work that ransacks history, draws freely from wide-rang-

The first part of this essay was published, in an earlier form, in *Theatre Design & Technology* (summer 1991). It should be placed in the context created by the first essay in this volume, "Postmodern Design." Twelve years later I talked to George Tsypin again. Rather than totally revise the original article, I have added an update at the end.

ing styles and periods, and bluntly mixes the stunningly beautiful with the harsh and ugly.

It is no accident that steel is his favorite material—"a material capable of sleek beauty and strength," but one also subject to distortion and decay.[1] Tsypin finds industrial ruins among the most beautiful things in the world. "I'm obsessed with metal," he told the *New Yorker*. "[It] is very hard and dangerous, but at the same time it's flexible, and you know, it rusts."[2]

Danger is a word heard again and again in relation to Tsypin's sets. There is often a physical danger, the risk of actors falling through gaps in the floor or tumbling from overhead structures, but there is also an artistic danger. His designs can be jarring, disconcerting, displeasing to the sense of symmetry or conventional aesthetics; they can make audiences uncomfortable. Yet Tsypin knows that visual disjunction must be carefully planned. "The stage is a dangerous machine," he says in his Russian-accented but meticulous English, "where you have to be very precise and careful."

While there is no Tsypin "style" as there is, say, an Oliver Smith or Jo Mielziner style, there is a sense of scale, space and verticality virtually unmatched in recent American design, except perhaps by Santo Loquasto. A Tsypin setting, with its towering images, skeletal scenic pieces made of metal, and moving elements, recalls the Russian constructivism that almost subconsciously shapes his work as well as his training as an architect at the Institute of Architecture in Moscow.

Perhaps because he came to theater relatively late—he received an MFA in design from New York University in 1984 at the age of thirty—he is remarkably unconcerned about theatrical tradition and propriety in his settings. "I'm really not trained," he insists. "I'm not interested in periods; I feel incredible freedom. I was never indoctrinated in the sense of, 'This is from this period, that is from that period.' I have total freedom to use whatever I like. I love, for example, medieval painting or sculpture, and I use it when I need to. I also use some elements of incredibly modern architecture, and somehow it exists on the same value level—I never give it a thought." And so *Don Giovanni* emerges in Harlem, *Ajax* is seen in a glass booth on a stage inundated with blood, *The Count of Monte Cristo* is a world of surreally moving Napoleonic armoires, *Tannhäuser* is set in a TV evangelist's crystal cathedral, and *Leon and Lena (and Lenz)* moves to a highway in the American Southwest.

For most spectators this "total freedom" is the hallmark of the so-called postmodern style. The freewheeling juxtaposition of historical and contemporary references, done in a self-conscious and pointed manner, typifies a particular approach to much theater production today, and much of

Tsypin's in particular. "Maybe it is a reflection of our times," he continues, "but it is also the history of art. Look at medieval paintings on biblical stories, obviously rendered with medieval costumes; they felt free to do that. And you look at a Renaissance painting of the same biblical story and all of a sudden it feels like the Renaissance. There is no way to get away from that—whatever we do is a reflection of our sensibilities."

Yet Tsypin insists that his approach is almost organic. "I don't feel that I'm breaking the rules; it's completely natural. I'm more interested in the essence of things, the textures, the shapes, the space, the historical elements as long as they serve the meaning." JoAnne Akalaitis concurs: "The point of view comes from embracing a lot of different worlds and exploring the possibility that different worlds can enter the world of the play, not just visually, but spiritually or psychologically or historically."

Henry IV at the Public captured the key elements of Tsypin's work. The basic set, capitalizing on the brick back wall and pillars that define the edges of the Newman Theater stage, suggested the ruins of a gothic cathedral or perhaps a crypt. Seeking a way to capture the history in the Henry plays, Tsypin thought of the gothic cathedrals of England, especially Westminster Abbey, which are filled with tombs and statues of kings and queens. "I wanted to create a space where you come in and history is there and your imagination comes alive," he explains. "It's like kings get out of those tombs." As if to reinforce his notion of the stage as dangerous machine, the relatively shallow depth and narrow wings of the Newman Theater spewed forth gantry-like platforms and towering walls with graceful case, quickly transforming the stage from the claustrophobic court to the densely smoke-filled tavern to the seemingly vast battlefields.

Interestingly, Tsypin's one stint as an assistant was on Neil Simon's *Biloxi Blues* with designer David Mitchell, the master of the cinematically fluid moving set. Tsypin's ease with the mechanical transformation of the stage is clearly influenced by Mitchell. The sense of depth and the multiplicity of locales at the Newman was further suggested by projections that played over the brick back wall, the wooden panels of the tavern, and a scrim on a traveler track. The projected images, both abstract and specific, had a fascinating effect. When broken up on the ruined cathedral construction or on the tavern wall, they functioned almost subliminally, creating a sense of something solid that was merely light, or, at other times, fragmenting solid scenery into vague patterns. Projections were used in a similar manner for *Cymbeline,* and Tsypin has also employed projections for the Chicago Lyric Opera production of *Tannhäuser.* The sense of scale is, of course, enhanced by his use of the vertical space of the stage. The vertical, he has explained, is his way of capturing the spiritual dimension of a work in visual terms, moving the setting beyond earthbound constraints. Even in the tavern scenes of *Henry IV* the walls were of a surprising height, so that characters perched high above the main action provided additional focal points for the spectators. The use of vertical space seems most prevalent in his work with Akalaitis. It was a key element of *Leon and Lena (and Lenz)* and Jean Genet's *The Screens,* both at the Guthrie Theater, and was even noticeable in Genet's *The Balcony* at American Repertory Theatre in Cambridge. For *Leon and Lena (and Lenz),* director JoAnne Akalaitis combined a play and novel by the visionary nineteenth-century writer Georg Büchner and transposed it to the American Southwest; the kingdom of the original play became an international corporate world. Through discussions and through studying images of the region and pop-culture icons (notably the *Cadillac Ranch* sculpture outside Amarillo, Texas), Tsypin came up with the idea of a highway going nowhere suspended above the thrust stage of the Guthrie. It appears to emerge out of a blazing sunset. Mark Bly, the Guthrie's dramaturg, described it in *Theatre:* "Suspended over the Guthrie thrust stage is a 60-foot highway, creating another whole level in the space, a road upon which people can travel. The highway is askew, reflecting the Guthrie auditorium itself, which is nonsymmetrical, filled with odd angles. The road has an astonishing power as it floats intrusively, jutting out ominously at the audience."[3]

Akalaitis's production of Genet's *The Screens* took the use of suspended scenic space even further. The stage floor was covered to resemble a desert, but above the entire stage was a net that represented the "land of the dead." (Tsypin wanted the net suspended over the entire auditorium.) The hanging net seemed to trap and oppress those below it, but when characters died, they burst through paper screens upstage and reemerged onto the suspended net, where they moved with slow deliberation "like a nightmarish vision of the Algerian desert," in Tsypin's words. The mechanics of hanging a tensile structure from the ceiling that would support the weight of up to forty moving bodies required the consultation of a German engineering firm.

Tsypin's use of steel was perhaps nowhere better demonstrated than in his setting for the opera *The Electrification of the Soviet Union,* directed by Peter Sellars at the Glyndebourne Festival in England. It also demonstrates the fluid relationship he has with his collaborators and the process of designing a set. The primary setting suggested the inside of train car, but Tsypin wanted it to be flexible like paper and soft "like a pillow," so that the actors could throw themselves against it. A working model was made of paper and given to Sellars to play with on the all-night flight from New York to London just before rehearsals began. Obviously, paper can twist and turn more than normal walls, and by the time he arrived, Sellars was so enamored of the flexibility that he insisted on a set that could function like the model. "One shop came up with the brilliant solution of flexible metal with applied foam," recalled Tsypin. "The walls moved; they were completely alive, you know, like in a dream where things move around you. They could squeeze people, then all of a sudden open up and change configuration completely. Peter created this unbelievable sculptural wall that completely transformed the space all the time, and the set took the abuse."

The sense of scale and height and the use of steel came together in a breathtaking manner for *The Death of Klinghoffer*. The opera is by John Adams, the composer of *Nixon in China* (which was designed by Adrianne Lobel), and Peter Sellars again directed. It was not meant as a documentary or realistic depiction of events on any level. As Tsypin described it:

> The real conflict of that opera takes place on a spiritual level. I was try-
> ing to capture a sense of place where nothing from this world exists;
> nothing is recognizable. It's a territory of the mind. What was important
> was to create an architecture or physical world that is almost immaterial,
> nonexistent. I studied some Middle Eastern and Islamic architecture, and
> it struck me how different the approach to architecture is from the West-
> ern approach which emphasizes structure—emphasizing the column, the
> beam. . . .
>
> The whole point of Western architecture is that you are supposed to
> understand how the building is put together. Of course, in Russian con-
> structivism, then in the deconstructivism of the last few years, it's all
> about structure, or destroying that structure. What Islamic architecture is
> trying to do is to diffuse the structure and make an understanding of how
> a building is put together impossible. It melts into the air, and there are
> layers and layers of patterns that prevent you from understanding where
> the building starts and where it ends. Or its sense of scale is completely
> obscured. It was very shocking to me to realize that. And of course, light
> plays a main role. The way the light is reflected and kind of swallowed
> by the millions of patterns. So, without actual references to Islamic archi-
> tecture—with the purely modern means at my disposal—I was trying to
> capture that whole different approach to the structure. I faced a purely
> technical problem: Because of the way the opera is structured, only
> dancers are allowed to be on the floor—there is choreography through-
> out the whole opera, which means I have to leave the floor empty. Yet
> I've got hundreds of people—a huge chorus that is very important,
> which means I've got to use all the vertical space. So the result is as if two

Islamic manuscripts stretched into space yet preserved the scale and verticality of it. And then make the light do the job: all the movement, all the changes, all the different locales are indicated with light.[4]

Among the striking things about Tsypin and his work is the thoroughness with which he talks about a production. Most designers are articulate—some might say surprisingly so given that they work in a visual medium—but Tsypin talks like a director. "I have to know a lot about the play, almost as much as the directors," he explains. "At the same time, I'm very sensitive to it and I welcome their ideas. I get very excited, and it makes me do something different. If you work by yourself all the time, you repeat yourself or your train of thought tends to become fixated on something, while conversation with the director could jolt you into something else. I find it invigorating. In fact, that's what makes your work different all the time. I feel that a set designer has the pleasure of collaborating, which is something few fine artists can do."

His description of a production covers literary metaphor, dramatic structure, historical and architectural references, and the relevance of play to the world today; it could be a lecture to a dramatic literature or directing class. This quality is equally true of Tsypin's NYU mentor, designer John Conklin. In fact, while Tsypin ultimately discusses the visual aspect of a production, that does not necessarily seem to be the starting point or the focus for him.

Henry IV is a case in point. Describing the setting, Tsypin provides a brief dissertation on Shakespearean production and the themes of the plays.

Shakespeare is so difficult because it has been done so much, it's really difficult to see it with fresh eyes. Also, it doesn't yield to interpretation—it's so complex. One doesn't want to oversimplify. We [director JoAnne Akalaitis] were looking for a very straightforward way [to present it]. You just create a place, you create an atmosphere, as opposed to a more usual production of Shakespeare, where the set is kind of generic and minimal and it's supposed to be like whatever Shakespeare had in mind, which is nowhere. JoAnne and I were determined to have more specific locations. But then, of course, what you have is theatrical space that you have to deal with. I felt it was important to be aware that you are in a theater watching Shakespeare. The stage itself is very much revealed. But then, I know the space pretty well; it's a colorful space by itself, and I just wanted to make it a little more interesting.

In medieval times the gothic cathedral represented the entire social and religious structures of the time. And the ruins of that gothic cathe-

18. Shakespeare's *Henry IV, Part 1,* New York Shakespeare Festival, Public Theater, 1991, director JoAnne Akalaitis, set design George Tsypin, costumes Gabriel Berry, lighting Jennifer Tipton. (Photo: George Tsypin.)

dral are very meaningful because we're in the war and the conflict is in the destruction. That's the basic setting. But the main conflict of the play is the order of law, social structure represented by Henry IV, and religion. Falstaff is incredibly irrational—he kind of represents subconscious, irrational behavior. The main character, of course, is Prince Hal, who's torn between the two. Whether we were in the palace or archbishop's cathedral, a lot of scenes could take place in that space. But then there is the tavern. Both parts 1 and 2 have these tavern scenes that are really key to the whole show. So I wanted the tavern to be there in the ruins of the gothic cathedral as if Falstaff and his mob actually happen to be in the cathedral. They desecrate the church. The sense of the tavern is so real— I have water, I have blood, they're shitting onstage, there's urine. The main inspiration is Brueghel—the life of the tavern was so juicy and dirty and real; it makes the play more horrible. Recent successful Shakespeare films demonstrate that reality is fine.

The basic elements of part 1 and part 2 are the same. My general image for part 1 was a cathedral that was burned down. There is fire in the show, a lot of fire. It's as if the battle took place in the cathedral and the cathedral burned down and collapsed. Meanwhile, part 2 has a whole other [feel]. It's like postwar, post passion. It's cool, it's snowing. I have dead leaves covering the entire stage. Falstaff is much older' the king is sick and he's dying. The whole feeling becomes much more surreal and also much stranger. Fluorescents are thrown around the stage; the period is not as rigorous. It's basically static. Among these dead leaves people are sitting in chairs and reflecting. There's very little action.

The Cabinet of Dr. Ramirez was Tsypin's first film, but the collaborators were familiar: director Peter Sellars and composer John Adams. It starred Mikhail Baryshnikov. Tsypin seemed the ideal designer for the film, not only because of his iconoclasm—he called what he did on the project "anti-design"—but because the film is about New York City and Tsypin has a clear and distinct vision of the city. "The original film is so famous because of the design," explained Tsypin. "To do something like that now is out of the question. Not only has it become the norm, but it is also trite and banal—wild angles and all that. How do you deal with that? All you have to do is define a way of looking at it." In part because he emigrated to this country as an adult, he has a view of American life that a native can never have. "Only by being a tourist can you experience a place," says a character in a Richard Foreman play. George Tsypin is a very insightful tourist, and New York holds great fascination for him. On the one hand the city is utterly exasperating; on the other, its sounds, its images, its angles and colors are a constant inspiration and source of wonder.

The movie "deals with madness, and modern city life, and money trading and trade scandals, the modern urban environment," Tsypin explains. "It's a film about the madness of contemporary urban life. Even though New York seems to be the most populated city in the world, it somehow is the loneliest, and I was trying to capture that sense of strange emptiness."

Film design was a new experience for Tsypin, and he had to learn the vocabulary at the same time that he was trying to find the proper approach for this specific project. "At first I thought that film was supposed to create very realistic things and use a lot of set decorating to really create a world that is believable. But then I realized that New York, in a way, is a ghost town," he said. "People are leaving. Even Wall Street now is kind of deserted. You see a lot of people, but there is something in the air. We just wanted to capture that, so I went with very strong color solutions."

Color became an interesting factor—the original film, of course, was in black and white:

How do you deal with color today? I'm not doing any of the usual *film* designing at all. All I'm doing is stripping things away rather than putting them in. In the original there are no props, nothing. So the main thing is the space and color. All the locations became these kind of strange empty places, and space itself became very charged. Film is such a flat medium, so it is very important to pierce that flatness with interesting spatial solutions. When a place is not cluttered, then space takes over, and the color. In this film I was trying to rethink black-and-whiteness in color terms, to really go to essentials in color where every color becomes a state of mind. I looked a lot at van Gogh—his color, his rooms. His paintings are devastating, so unbearable. His colors are incredibly intense and yet somehow dead and suffocating. In his self-portrait with the cut-off ear, for instance, he's trapped in this blue-green-white color. Eventually we find ourselves in the mental institution, which is very beautiful. There's nature, beauty, everything is very serene, except for chains and locks on windows and doors. It's a metaphor of modern life.

Tsypin was not sure that he wanted to do more films. "You see, films take a lot of time, and I don't think it's that satisfying creatively. If it's a regular commercial film, basically all you're required to do is create real places. The biggest compliment a film designer can get is, 'Oh, this looks just like . . .' So what?" What does interest Tsypin are his sculptures. There are several artists who design for the theater, and many designers who also paint, but Tsypin has created a form of sculpture based on conceptual set models that can exist independently as provocative works of art in their own right, as was evident at the Twining Gallery show.

At first glance, the sculptures look like set models placed upon pedestals. But this turns out to be deceptive. First, the "models" were often bewildering if seen as plans for a stage production. The *Cymbeline* "model," for instance, had no floor on which performers could move. Anyone who has seen the renderings produced by Soviet designers know that the tradition there is to produce conceptual renderings that can stand alone as works of art, not working shop drawings. Though his Soviet training was in architecture, not theater, Tsypin seems to have inherited this sense of theater artistry. Second, the models and the "bases" form a unit. The bases are often made of steel that has been rusted, twisted, and distressed, and the model portion often sits within rather than merely perched atop the base. These bases represent, in a sense, the nonvisible part of the world of the play. "Whenever you build a set," Tsypin explains, "whatever is not onstage is just as important as what is. Sometimes, the imaginary space that you don't actually see onstage is the actual life essence of the show. For example, in *Don Giovanni,* it's the space below, it's the underworld that haunts our imagination. And in the sculptures, I have the freedom to actually create this. I have a space that is bigger than the stage itself. So in a way, it is the world around them or the space around them that makes the sculptures."

The sculptures are certainly inspired by the plays, but they are concepts or essences, and significantly, they are often completed after a show is over. "When I work on a real show, I don't have time to do something like this. That's why I needed to do these sculptures, so I could eventually realize that need that was taken away months ago," he says, laughing. "You see something in your mind that is not necessarily possible in that particular theater. It's an idealized world that exists only in your imagination. That's what makes it interesting in a way. But here, it takes another leap."

By coming back to the sculptures after the completion of a show, Tsypin creates a sort of memorial or monument to the show, as he describes it: "The show happened. Usually I've dealt with wonderful works of literature or music, yet it just came and went. That's all that's left. There's a tension between the fact that I work with this very solid material and yet it just goes away like this, *whoosh.* You see your sets destroyed and burned. In a way, it's Manhattan."

The gallery show was more than a simple display, however. It was a total environment that reflected Tsypin's vision of New York as a multilayered city. Part of the gallery floor was covered with metal plates—the kind used to cover excavation sites in city streets. Anyone familiar with the city has heard the metallic thumping of cars and trucks riding over improperly secured plates. Visitors to the gallery walking across these plates triggered a taped sound score composed by Bruce Odland, part of which consisted of sounds collected by riding around the city with a microphone attached to the underside of a car. Tsypin referred to these as "underworld" sounds. "Nowhere else in the world do you have such a strong sense of an underworld as in New York—layers and layers. That connects with the whole sense, especially in *Don Giovanni,* of abyss and underworld." Above the gallery space, golden threads, based on *Klinghoffer,* also create sounds. "In a way," he continues, "it's a theater, but there are no actors—you become an actor."

The fact that Tsypin takes the time to create these "monuments" sets him apart from almost all American designers, who keep virtually no records of their work. But Tsypin feels that this is a necessary part of his artistic process. "I don't know how they do it, fifteen or twenty shows in a row every year, one after the other," he marvels. "Then it becomes a job, and you hate it.

It's a routine and you're exhausted. I have to get some other perspective."
Tsypin's increasing popularity and the demands on his time may, unfortunately, begin to change some of this.

Tsypin claims that the sculptures and the working models are often very
similar, though. "Strangely enough, you aim for that kind of conceptual
essence of the model, and almost always, if the idea is strong enough, you can
do it. The stronger it is, the easier it is to do it. But what do I give the shop?
I complete the model. I find that if you like a model and really work on a
model, the more energy and kind of love you give to the model, it will all
transfer to the real work. You might build people, and then you will see
those people onstage. I always found that if I actually took care and built people, I will see them onstage. I don't know how—it just gets ingrained in
everybody's mind. You might build in lighting, and you'll see that lighting."

For many designers, the mechanics of preparing drawings for the shop
are tedious and are generally left to assistants. At best, most designers consider it technical, not artistic, work. But here, too, Tsypin is different; he
may be the only designer to refer to mechanical drawing as "beautiful."
"Ideally I would like to do all my own drawings because I work out eleva-
tions myself, I work out proportions myself. I like to make drawings very
beautiful. *That* also transfers onstage. Unfortunately, there's not always time.
I have to use assistants, and it's very hard to find assistants who draw beautifully. There are a lot of assistants who draw well and fast, but drafting
beautifully is something that, unfortunately, is not taught in theater
schools." "The art of drawing is very important," he continued. "The plan
has to be beautiful, the ground plan has to be beautiful. Like Le Corbusier's
famous theory—if the plan of the building is beautiful, then the building
will be beautiful. Of course, that philosophy doesn't translate onstage. People come up with very awkward and ugly ground plans, uninteresting
schemes, but then you actually see it on stage because it shows. Unfortunately the reality of theatrical practice is that there is no time."

Tsypin has been fortunate. His student work at the late League of Pro-
fessional Theatre Training Schools portfolio review led to his first job, *The
Power and the Glory* directed by William Woodman at the Philadelphia
Drama Guild, and his second job, with Peter Sellars at the American
National Theatre in Washington. Since then, working with Sellars,
Akalaitis and Robert Falls, and lighting designers Jennifer Tipton and Jim
Ingalls, he has been at the cutting edge of American theater. "George is an
artist," declared Akalaitis. Perhaps, if he continues to work in this way, he
will succeed in eroding the critical prejudice that there is some sort of

dichotomy between "real" artists, like David Hockney or David Salle, who design for the theater, and "mere" designers.

Twelve Years Later

In the 1990s, Tsypin's career soared, and he designed some thirty productions (mostly operas, but also a few theater pieces and some television concerts, the latter mostly for Japanese television) in Austria, Japan, Italy, the Netherlands, Switzerland, Russia, England, Germany, and France. Significantly, although a few of the operas ultimately played in the United States, he has designed very little in this country. The last theater piece was *The Rover* at the Guthrie in 1994; he designed *The Flying Dutchman* for the Los Angeles Opera in 1995; in 1997 he designed an *Othello* for the American Ballet Theatre; in 1999 the *MTV Music Video Awards* from the Metropolitan Opera; and in 2003 the Metropolitan Opera production of *Benvenuto Cellini,* directed by Andrei Serban. Since 2000 he has designed several productions for the Mariinsky Theater of St. Petersburg with conductor Valery Gergiev. Increasingly, though, Tsypin's work has not been limited to theater. The materials of his more recent productions—light and glass—have become the primary materials of elaborate sculptures that have been exhibited in gallery shows. For the British Millennium Project he created a major installation, *Earth Center,* for an English arts center. In conversation one clearly senses a tension between the collaborative work of the theater and the total creative control of the individual artist.

The notion of danger surfaced unintentionally in the spring of 2002 with the Metropolitan Opera production of *War and Peace.* The setting was literally the world. A large dome mounted on a turntable was set at the front of the stage. "It's like a fisheye in the movies that provides a wide-angle view," he explained. "It feels like the world is on the edge of a precipice."[5] On opening night, a performer, one of the supers, tumbled from the dome into the orchestra pit, temporarily halting the performance. The reviews and subsequent articles in the New York press were often more focused on the danger posed by the set than on the production or the singers. But, as Tsypin pointed out, *War and Peace* opened in St. Petersburg, then played Covent Garden, La Scala, and Madrid, racking up some fifty performances without a mishap before New York. "What I believe," he mused, "is that it wasn't really dangerous, but there was something getting into people's subconscious. There was a perceived danger in the design." This was actually exciting for him. For Tsypin, finding the balance between "real danger

19. Model of *War and Peace,* Mariinsky Theater, St. Petersburg, 2000, and Metropolitan Opera, New York, 2002, designed by George Tsypin. (Photo: George Tsypin.)

and theatrical danger" is an ongoing effort. One of the reasons he has moved away from theater (and from production in the United States) is that the productions are too safe—both aesthetically as well as practically—and this leads to boredom. "Theater does not exist without danger," he declares. But even in Europe, he notes, safety regulations and soaring budgets are increasingly restricting what directors and companies are willing to risk, though by and large, European productions are still more daring on many levels than their American counterparts.

The major undertaking of the past decade was a production of Wagner's *The Ring of the Nibelungs* at the Netherlands Opera (1997–98) directed by Pierre Audi. For Tsypin, this was a chance to fully realize his conception of theater as a spatial art. "People continue to go to the theater because it all happens in space; all other forms of art are 'flat,'" he explains.[6] For this production of the *Ring,* Tsypin created an environment in which the audience and the stage were intertwined, with some of the audience sitting on galleries constructed over the stage, or the stage projected over the audience. The result, according to Tsypin was "antitheatrical," which he sees as a positive quality in the spirit of the symbolists who demanded the "detheatrical-

20. *Götterdammerung* at the Netherlands Opera, 1998, designed by George Tsypin. (Photo: George Tsypin.)

ization" of the stage in the late nineteenth century. The sheer scale of the production meant, in Tsypin's words, that all of Amsterdam was taken over: sets were stored throughout the city, scene changes required moving sets from the stage to the lobby and into the street. The theater became a kind of enveloping experience.

The design, in a sense, was about "the clash of materials": wood, steel, glass, stone, an "alchemy of the creation of the world." *Das Rheingold* employed three platforms representing the Nibelungs beneath the ground, the giants on earth, and the gods in the heavens. They also represented the elements of water, earth, and air; the water and sky were glass, the earth was steel. The first note of the opera sounds in darkness, and then there was "an 'explosion' of glass and metal. The platforms begin moving and action immediately becomes spatial."[7] Because part of the action of the opera involves the gods constructing Valhalla, the setting was conceived as a construction site. *Die Walküre*, on the other hand, was conceived as more pastoral, and everything was constructed of wood. The circular platform that surrounded the orchestra and created a playing space between the orchestra and auditorium was intended to resemble the rings of a section of a tree trunk. (At the same time, the vastness and minimalism of the set, together with the saturated color of the lighting, created a futuristic look.) Although Wagner called for a tree in which Wotan's sword is stuck, "My set has no tree, only a tree trunk. There are steel constructions sticking out of it; they stand for the sword. Wotan's spear hangs over the audience."[8]

Siegfried became a series of crossing paths in a forest, a representation of the hero's mind. One of the platforms, through the use of flexible metal, turned into the dragon. While both *Die Walküre* and *Siegfried* incorporated shafts of fire shooting up through the stage, Tsypin used glass to represent fire as well. Brunhilde, for example, is supposed to be surrounded by a ring of fire as she sleeps, but Tsypin created a fan of glass that opened around the orchestra, thus creating a more metaphoric sense of fire. *Götterdammerung,* of course, depicts the destruction of Valhalla.

> The space was circular, enclosed and collapsing. There was a steel wall, a wooden one and still another wooden one. The audience was in the balconies. All of this inclined forward like a falling tower of Babylon. If *Siegfried* was an ever-opening path, in *Götterdammerung* everything collapses inward.
>
> All materials were present here, too, but there was no foundation. This is twilight, the end—everything is destroyed. A huge stone mass hung directly above the audience. It descended gradually and broke the glass on the floor of the stage. In the final conflagration the theatre itself "burned up." Flames shot out from everywhere. A gigantic spear penetrated the wooden wall with a fearful crash and also burned. I put red lamps on the balconies. People sat there and suddenly saw all the balconies, all the audience members, lit up with red light. It really seemed like the theatre was burning. The gods' Valhalla was the theatre. It is inside us. Everything closes into our own consciousness. The flood at the end was represented by raising the floor on which there were heaps of broken glass—this was the remains of the waves and the cliff.[9]

Tsypin could not use real glass for these sets because the weight would have been extreme. So he was able to work with other materials to create "an optical illusion" of glass. Glass has come to replace steel in both his sets and sculptures. What is appealing to Tsypin is its transparency. "Glass has a lot of poetry in it. It goes to the very heart of theater, strangely enough, because it takes light in such a beautiful way. Basically, theater is about light and how things emerge out of darkness. At the moment I have trouble considering anything that is *not* transparent."

The *Earth Center* (1998–99) was, in a way, an extension of the ideas and motifs found in the *Ring*. It was not simply an art installation but was thematically focused on ecological concerns and finding ways of creating strategies for sustainable living on the planet. It was located in a former mining district, so the idea of both exploitation and reclamation of the land was inherent in the site itself. The space contained an almost imperceptibly revolving turntable (suggesting the rotation of the earth) and a skylight. When the sun was at a particular angle, the rays of light fell into a well as a prism broke the light into its component parts. There were two hundred sculptures, a Stonehenge of glass, video projections, music. The elements of fire, water, earth, and air were the guiding themes. Inspiration also came from Hieronymus Bosch's *Garden of Earthly Delights* (a paradise with something askew) and Japanese haiku (the idea of momentary descriptions of nature). Sensors in the room, attached to computers, caused changes in the room in response to the movements of visitors.

> When a certain number of people act in a certain way, critical mass is attained and the room "explodes"—for instance, it fills up with a nightmarish barrage of advertising, or overflows in a gigantic wave. You sense the beauty and scale of the ocean, but feel that somehow something is not right and understand: the water is poisoned. These mega-moments can end variously. The earth perishes or . . . (it is easy to show destruction). "New beginnings" are much harder. Sunlight serves this aim. Suddenly everything disappears and sunlight streams in—a complex construction "unfolds" to catch the sun's rays and a symphony of light begins. This is catharsis.[10]

Perhaps most interesting in listening to Tsypin talk about the creation of the space was to hear him revel in the almost Wagnerian control. "I had to design the space, conceptualize the whole approach. . . . I had to create theater with no actors, no director. There was just the theatrical experience that you enter, stay, and move through. It had all the components [of theater]: the sets moved; you moved with the sets and through the sets. There was music and lights and video—a total experience." In a sense, the spectators became the performers. In this regard the installation harks back to the proto-Happenings and events created by Allan Kaprow and certain Fluxus artists—an all-encompassing, total work of art that, by its use of movement and spectator-performers, is inevitably performative.

Tsypin continues to work with directors and other collaborators (he has, since 1991, begun to collaborate on projects with architect Eugene Mon-

akhov) and expresses admiration for directors. But clearly, Tsypin is interested in creating a world in his art. The problem with directors, actors, and
other designers is that they inevitably envision the world differently.
"Sometimes you operate in one world, and then all of a sudden come the
actors and the director and you realize they are doing the same old thing
within this other world that you're trying to create. So to find a language of
performing that matches the language of the space is the biggest challenge."

Can Tsypin still be called a postmodernist? His influences remain modernist, in particular the constructivists of the early twentieth century, whose
influence can be seen in *The Death of Klinghoffer, St. Francis of Assisi,* and *The
Ring.* It even showed up in the MTV award show in which the central
object was based on the famous Soviet project by Vladimir Tatlin, the *Monument to the Third International.* The fact that the tower seemed to be contained within the Statue of Liberty may have read as postmodern appropriation, but it could be seen equally as modern liberal political statement.
Whereas Tsypin's work from the late 1980s and early 1990s tended to have
the hallmarks of postmodernism, pastiche, historical quotation and juxtaposition, discontinuity, aesthetic discordance, and so on, his more recent work
seems to sit firmly within the modernist tradition. The very fact that he creates "worlds" (read "metanarrative") fixes him as a modernist. His reasser-
tion of the single controlling artist places him alongside Wagner and Gordon Craig. His increasing use of technology and new media—but often in
a social or political context—again places him in the tradition of the modern. It is as if George Tsypin moved through the postmodern looking glass
and has reemerged as an energized, original, iconoclastic modernist.

Notes

1. All quotations not otherwise attributed are from personal interviews by the
author, March 2002.

2. *New Yorker,* May 14, 1990, 36–37.

3. Mark Bly, "JoAnne Akalaitis's *Leon and Lena and (lenz):* A Log from the Dramaturgy," *Theatre* (winter/spring 1990), 94.

4. Jim Ingalls was the lighting designer.

5. Ellen Lampert-Gréaux, "Is Moscow Burning?" *Entertainment Design,* July 1,
2002, 19, 21.

6. Interview by Eugenia Kikoulina in *George Tsypin* (Moscow: A-Fond Publishers,
2000), 3.

7. Tsypin, interview by Kikoulina, 10.

8. Tsypin, interview by Kikoulina, 12.

9. Tsypin, interview by Kikoulina, 14.

10. Tsypin, interview by Kikoulina, 20.

Afterword

The big event looming upon the 21st century in connection with . . . absolute speed, is the invention of a perspective of real time, that will supersede the perspective of real space, which in its turn was invented by Italian artists in the Quattrocento.

—Paul Virilio

Modern Western scenography is largely the child of Renaissance perspective. In a sense, all illusionistic decor can be said to date from Sebastiano Serlio's three stock settings, and since that time, all stage design has been, in one form or another, about space. Perspective created a science of spatial perception in which artists and spectators alike believed that they were viewing an accurate re-creation of the visible world or at least its simulacrum. In reality, of course, perspective painting and design did not reflect the world so much as create a particular way of seeing it; simply put, it transformed Western consciousness. Some five hundred years later, this consciousness is undergoing another transformation. Foucault understood this when he declared that we are now "in the epoch of simultaneity: we are in the epoch of juxtaposition,"[1] but he saw this as a triumph of space over linear time as a means of apprehending the world; it was a substitution of late-twentieth-century physics for early modern physics. Philosopher Paul Virilio, who writes extensively on technology and society, addressed the same phenomenon, but he understood it as a shift away from spatial sensibility to a temporal one, though a most definitely nonlinear temporality. "Cyberspace is a new form of perspective," he declared, identifying both the link to, and break with, the Renaissance.

It does not coincide with the audio-visual perspective which we already know. It is a fully new perspective, free of any previous reference: it is a tactile perspective. To see at a distance, to hear at a distance: that was the essence of the audio-visual perspective of old. But to reach at a distance, to feel at a distance, that amounts to shifting the perspective towards a domain it did not yet encompass: that of contact, of contact-at-a-distance: tele-contact. . . .

For the first time, history is going to unfold within a one-time-system: global time. Up to now, history has taken place within local times, local frames, regions and nations. But now, in a certain way, globalization and virtualization are inaugurating a global time that prefigures a new form of tyranny. If history is so rich, it is because it was local, it was thanks to the existence of spatially bounded times which overrode something that up to now occurred only in astronomy: universal time. But in the very near future, our history will happen in universal time, itself the outcome of instantaneity—and there only.

Thus we see on one side real time superseding real space. A phenomenon that is making both distances and surfaces irrelevant in favor of the time-span, and an extremely short time-span at that. And on the other hand, we have global time, belonging to the multimedia, to cyberspace, increasingly dominating the local time-frame of our cities, our neighborhoods.[2]

If Virilio is right, and I think he probably is, a fundamental reshaping of the perception of the world is at hand with profound implications for everything from communications to politics. The scientific and perceptual revolutions of the Renaissance were not merely agents for change in the theater but were in fact instrumental in the very creation of modern Western theater. By implication, then, these recent shifts and developments should have an equally significant impact on future theatrical developments. As some of the preceding essays have suggested, our way of thinking and perceiving is, indeed, transforming, and this will most certainly have an effect on developments in theater content, form, and presentation. But theater is stubbornly old fashioned, limited by its fundamental dependence on live presence; it remains "local," it exists in the here and now. Until some future date when science fiction devices such as *Star Trek*'s transporters and warp speed travel are reality, or even in the not too distant future when large-scale holograms capable of filling a stage and being viewed from all points in an auditorium are available, theater (as opposed to media) remains connected to the corporeal presence of the performer, the stage space, and the spectators.

This afterword is being written in Seoul, Korea. The fact that I can communicate with ease around the world, listen to familiar radio stations, read American newspapers online, and see well-known trademarks and advertising images on billboards and in stores indicates that some version of Virilio's world is already commonplace. But the local still emerges from beneath the surface and acts both psychologically and physically to thwart the hegemony of the global. On a personal level, I must plan phone calls home carefully because of the fourteen-hour time difference; similarly, my e-mails reach colleagues in the middle of their night and vice versa. But more to the point, the look of the city—its scenography—reveals the tension between the global and the local. The surrounding mountains and, of course, the *hangeul* alphabet on all signage would identify the location to a knowledgeable viewer immediately. But from many angles Seoul is indistinguishable from countless other global cities. With the exception of one or two signature buildings unique to this metropolis, the postmodern commercial style of its high-rise hotels and offices is an architectural lingua franca creating a sense of both anonymity and familiarity. (And even the "unique" buildings of one city blur into the "unique" buildings of other cities so that skylines are no longer site-specific.) But despite the omnipresent construction cranes and heavy machinery rapidly transforming the unremarkable postwar neighborhoods, the older city lurks just behind the glass and granite monoliths. Narrow, twisting streets and alleys crowded with people, shops, and vendors' stalls—which lack even the slightest hint of design or plan—sit in marked juxtaposition to the postmodernist facades that surround them. Unlike the vertical layers of history typical of ancient cities, this city (and many just like it) is layered horizontally, as it were; a recent past coexists in time and space with an imagined future. We might even think of them as fractal cities—worlds within worlds. And while global corporate business occurs in these postmodern edifices, urban life still unfolds in the boisterous labyrinths of the older, unplanned city.

This is not unlike the situation of scenography today. The "globalization" of directors, designers, choreographers, and conductors, particularly in opera and dance, is leading to a scenographic equivalent of postmodern commercial architecture—an almost universal style that can be seen at opera houses and theaters around the world with parallels in fashion advertising and graphic art. But because, at least for now, theater occurs in specific locales—specific theaters within particular cities—the rougher, less polished imagery of recent history and practice is there beneath the surface. If one looks at a photo of a production from a major opera house there is almost no way of telling what country or city it is from. The same is largely true for the replicas of Broadway and West End musicals produced around the world. But in the small theaters, local texture comes through. Everything from materials to mechanics to union regulations or specific work customs affects the look and style and presentation of a work. This is true whether it is a homegrown piece of theater or an attempt to replicate the work of a different culture.

This is not to say that local work is anachronistic. Any form of theater must inevitably reflect its time if it is to be accepted and understood by an audience. (There are exceptions, of course. At New York's Metropolitan Opera, for instance, there is a contingent of spectators who lustily hurl boos and hisses at the directors and designers of any production that they deem too contemporary.) So contemporary scenography must find some way to encompass the "new perspective" engendered by new technologies so that audiences will understand it as part of the present-day world in which they live. But the denizens of the global community still live in real, tangible, physical locales with particular textures, smells, visual identities, and human rhythms. The new scenography must recognize that as well.

Notes

1. Michel Foucault, "Of Other Spaces," *Diacritics* 16 (1986): 22.
2. Paul Virilio, "Speed and Information: Cyberspace Alarm!" trans. Patrice Riemens, *Theory* 18 (August 27, 1995). <www.ctheory.net/text_file.asp?pick=72>

Index

Obolensky, Chloe, 130

Octoroon, The (Boucicault), 76

Odets, Clifford, 187

Odland, Bruce, 215

Oedipus (Sophocles), 69

Oenslager, Donald, 158

Offenbach, Jacques, 144

off-off-Broadway, 1, 25, 79, 171

Olivier, Laurence, 124

O'Neill, Eugene, 157, 180, 187

On the Art of the Theatre (Craig), 158

Ontological-Hysteric Theatre, 111. *See also* Foreman, Richard

Open Theater, 171

Order of Things, The: An Archaeology of the Human Sciences (Foucault), 97

Oresteia, The (Aeschylus), 3, 55–56, 71

Ormerod, Nick, 183

Otello (Verdi), 150

Othello (Shakespeare), 217

Otway, Thomas, 62

Our Town (Wilder), 176, 186, 191

Pandering to the Masses (Foreman), 176

Paramount Theatre, 151–52

Paris Exposition of 1900, 138

Paris Opéra, 201–2

Parker, H. T., 137, 145

Parks, Suzan-Lori, 77

Parsifal (Wagner), 45, 146, 150–51

Parthenon, 55

Pearls for Pigs (Foreman), 162

Pelléas et Mélisande (Debussy), 142–43

Perestroika (Kushner), 183, 185, 190, 193

Performance Group, 103, 171, 176

Performing Garage, 78, 130, 171–72, 180–81

Permanent Brain Damage (Foreman), 165

Persians, The (Aeschylus), 55

Phèdre (Racine), 176

Philadelphia Drama Guild, 216

Picabia, Francis, 22

Picasso, Pablo, 15,

Pigmeat Markham, 178

Pinckney, Darryl, 84

Piscator, Erwin, 47, 86, 118

platform stage, 17, 35, 39, 72, 130

Plato, 68, 83, 101

Plautus, 67

pneuma, 49

Pod Restaurant, 194

Poe, Edgar Allan, 135

Poelzig, Hans, 142

Poetics (Aristotle), 3, 195

Poetics of Space, The (Bachelard), 8, 41, 59, 135

Point Judith (Wooster Group), 176

Polieri, Jacques, 39, 70

Postmodern Geographies (Soja), 111

Power and the Glory, The (Greene), 216

Prado, 98

Production of Space, The (Lefebvre), 190

Prometheus Bound (Aeschylus), 55

Propylaea, 18, 19

proscenium, 25, 26, 34, 38, 40, 72, 76, 78, 90, 104–5, 121, 139, 140, 142, 144, 192, 202–3

Provincetown Playhouse, 157

Psalm 121, 60

Public Theater, 129, 206, 208, 212

Puccini, Giacomo, 146

Purgatorio (Dante), 60

Quillard, Paul, 119, 120, 132, 135

Racine, Jean, 61, 174

Radio City Music Hall, 202

Radio Hole, 95

Ramlila, 40

Rathauskeller, 139

Rauschenberg, Robert, 24, 46

Red Desert (film), 204

Redlich Villa, 147

Reed, Lou, 84

Reichl, Ruth, 204

Reinhardt, Max, 142

Relâche (Satie/Picabia), 22

Rheingold, Das (Wagner), 18–19, 219–20

Rhoda in Potatoland (Foreman), 164, 175

Rhode Island Trilogy (Foreman), 176

Rice, Elmer, 190

Ringling Brothers, 204

Ring of the Nibelungs, The (Wagner), 18–19, 218, 221